THE FAMILY THAT OVERTOOK CHRIST

the family that overtook CHRIST

M. Raymond, OCSO

Pauline
St. Paul Books & Media

Cum permissu reverendissimi D. Hermanni—Joseph Smets, Abbatis— Generalis Ordinis Cisterciensium Strictoris Observantiae.

Nihil Obstat: M. Albert Wulf, OCSO
M. Maurice Malloy, OCSO

Imprimi Potest: ✠Frederick M. Dunne, OCSO

Nihil Obstat: Arthur J. Scanlan, STD

Imprimatur: ✠Francis Joseph Spellman, DD

Library of Congress Cataloging-in-Publication Data

M. Raymond, Father, OCSO, 1903-
The family that overtook Christ.

Contents: The grand old warrior, Venerable Tescelin — The mother who became a saint, Blessed Alice — Bernard's big brother, Blessed Guy — [etc.]

1. Bernard, of Clairvaux, Saint, 1090 or 91-1153. 2. Bernard, of Clairvaux, Saint, 1090 or 91-1153 — Family. I. Title.
BX4700.B5M23   1986   282'.092'2 [B]   86-19670
ISBN 0-8198-2625-1

Previously published by P. J. Kenedy & Sons, NY.

Cover Art: Giraudon/Art Resource, NY CRL 26.772.
Jean FOUQUET. Heures d'Etienne Chevalier.
St. Bernard, abbe de Clairvaux. Ms. 71 F° 36.
Chantilly, Mus. Conde.

Printed and published in the U.S.A. by St. Paul Books & Media, 50 St. Paul's Avenue, Boston, MA 02130.

St. Paul Books & Media is the publishing house of the Daughters of St. Paul, an international congregation of women religious serving the Church with the communications media.

2 3 4 5 6 7 8 9   99 98 97 96 95

In gratitude to
my heavenly Father
GOD
who gave me His only Son as model;
and to my earthly father,
P.J.F.,
who showed me how to model on Him;
praying that we shall meet in heaven.

Acknowledgments

Making acknowledgments is a difficult thing, for words can never express our indebtedness first to Rev. John P. Flanagan, S.J., of Boston, MA, who in his Jesuit generosity and Christ-like charity, painstakingly went over and over every line of the manuscript, expertly evaluating, judiciously correcting and continually offering scholarly suggestions for the improvement of the work. In the midst of the hurried life of an over-busy missioner and retreat-director, he made time—stealing it from needed rest—to aid those who needed aid and to improve what needed improvement. The intellect of the man we appreciate, the heart of the brotherly priest we love, and we tell the readers of this work that to him and his encouragement *The Saga of Citeaux* is greatly due.

Then there is Father Mary Maurice, O.C.S.O., of the monastery of Our Lady of the Valley, Lonsdale, RI, the "censor deputatus," who proved more than a censor with his meticulous care for all the proprieties. He was more than conscientious. He did much more than his duty. He was a brotherly cooperator.

To Father Mary Amedeus, O.C.S.O., of the Monastery of Our Lady of Gethsemani, a gigantic debt of gratitude is due. In fact, the major part of the basic facts of this work is the fruit of his long hours of heroically patient research; digging into ancient manuscripts, original records and documents, and century-old tomes—bringing to light valuable, 'sine-qua-non' information—displaying indefatigable labor and zeal; and all, in a true spirit of brotherly collaboration and love.

To the first "censor deputatus," Father Mary Alberic, O.C.S.O., of the Monastery of Our Lady of Gethsemani, also, acknowledgment is gratefully made for his generous assistance, helpful suggestions, and fraternal cooperation.

To America Press acknowledgment is gratefully made for permission to quote from Rev. Alfred Barrett's poem on St. Bernard which appears in Father Barrett's book of poems, *Mint By Night.*

Finally, we must thank Our Lady of Citeaux. So often did she answer our appeals for help! May she guide this "Saga" and all who read, leading them, through it, to the heart of Citeaux's inspiring Hero—her Son, our Lord, Jesus Christ.

CONTENTS

Introduction

Sister Superior put the book down gingerly. It was a "Life of St. Bernard of Clairvaux." Then in a disgusted tone she said, "I could give that author a good shove."

Her brother looked at her with an amused twinkle in his eye and said, "Why, Sister Superior, such language, and in such a tone! Just what do you find wrong with the book?"

"The author has made a saint of God anything but a saint. He has taken Bernard's boyish oddities and novice-ship extravagances and written of them as if they were the heroic acts of a saint. Just imagine this!" Picking up the book, she flipped over a few pages and read: "'Such was his heroic modesty of the eyes that at the end of his year of novitiate he could not say how many windows there were in the chapel.' —Such nonsense! Who can? I was a novice for two years; I've been back to the novitiate every summer for twenty-two years, and I can't tell you now how many windows there are in our chapel. But no one will ever credit me with heroic modesty of the eyes, and I don't think anyone will canonize me. At least," she added with a smile, "not just yet."

"No," laughed her brother, "not just yet. But come, isn't that a very little thing on which to condemn a whole book? I admit that too many authors of lives of saints, not knowing religious life or the spiritual life intimately, make similar blunders; but are you going to put that book on your 'Index' just because of that one blunder?"

"Oh, that is only an instance," said Sister; "the whole book disgusts me. It tells me what Bernard did, not what he was."

"Ah! but Sister," countered her brother, "you must never forget your philosophy—'agere sequitur esse.' Tell me what a man or woman does, and I'll tell you what they are."

"No you won't," retorted Sister quickly. "As long as human nature is human nature you'll have scribes and pharisees, publicans and sinners; and if you know only what they do, you'll never know what they are. For if I read my New Testament aright, many of the pharisees and scribes were the greatest sinners, while some of the publicans and sinners became the real saints. You see, Father, too many authors miss the whole point of sanctity. They write as if it were something exterior, telling of the wonders the saints performed, endlessly talking of the miracles that they wrought, intimating all the time, of course, that they were saints because of these marvels."

"But, Sister, don't you admit that miracles are the stamp of divine approval?"

"Of course I do. But please grasp my point! You theologians settle the whole matter with a neat distinction between 'gratiae gratis datae' and 'gratiae gratum facientes.' But to put it in English, let me say that miracles may show me the saint; they do not show me how he became a saint; and that is what I want to see. It is not the completed process that intrigues me; it is the process itself; for, you see, my work is not to be a saint, but to become one. If that doesn't sound too paradoxical for you."

"Not a bit," answered her brother. "I grasp your point on the miracles, too."

"You know, Father, every time I read a book that is replete with the miraculous I feel like writing to the author and telling him of an old retreat master of ours, a man with a keen sense of humor and a profound sense of theology. Speaking on this very point, he said that if miracles were the only proof of sanctity, we would have to conclude that Balaam's donkey was a greater saint than St. Joseph or our Blessed Lady. The donkey did the miraculous. He spoke. While neither Joseph nor Mary have a single miracle to their credit. But the wise retreat master added: 'However, I am fully convinced that doing the miraculous did not make Balaam's donkey any more of a jackass than he was.'"

Her brother laughed heartily, then said, "Sister, I've never seen you in such a mood before. You are fluent, facile and felicitous. Tell me now, just what sort of life of a saint would you like."

"One that tells the truth truthfully. One that shows the man becoming a saint, not already made a saint. One that shows him modeling on Jesus Christ, not on the absurdities of a school of hagiographers. Do you know what that means, Father? It means show me a saint that was human! Jesus Christ was such. Oh, those biographies that make the supernatural consist in the unnatural! May God forgive the authors. They have done a whole world of mischief. Don't you theologians say that 'grace perfects nature, it does not destroy it'?"

"Yes."

"Then why do so many authors portray their subjects as engaged in nothing so much as 'slaying their passions' and 'annihilating self'?"

"But, Sister, we must have penance and purgation."

"Are you telling me? As novices didn't we all try to 'slay a passion a day'?"

"We did," laughed her brother. "It was the novice-ship practice."

"It was the noviceship malpractice, you mean," snapped Sister Superior. "And it was brought about by just such biographies as we have been discussing. When we found that our passions would not remain slain, that they were worse than Banquo's ghost, and had as many lives as a cat, didn't we despair of ever becoming saints? And as for the annihilation of self—listen, Father, I used to make novenas of self-annihilations. Honestly. Before every great feast. But when I learned a little philosophy and some theology, when I learned about the identity of self and soul, about the incommunicability of our individual personalities and the immortality of our personal souls, then I began to understand the sterility of my novenas, the absurdities of many ascetical writers who never clearly distinguish, and the real wisdom of Saint Francis de Sales."

"What was that?" asked her brother.

"He said something to the effect that self will die just fifteen minutes after we do; and I sometimes suspect that even his calculations are a wee bit premature. I hold for certain that self will die three days after we are in the grave; any other opinion to me is only highly probable."

"You are safe in your opinion, Sister, but so far you have told me what you don't want in a life of a saint; you haven't told me what you do want."

"You know, I think you're just teasing me. But since you claim to be something of an author, I challenge you. Write me a true life of a saint; and my whole emphasis is on the word 'true.' Give me the inner life of a great man who became a great saint. Tell me what was churning in his soul as he battled his way up from selfishness and the allurements of sin to the great heart of God. Make it a lyric, if you will; but don't give me any legend. Tell it lovingly, by all means; but give me no extravagances or silly bursts of sentimentality. Be easy and popular in your style while ever maintaining your dignity. Be just sufficiently elevated to be genuinely good. Be scholarly always, but never pedantic. Tell the real story of a man who became a saint, and tell it with a charm that grips me from the beginning and holds me to the end. To do that, make your subject supernatural, not unnatural; bring your every fact to the touchstone of accepted theology, sound philosophy and, above all, true human psychology. In other words, brother mine, tell the truth! Let there never be a disillusionment connected with your work; never allow me to embrace gladly what you write only to learn in my more mature years that I have hugged a shadow, grasped at fancy and been nursing sentimentality. Let your saint be a broad highway for me to the Divinity. I don't care how long, wearying or steep he be, as long as he leads me to my God. But I beg you give me no by-path that is luring and lovely, but leads me nowhere except to sentimental pietism."

That was a tremendous task you set me, Sister Mary Clare; but here is my honest effort. If it has any merit, it belongs to you; the defects I claim for myself.

I just want to give you one warning. It is this: *Don't Be Deceived!*

Because of the mold in which I have cast it, this may read like a novel; but don't be deceived. *It is history!* The facts are *facts*. Many of the words are *Bernard's own words;* culled either from his sermons or his letters. I have dramatized much; I have fictionalized little or nothing. So, take it for what it is—a perfectly *reliable* story.

You may ask: Why the story form? My only answer is that we have had plenty of historical novels and plenty of biographical novels; so why not have some novel history in a novel biography? This family *lived!* Why not represent them then, as *lifelike?* Furthermore, since it is only in and by your everyday living that you are going to *become* a saint, I had to give you a safe model. I am sure that you and I and all of us can learn much from this 'everyday living' of Bernard's family. They show us how we can supernaturalize the natural. What a family!

Now, remember, I have given you only sketches, not full-length lives. Bernard alone would take a volume twice this size! But I hope that the sketches will satisfy and stimulate. I never met such a family before; I feel sure you will enjoy the introduction I give you.

Fr. M. Raymond, O.C.S.O.

Part 1

THE PARENTS

The Grand Old Warrior

"...his honesty bends."

"What's the matter with you? You've got a face a league long; you're grumbling to yourself; and you're ruining the toes of a good pair of riding boots kicking the dirt that way. What's the matter with you, anyhow?"

"Oh, nothing! Nothing! Nothing! Go away and don't bother me," and Gerard of Fontaines turned on his heel and started to walk away.

"Not so fast, young fellow," said his older brother Guy as he stretched out his hand and caught Gerard by the shoulder. "The grooms told me that your horse was lathered in sweat when you came in; that you vaulted from the saddle and bolted away without a single world. You're old enough to know that is no way to treat a horse. And I'm old enough to know that something is very wrong with you. Out with it. What is it?"

"Aw, something would be wrong with you, too, if you saw what I just saw."

"What did you see?"

"I saw Father play the coward."

The blood fled from Guy's face; his eyes narrowed as his jaw squared and his upper lip trembled; then between clenched teeth he squeezed out the words, "If you weren't my brother I'd throttle you for that statement. Now tell me what you mean, and tell me quickly or I'll thrash you."

Gerard squirmed beneath the fiercely gripping hands of his older brother, his face was crimson and his eyes held fire as he said, "Thrash me! Go ahead and thrash me! I don't care what happens to me now. I'm sick down to my toes; and I'm ashamed as deep as my soul. And you'll be too, when you hear the awful truth. But I'll not tell you. It would choke me." With that he gave a quick lift to his arm and broke the grip Guy had on his right shoulder. But Guy was angry now; wheeling the twisting youngster around he brought his eyes down level with Gerard's and said, "I'll choke you if you don't tell me! What did Father do?"

Tears gushed from Gerard's eyes; they were tears of anger; He blurted out, "He played the coward."

Guy gave him a violent shake and said in a deadly tone, "Gerard, if you say that once again, I'll wallop you." Then tightening the grip on his brother's shoulders until his own knuckles showed white, he shook him again and said, "Tell me the story."

Gerard broke under the grip and the shaking. Tears flooded his pain-filled eyes as he said, "Father wouldn't fight. He shook hands with his enemy. We're disgraced."

Guy's eyes opened wide as his lower jaw dropped. His whole person seemed to undergo a change as he gasped, "Father wouldn't fight? Gerard, Gerard, what are you saying? Tell me what you mean." His tones were pleading. He was no longer the angry older brother, he was an anxious, awe-struck suppliant.

"Oh, Guy, I don't know what happened," cried Gerard. "I heard the grooms whispering the other day that Father was to fight a duel. I nosed about until I found the place and the time. Today, I stole out to that hollow in the woods where Alfred has his hut. I hid in the thicket. I knew my horse would be quiet. Then they came: Father with his two attendants, and a lowly knight with his two. Father could have flattened him with a look. But what did he do? What did great Tescelin the Tawny, Counsellor of the Duke and one of the most famous knights in the Duchy do? What did Father do? My father.... Do you hear, Guy?... My father—he put out his right hand, spoke some soft words to this sorry knight, whoever he was—one that I could conquer—and they clasped hands. Then they walked to the hut and signed some papers. I saw the knight ride away. I wanted to ride after him and strangle him; I could have, too! But I was so filled with shame, I galloped home. Guy, Guy, how can we ever show our faces in the Duchy again? Our father, a coward."

The back of Guy's hand flipped to Gerard's mouth. It was a sharp, stinging blow, one that drove the upper lip against the teeth and drew blood. Gerard was more bewildered by the fact that his brother should strike him than he was stung by the blow; he just looked in openmouthed amazement as the blood trickled down his chin.

As soon as Guy saw the blood, his arm circled Gerard's shoulders and pressing the younger brother to his side, he said, "Oh, I'm sorry, Gerard, really sorry. That blow was involuntary; it was completely automatic and instinctive. Forgive me, please. But don't you ever, ever, ever say that about Father! He's not that. He could not be that. Never! There are no cowards in the Duke's bodyguard, and Father has been in that guard since before you or I were born. I don't know what happened in the wood. I accept your word that Father didn't fight; but never say that Father wouldn't fight. There is some explanation. Trust him. I'm ashamed of you for even having had these thoughts. But forgive me for that slap in the face."

"Huh," grunted Gerard, "do you think a little slap in the face matters now? Nothing matters. I saw what happened in the wood. Father wouldn't fight."

Guy's lips tightened; so too did his fists. "Gerard," he said, "I'll..." But that was as far as he got, for just at that moment his father came around the corner from the stables. He stopped short as he caught sight of the attitudes of his sons. Glancing quickly from one to the other he asked, "What's wrong here?" It was a quiet question, put in a deep, cool voice, but Guy noticed that the voice sounded weary. He looked more closely at his father and noted that there was a sag to his whole countenance: the lines in the forehead were jagged and deep, the eyes were sunken, the mouth appeared loosed and the cheeks somewhat hollow. Guy frowned, peered even more intently and saw that his father looked old and very tired. He gasped then and said, "I think that we should ask that question of you, Father. What's wrong with you? You look ill."

His father straightened at the statement. His head came up, his mouth snapped shut and his lips showed one straight line. He was the warrior again, in perfect command of himself; but the effort had been noticeable. Without answering Guy, he looked at Gerard who had turned away and was apparently disinterested. "Gerard," he said, "what's wrong?"

"Nothing," came the sulky answer as he kicked sharply into the loose dirt.

"Turn around here and tell me...," but there he stopped, for Gerard had turned and there on his chin was the tell-tale blood. "What?" exclaimed the father, "have you two been quarreling?"

"Not exactly, Father," put in Guy. "I struck him on the mouth, but it was a blow that was not premeditated. He has forgiven me."

"But why did you strike him?"

"I would rather have him tell you that, Father."

Tescelin looked at Gerard, but only got a deep crimson blush by way of enlightenment. He waited. The silence grew embarrassing. Guy shifted from foot to foot; Gerard kept kicking the dirt and blushing, while the father looked from one to the other and frowned. "Come," he finally said, "this is no way for my sons to act."

"Well, Father," said Guy, "Gerard said something about you...."

"Oh," interrupted the father, "so I am the cause of it, am I? What did he say about me?"

"Well," said Guy very hesitatingly, "he said that you wouldn't fight...."

Tescelin's eyes closed. It was as if he had been struck in the face. He blanched as he said, "Wouldn't fight whom?"

"That he could not tell; he says it was some sorry knight...."

"Gerard," broke in the father, "were you in the woods today?" The question was heavy with sadness.

"I was," came the hot reply. "I was and I saw it all; and I told Guy that you played the coward. That's why he struck me."

Tescelin seemed to sway. His face grew ashen grey. The muscles on either side of his face were seen to flex as he clenched his teeth. With a deep sigh he said, "There are others who will say the same." Then walking over to Gerard, he put his arm around his shoulder as he wiped away the blood from his mouth and said, "My boy, I want you to love me always the way you do this moment. It is your deep loyalty and love that Guy takes to be disloyalty; and it is his loyalty and love that made him strike you. I am sorry that you were in the woods today; sorrier still that you have spoken about it; but since you have, you must come along to my room and allow me to explain. I will try to teach you both a deeper loyalty and a greater love."

In silence the three turned from the yard and headed for the castle; in silence they walked the corridor and mounted the stairs, and in silence they entered Tescelin's room. When he had quietly closed the door, the father waved the boys to two chairs and reaching up, took from its hooks on the wall a splintered spear. Walking over to Gerard he placed it in his hands and asked, "Do you know when that spear was splintered and how?"

"Yes, Father, I do," came the quick and uncompromising reply. Gerard had not lost any of his fire as yet.

"Then you know, my son, that I almost lost my life by that spear; you know that it struck me here on the right side, and had not that shaft splintered it would have driven on, into and through my heart. That is the only trophy I keep of all the battles I have fought. Do you know why?"

"No, Father, I don't." Gerard cooled a little, but only a little.

"Do you know, Guy?"

"No, Father, I don't; but I have often wondered. You have been victorious in countless battles, and yet you keep as memento only this spear that almost caused your death."

"Yes, and it is the only trophy I will ever treasure. I keep that splintered spear to remind me to be grateful to God. I have faced death numberless times, as you know; but if that shaft had not splintered that memorable day, I would have faced God! And had I met Him then, I fear that I would have been empty-handed. So that spear is my admonisher. It tells me that I'll have to face God one day and that I must not be empty-handed. It tells me to be grateful for life as it reminds me how close I was to death. I keep no trophies of my own successes; I keep only this treasure as a memento of God's great mercy. Have you followed, Gerard?"

"I have," came the sullen reply. Gerard was far from friendly even yet.

"All right, son. Now I want you to look at another Man who also had a spear driven into His side; but this time the shaft did not splinter! It went up and on and into His very heart." As he spoke Tescelin lifted a large crucifix from the wall and brought it close to Gerard. The boy looked up almost in fright. His father had never spoken as solemnly as this to him before. Guy, too, was all attention, for although he was the eldest son and first-born, he had never seen his father in such a mood as this.

Tescelin the Tawny was a man of deep emotions; but he kept them deeply hid. He was known as the quiet and ever congenial Lord of Fontaines, whose fire was seen only in battle. In fact, the metamorphosis that seemed to take place as the tawny one went into a fray puzzled most; for they never knew that the Duke of Burgundy's most reputed Counsellor was a man who had fought for and won the mastery of the very deep and very powerful emotions of his soul. As he now stood before his two oldest boys, holding a large crucifix in his hands and pointing to the wound in Christ's side, he was manifesting more feeling than they had ever seen him show in all their years, even though Guy was eighteen and Gerard just sixteen.

"My boy," said the father, "look at this wound often, and let it speak to you. Let it tell you that there is a victory greater than that of vanquishing a foe, a fiercer enemy for you to conquer than the one who comes to you from without, clothed in armor and armed with steel, that there is a battle more bitter to fight than the one fought in open field. You say that I would not fight a sorry knight today. You are right, son of mine, I would not fight. And here is my reason." Saying which he held out the crucifix. "You call me coward. In that I hope that you are not right, my boy. My opponent was hardly worthy of my steel. It was not fear of man that made me hold out the hand of friendship, Gerard; I meant it to be love for God. Yes, my boy, let me tell you that there is a greater victory than vanquishing a foe; and let me insist that it costs much more! Do you begin to understand?"

"I do, Father," broke in Guy, "you forgave your enemy for love of Christ."

"Right, my boy, for love of Christ. And you, Gerard, do you understand?"

"No," blurted the younger brother, "a duel is a trial before God. I wish that you had fought."

Tescelin sighed as he put the crucifix back on the wall. He looked at it lovingly, then took the spear from Gerard and hung it close to the crucifix. After that he turned and said, "You will understand one day, Gerard; but until that day dawns just remember that Christ did not come down from the cross although His enemies taunted Him with this as a proof that God had abandoned Him. I am sorry, son, that I have wounded you so deeply by my action today, and as a balm for your wound I give you permission to enter this room of mine any time at all, so that you can look at the cross and my splintered spear. They may yet teach you the lesson that I have failed to teach."

Gerard sprang from his chair, flung himself into his father's arms and sobbed, "Oh, Father, Father, I believe in you. I trust you. I love you. But why, oh, why didn't you fight?"

Tescelin patted the boy's shoulder and smiled; it was a sad little smile for he was sorry for this son of his and fully sympathized with the tempestuous little heart that wanted to be loyal but could not give up its preconceived ideas. "Come, son of mine," he said after he allowed the crest of Gerard's grief to spend itself, "mother must not know what happened today, nor anyone else in the house. Promise me that?"

"I promise," came the sob.

"Very good, then. Now go with Guy and wash away every last trace of your tears. One day you'll understand it all." Patting them on the back, he sent them from his room and closed the door behind them; then leaning against the door and looking to the crucifix he said aloud, "It hurts to be thought a coward, Lord, and that by your own son; but I bear it for You. Give me strength to brave it all for You."

Scars for Memory

Gerard kept his promise; hence, the rest of the family never heard how Tescelin, by a display of surpassing moral courage, earned for himself the name of coward with his second oldest son. One day, many months after, he found Gerard in his room studying the crucifix and the splintered spear. When he asked the boy what he was doing, he was surprised with the answer, "Trying to read enigmas; but I can't make anything out of them yet." And with that the boy was gone. Tescelin laughed then and said to the unheeding walls, "That boy is going to be a man of one idea. I hope it's a big one!"

The Lord of Fontaines failed in teaching Gerard the lesson he wished to teach; but the trouble was psychological, not pedagogical. Gerard's mind, memory and imagination were crowded to capacity; hence, there would have to be an evacuation before there could be an entrance, and the present occupants were proving most tenacious of their lease. His ideas of chivalry would not yield to those of charity. Already Gerard was showing himself a man of one idea. But Tescelin was much more successful with the rest of the family and especially so with Humbeline, the only girl in a family of seven; and while it is true that the preponderating male element made something of a tomboy out of her, it is equally true that her isolated femininity made a courtier out of her father. He called her his "Little Queen," and she accepted the homage with all the grace of one.

One day he came upon her as she knelt before the shrine of St. Ambrosian which he had had erected on his grounds. He looked at her in amazement, then cried out, "Oh, Humbeline, my Little Queen, for a moment you took twenty years from my life. As you knelt there I thought I was looking at a girl I loved much."

"Ooo, tell me about her, Father." Humbeline was just fifteen, an age when the very word "love" connotes worlds of romantic mystery.

Tescelin smiled as he said, "Come here and sit by me, and I'll tell you all about her." Humbeline turned from the prie-dieu and walked to the rustic bench on which her father sat. Once she had nestled close to him, he began, "She had hair just like yours, Little Queen, soft, silky and bewitchingly black; she had eyes just like yours, wherein tall candles were always lit and star radiance always lingered; and her skin was as snowy and transparent as your own; her mouth was a rosebud, even as your own, and when she smiled, the same even, white line of pearliness shone. Yes, Humbeline, she looked exactly like you, even to this precious dimple, which they tell me is left from an angel's kiss."

"Ooo," exclaimed Humbeline in a kind of breathless awe, "she must have been beautiful!"

Her father's laugh was light, liquid and airy. He knew that his little queen had not meant the complacency that was in the exclamation; but his sense of humor was such that he could not allow such naïveté to pass. "That's what I've been telling you, Humbeline. She was very beautiful, for she looked just like you."

"Was she rich?"

The question had come so quickly that Tescelin saw that his daughter was so completely absorbed in this other woman that she was entirely oblivious of self, so he went on, "Yes, she was very rich. She was the daughter of a wealthy lord who saw to it that she was educated in such a way that her mind, memory and will would be as beautiful as her outward form. She was as rich in ideas and ideals as he was rich in estates. All in all she was a very lovely little lady."

"And did you love her greatly, Father?"

Tescelin was now enjoying himself; he saw that his little queen was lost in the tale. "With all my heart and soul I loved her," he said.

"What was her name?"

"Oh, a beautiful name; one that described her perfectly, for it is a name that means 'truth'; a name that flows from the lips of a lover with limpid gracefulness, for it is composed of an exclamation and a sigh. You see, my Little Queen, your name is a song on a lover's lips; but this girl's was an exclamation of admiration and a sigh of longing. You just breathed it in wonder and worship."

"Ooo, how exquisite!" said Humbeline. "Breathe it for me, Father."

"Ah—liss," breathed her father and made it sound like a caress.

Humbeline sat bolt upright and said, "Why, that's mother's name."

"Yes," said her father, "and the girl I've been describing, the one you reminded me of so forcefully, the one I loved then as I love now is your mother."

Humbeline gasped, then laughed aloud as she said, "Oh, you old tease! I thought you were letting me in on some intrigue. You fooled me. But how beautifully you speak of mother."

"I've been saying a few things about her daughter, too," said Tescelin with a smile. "Honestly, my Little Queen, you look just like your mother when I courted her. When I saw you praying there at the shrine I thought I was back at Montbar, twenty-two years ago, looking at Alice, my lovely Alice. Tell me, for whom were you just praying?"

"I was thanking St. Ambrosian for saving your life. Were you terribly sick that time, Father?"

"So sick, child, that I didn't know where I was, what I was, or if I was; and I didn't care."

"Tell me about it."

"We were coming back from Jerusalem...."

"Now, Father, that is no way to begin! Who are 'we,' and what were you doing in Jerusalem?"

"Oh, you want the whole story. Very well. It was 1075. The world was in a pretty messy state at the time and everyone was nervous, anxious and quite restless. I was just twenty-five years old and in the full lustihood of my young powers. Oh, how I was twisted and torn those days! England called to me, for William the Conqueror, one-time Duke of Normandy, had been crowned king there, and French knights were very welcome under the new regime. Excitement was promised aplenty, for the Saxons were holding on to old customs and their lands; fighting was common. At the same time Germany called to me, but for a very different reason. There young Henry IV was Emperor, and I would have given my right eye if I could but meet him in single combat. He was outraging the very name of nobility as he rebelled against

Hildebrand, the man who had tutored him when still a boy, and who but two short years before had been elected Pope.

"They were times that stirred the blood, Humbeline, and there was fighting on all sides. Even our own France was not perfectly peaceful; for many of her bishops and princes resented the Pope's decree against the awful conduct of the clergy. As I told you, Humbeline, my blood was hot; I wanted to fight, but I did not know with whom or against whom. Those were sad days, too, Little Queen, sad for the Church and for the State. Well, just at that time the Bishop of Langres, Raynard by name, asked me a question that changed my whole life. He saw the situation and he saw into my soul, so he very quietly asked me if I had ever thought of fighting for God. I didn't know what to answer. The question filled me with awe; it held such wondrous possibilities. The Bishop sensed my reaction, so he said, 'Let's fight Henry IV in the Holy Land. Let us fight for Hildebrand with the spiritual weapons of prayers and a pilgrimage. Let us do something for God, since so many seem intent upon doing all they can against Him.'

"I joined him, Humbeline. With a small group we made our way to the Sepulcher of Christ and prayed for His Body, which is the Church. It was the first bloodless battle that I had ever fought; but God was not going to leave me without a scar. No, indeed. So on our way back, as we were passing through Constantinople, I was seized with a fever. No one could do anything with it. It burned up my body, and my brain went wandering; but I did remember enough to call for a relic of St. Ambrosian. I don't know what happened after that. My companions say that they had despaired of my life; but the Bishop obtained a relic and applied it to my head. The next morning I was kneeling at the saint's shrine, saying what you were just saying—'Thank you.'"

"Were you completely cured?" put in Humbeline with a gasp.

"Completely, Little Queen. I felt rather weak, it is true; but we went on with our journey and every day I grew stronger. The relic was always in my possession, and it is there in the shrine now. Wasn't God good to me?"

"Was it because you had been good to Him, Father?"

"Oh, ho, I would that I could be good to God! But I know what you mean, Little Queen; and you are right. God never forgets a single effort. So every time that you kneel at this shrine you must do two things; you must say 'thank you' to St. Ambrosian for his cure, and you must also pray as I prayed in Palestine thirty-two years ago; pray for God's Church, Humbeline. All is not well with it yet. And pray for our princes and prelates; much depends on them."

"I shall, Father; but now tell me how did it feel to be on Mt. Calvary?"

"Oh, girl of mine, words can never tell that," said Tescelin and his tone was as solemn as a sacred chant.

"Well, you can tell me this, Father: why didn't you go with the Crusaders in 1098?"

Tescelin smiled a slow, sad smile, shook his head and said, "How I wanted to go! How I wanted to go!"

"What kept you back?" questioned Humbeline.

Tescelin looked at her intently, then broke into a pleasant chuckle as he said, "A little queen with golden gleams in her raven black hair, and star radiance in her eyes. A little queen whom most people call 'Humbeline,' but whom I am often tempted to call 'Alice.' She kept me back. My heart prompted me to go, but stern duty said, 'Stay!'—Are you sorry?"

"Of course not, Father. Whatever you do is right. But I have often wondered. Show me the scar God gave you for your pilgrimage."

"I have just shown it to you, child. It is in my memory, a scar that will never fade. You know, Little Queen, scar tissue is always tougher than ordinary tissue; that is why I say that the scar God gave me at Constantinople will never fade. It is deep and jagged and very, very tough. I am ever mindful of the fact that He almost called me home when I was but twenty-five. I wouldn't have had much to show Him, would I?"

"I don't know, Father."

"Well, at least I wouldn't have had you, nor that other girl that looked so like you; nor any of the boys."

"Are we going to help you get to heaven?"

"More than my pilgrimage, my title or estates! In fact, Humbeline, if I don't get to heaven by what I have done with you and for you, I'm afraid that I'll never get there at all. For, you see, the only ladder to heaven that I know of, outside of Jacob's ladder, is the ladder of stern duty. I've always tried to climb that; and you and the boys are the solid rungs. Or to put it another way: I look on life as another pilgrimage. My first was to the earthly Jerusalem; my second is to the heavenly one. And just as my companions saved my life by obtaining a relic of St. Ambrosian in the first, so will my companions in the second save my soul. Do you know my companions, Humbeline?"

"The girl with the name like an exclamation and a sigh, six boys who are often rough and rowdy, and a little queen."

"Good for you! And what must the Little Queen do here at the shrine?"

"Thank St. Ambrosian for giving my mother my father, and pray for the Church."

"Excellent!" exclaimed Tescelin. "You are an apt scholar. I wish that I could say the same for all of your brothers."

"Surely you're not thinking of Bernard," said Humbeline. "He is the leader of his whole school."

"No," laughed her father, "I was thinking of Gerard. But I must leave you now; the Duke is waiting for me. Put your lesson into immediate practice, for, today, I have to judge a case concerning the Church. Pray that I do it rightly." With that he kissed his daughter, whispered, "Alice—Humbeline—my Little Queen," and was gone.

The Duke Rages

Some ten hours after Tescelin had kissed his daughter and whispered her name so lovingly, the Duke of Burgundy was heard in angry outburst and the name most frequently on his lips was Tescelin the Tawny. It was early evening; the ducal household was quietly completing the tasks of the day, but in the Duke's private council room nothing was quiet. The Duke was pacing the floor like a caged lion and, addressing no one in particular, was saying, "I like men who are upright; but I don't care for men who are so upright that they bend backwards. I believe in having clean hands; but that doesn't mean that you have to scrape off the skin. I know that honesty pays; but that doesn't mean that I have to go destitute; and that is just what I'll be if that Tescelin the Tawny keeps on giving decisions against me. That man hasn't got a tender conscience; he's got a bashful one. It pales at the very idea of partiality and blushes at the mere mention of favoritism. The goddess of justice may have been blindfolded and even-handed, but she can meet one more blindfolded and more even-handed in the Lord of Fontaines."

"But, Your Excellency, it is only a question of a few fields. After all, the monks need the land and the tithes therefrom," said Seguin of Volnay soothingly.

"I'd give them the fields and the woods; I'd give them the tithes and the harvests. It is not those things that bite, Seguin. No! It's losing a battle; and with your own Counsellor as judge. That's what hurts! Didn't I practically found that Abbey of St. Benignus de Dijon? Didn't my father, Odo I, and my uncle, Hugh I, after whom I am named, give and give and give to the Church? No, Seguin, understand me clearly. It's not the lands that I mind losing; it's the battle. And I blame Tescelin the Tawny. He's too straight!"

"Well," Ranier the Seneschal soothed, "there's a way to end that, Your Excellency. Tescelin was not born a member of your council, nor does he have to die such."

"Humph," grunted Hugh, "that's a brilliant bit of advice. Get rid of one of the bravest warriors the Duchy ever knew, a knight who seemingly knows no fear but the fear of God; get rid of the deepest man in the whole realm, a man who sees as keenly as an eagle—and why? Just to keep a few fields I never use or collect some tithes I don't need! No, Ranier, it won't do. Tawny-beard stays in the council, but I wish I could keep him off the judge's bench, or at least get him to bend a fraction of an inch. He's too honest!"

Ranier laughed as he said, "Your Excellency, you remind me more of your uncle than you do of your father. Hugh I always wanted to 'eat his cake and have it, too.' It can't be done, my Lord. If you want Tescelin for a warrior and a counsellor, you've got to take him as judge. If you will have his fearlessness and his longsightedness, you will also have to take his unbending honesty."

"Ah, but that's my complaint," growled the Duke, "his honesty does bend; it bends backwards! Couldn't you have given me the decision today? Wasn't it all but a matter of a mere technicality? Couldn't you have arranged to have said that I was right in the past but that for the future the monks of St. Benignus de Dijon could have the lands and the tithes? Couldn't you?"

"I could have, but I'm not Tescelin."

"Aren't you honest?"

"Yes, but with a touch of the sycophant. Tescelin is not. You say he bends backwards; I understand you, but I envy him! Would that I could be so utterly independent of men that I would look, as Tescelin always looks, only at God. He's always been that way, Your Excellency. He was that way with your father before you, and with your uncle before him. Tescelin has been that way since first I knew him, and that was when he was hardly more than a boy, just back from the Holy Land. Tawny-beard is all that you say he is, Your Excellency; he's brave, fearless, straightforward, far-seeing, deep. But you haven't said all, nor have you said half. And what you have omitted, many miss—Tescelin is holy!"

The Duke stopped in the middle of his stride, looked at Ranier sharply, then almost shouted, "By heavens, you're right! And it is that which makes him different. He's as quiet and controlled in that as he is in everything else except battle; but when I reflect on his shrine to St. Ambrosian, his pilgrimage to Jerusalem, his unwavering honesty almost to hostility, and his devotion to his family—there's only one explanation, and you have given it. There's more gold to Tescelin than his hair and beard! And still I must say that I wish he weren't quite so honest when I am defendant in a case."

The council room rang with laughter as Seguin and Ranier appreciated their liege lord's predicament and contradictory sentiments.

"Laugh," said the Duke, "go on and laugh; but you won't change me, and I won't change Tescelin. I'm a poor loser and he...well, I'll use your word, Ranier, he's holy. So let's drink a toast to the holy one who serves his duke so well that he makes him mad."

They drank the toast, and amid the jests and laughter, Hugh II of Burgundy regained his noisy, good-natured self.

Silver Jubilee

It was several years later that the castle of Fontaines stood silhouetted one night, against a blue-black and silver-spangled sky. From within but one single light shone. The night was deep and its quiet was broken only by the long, low howl of a distant dog as it bayed the moon. The looming outlines of the castle seen beneath the light of that high moon seemed to speak of confident strength and promise substantial peace. There was that about it that made it seem like a living thing. Beneath the one light that shone within, sat Tescelin the Tawny and his wife, Alice of Montbar. They had just celebrated their silver anniversary, and now, as the high moon walked her silver way in the blue-black sky, they were enjoying the echoes of the day and the memories of the years.

"Does it seem twenty-five years to you, Alice mine?" asked Tescelin.

"No; nor like twenty-five months," came the speedy reply. "And yet," she went on, "it seems that it has always been, that never was there any other life but this one here in the castle with you, the boys and Humbeline. I know that that sounds contradictory," she laughed, "but it really isn't. You see, sometimes it seems like yesterday that my father told me that you had asked for my hand; but then, when I think of my little ones, it seems that I never had any other life or any other love."

"What you are saying, Alice, is that you have become 'all mother'; that girlhood is but a vague and very misty memory; and I can readily understand that. Your girlhood was short; you were a mother almost before it had ended. You were only fifteen, you know, when we married. It does seem but a short while ago, doesn't it?"

"Like yesterday, Tescelin; and yet, when I look at Humbeline and reflect that I was the mother of Guy and Gerard at her age, I begin to think that I am very old."

Tescelin chuckled as he said, "Well, what does that make me? I was more than twice your age when we married; if you are ancient now, I must be some sort of an antique. But no, Alice, God has been good to both of us. To me you look as lovely today as you did twenty-five years ago."

"Yes, but you're looking through lover's eyes; my mirror tells me a more truthful story. But as you say, God has been very good to us. Tell me, Tescelin, do you worry as much about God's world today as you did twenty-five years ago?"

"Every bit, Alice. It has not mended any. Do you remember what happened the year we were married?"

"You mean the death of Hildebrand?"

"Yes, and all that led up to it and all that followed. I used to fret in those days and worry about the Pope. I had reason to. Think of it! Christ's vicar had to die in exile, driven there by those who called him 'Holy Father.' Think of that ingrate Henry IV. Hildebrand did all that a father or a mother could do for that man, and yet look at the return the ingrate made. Oh, the sacrilege of it all! To have the satanic arrogance to dethrone the Pope and set up a creature of his own. My blood boils even as I think of it."

Alice smiled a little as she said, "I'm afraid the Lord of Fontaines has not learned his lesson yet. You are no better today at looking at the whole picture than you were twenty-five years ago. What a dull pupil you make; or is it that I am a poor teacher?"

"Oh, I know. I know," answered Tescelin quickly. "You say that God always balances things, and you're right. Hildebrand had his Countess Matilda of Tuscany, a second Deborah if ever there was one, while at the same time, a Peter Damien in Italy, a Lanfranc in England, a Stephen of Muret, a Hugh of Cluny and a Bruno with his companions and Chartreuse in this our own land told us clearly that man had not entirely forsaken God, nor had God abandoned the world to its wickedness. But I suppose that we could take up our argument just where we began twenty-five years ago and get just as far as we did then. We never decided who was looking at the shadows and who at the lights, did we?" He smiled as he said it and her returning smile was one of complete understanding. Then he added, "There is consolation though, in looking at the whole picture, Alice; but I still hold that more immediate harm comes from the actions of sinners than good from the actions of saints. Why, look, for one who is ready to imitate Bruno and his Carthusians, I find two hundred, if not two thousand, to imitate our King and his wantonness."

"Look at the highlights!" cried his wife. "Philip was a disgrace to nobility. That is unquestionable. He was every bit as bad, if not worse than Herod of old. But look at the balance! Philip puts away his lawful wife and steals for himself the wife of the Count of Anjou, but immediately there rises up a second John the Baptist in the person of Yvo of Chartres. Philip showed the beast that lurks in man, Yvo showed the angel. And despite what you say about your two hundred or your two thousand, I maintain that the universal protest that arose against the King shows how good can come from evil."

"I wish that I could catch your optimism, Alice; but even when I look at the whole picture I get scared. Perhaps I'm not spiritual enough, for although I see God's balancing in England, I fear that things are still off balance in that land. William Rufus plunders the property of the Church and almost immediately there arises an Anselm. 'Balance,' you say. But I say, 'off balance'; for while Anselm had to go into exile, Rufus still reigns."

"Oh, Tescelin, you're as nearsighted as ever! One saintly man is worth a hundred or a thousand of your monarchs. Anselm will be influencing people to do good, when your Rufus is no more than a very, very dim name in history. You live too close to sovereigns, Tescelin; you think them all-powerful. They are not! They make a lot of noise, but so does a hollow drum. They cause quite a commotion, but so does a passing wind."

"Yes, my dear," quickly countered her husband, "but I have known hollow drums that summoned devastating armies, and passing winds that leveled whole countrysides."

"If so, it was the will of God; and where those armies devastated cities, civilizations flourished again; and where those winds leveled there came a new growth."

"But what if the winds and the armies persist?"

"They won't."

Tescelin laughed at his wife's positive statement and said, "We're back just where we were twenty-five years ago. We come to a certain point and you no longer discuss, you assert; and that ultimate assertion is always— God. And, of course, you are perfectly right, Alice; the last word is always—God. But, my dear, in all seriousness, I do fear for His Church. Oh, I know that the gates of hell shall not prevail; but they can and they do cause a lot of damage. The Church will remain; we have God's word for it; but what we haven't got His word for is in what state it will remain. And that is what gives me concern.

"At this very moment things, to my eyes, are in as bad a state as they were under Hildebrand. Henry V of Germany is every bit as arrogant as was Henry IV, and I predict suffering for Pascal II every iota as sacrilegious as that inflicted on Gregory VII. Henry I of England is a menace. That man is a calculating, scheming politician. I wouldn't trust him as far as I could throw him. And here in France.... Well, I only hope that the combination of Louis VI and Philip I will be less bad than was the reign of Philip alone; but I have only loose and shifting sands on which to base that hope. Sovereigns want too much power over the prelates of the Church. There's the trouble. This matter of lay investiture is a scandal."

"If you ask me," put in Alice, "I'd say that the trouble lay in the Holy Roman Empire, that thing which is not an empire, by no means Roman, and most certainly not holy. But what was it that we decided just about twenty-five years ago tonight? Didn't we find a way to change the whole world?"

Tescelin stopped, looked at his smiling wife, thought a bit, then laughed as he said, "I remember. We decided that there was a way to change the whole world and that was by changing ourselves. We determined on the cardinal principle that the soul of all reformation is the reformation of the individual soul. We decided that God had placed us in this tiny speck of the universe that we call Fontaines, for the one purpose of making that tiny speck beautiful for Him. Yes, Alice, I remember. I have never forgotten. And yet, I must think of those other tiny specks."

"Yes, but you think about them too much. Pray more for them and you'll be more peaceful."

"You win," laughed Tescelin. "You always have. What you say is true. I should pray more; and I have noticed that Humbeline is taking after her mother."

"Yes, and most of the boys are taking after their father. You're bringing up a fine family of knights, when I wanted priests or prelates."

"Doesn't your balance work both ways, Alice? Mustn't there be a hundred or a thousand knights to one saintly soul?"

"Not in the one family," answered Alice. "But I'm not complaining. I'm really proud of Guy and Gerard; and I'm sure that Andrew will win his knighthood early. But Bernard belongs to me."

"Don't be too sure of that," said Tescelin. "He's not robust, but he has a more daring spirit than any of the rest. Further, the way he is winning honors at school, sometimes makes me wonder."

"Well, don't go putting ideas into his head. Leave that to me. You've left most of it to me for the last twenty-five years. Don't stop now. Bernard is mine. You can have the rest."

"And I suppose you call that balance," teased her husband.

"Indeed I don't," answered Alice. "I'm cheating. You don't know the fire that burns in the soul of that boy. Train your knights; they'll be worthy of you. But leave me my boy."

"Well, if Bernard has fire," said Tescelin, "I know where he got it; it is not all from the Lord of Fontaines; the little Lady of the castle has a spark or two. All I say now about Bernard is: God's will be done."

"And I say, do it!" put in Alice quickly. "Everything about him shows where God wants him."

Tescelin looked at his little wife admiringly. "Twenty-five years have not changed you a bit; and I thank God for it!"

"Yes and I say 'Thank God' for the twenty-five years."

"Before I join you in that prayer, Alice," said Tescelin, "I want to ask you a very personal question."

"What is it?" said his little wife.

"This: Twenty-five years ago I rode to Montbar and asked your illustrious father, Bernard, if I could have you for my own. He hesitated; shook his head; then said, 'I don't know. I think that she belongs to God. I had intended her for the convent.' Tell me honestly, on this our twenty-fifth anniversary, are you sorry that your father changed his mind?"

Alice did not answer immediately. She closed her eyes, folded her hands on her lap and allowed her head to bow forward. It was as if she were trying to look into the depths of her heart. She stayed in this posture for what seemed a very long time to Tescelin, but actually was only a minute; then her head came up, her eyes opened wide, large, blue, beautiful eyes, with tall candles aglow in their depths; then her arms opened, and she walked over and embraced her husband.

"For twenty-five years," she said, "I have been just where God wanted me to be, doing just what He wanted me to do; could I be other than happy? I am positive that it is the will of God that I love you and rear your children and His. Tawny Tescelin of Fontaines, I am happy this moment and have been happy for every moment of the twenty-five years that have fled, happy that my father changed his mind, for I am sure that that was the will of God." They embraced on the last word. It was a young lovers' embrace. "Tescelin, I hear your heart. I wonder if it can spell me a riddle," Alice said, holding her raven head against her husband's breast.

"It will try," said Tescelin softly.

"Then tell me why they celebrate such gloriously golden years by a jubilee that they call silver."

"That's what I call Alice of Montbar's delicate tribute, and my heart says, 'Thank you.' Now, my little lady, off with you to the land of dreams; and may they be golden on your silver jubilee!"

Can't You Pray?

Eight years later Tescelin was again seated 'neath a solitary light; but this time it burned in the castle of the Duke of Burgundy, not Fontaines; while across from him sat, not Alice, but the noisy and somewhat angry Hugh II.

"But, Tawny, you're too old for that sort of thing," growled the Duke. "Your decision makes me think that you are getting childish."

"Well, Your Excellency," answered Tescelin with a laugh, "did not our Lord say something would happen to us if we all did not become like little children?"

"Yes," came the quick and gruff reply, "but He wasn't talking about second childhood! It's simplicity that He wants, not senility; and senility is all that I can see in this act of yours. Come, be yourself!"

"Isn't it strange, my Lord, that you should make use of the very expression my boy, Bernard, used? His answer to every objection and his final exhortation was, 'Come, be yourself!'"

"That Bernard of yours has caused me more trouble in the past five years than a besieging army. He began by taking thirty of my best men to Citeaux. Since then my Duchy has gone fanatic; every knight that was or was-to-be goes to Citeaux, Clairvaux, or one of their filiations. Now he's taking you, my best counsellor. When and where will he stop? Will it be my turn next?"

There was an undercurrent of humor in Tescelin's voice as he made answer saying, "Hugh I ended his days at Cluny; why shouldn't Hugh II go to Clairvaux?"

"Because it's madness! That's why. Sheer madness. Come, Tescelin, you're almost seventy years old. What can you do at the Abbey?"

Tescelin arose at that question, clasped his hands behind his back, and started to pace up and down in front of Burgundy's Duke. "Your Excellency," he finally said, "I'm going to tell you a story. Don't interrupt unless you have to. As you say, I'm almost seventy years old. I've had a full life, a long life, a happy life. Oh, there have been shadows and sorrows and bitter disappointments; but looking at it whole and entire, it has been happy. I was born of noble parents; for that I have to thank God. From my father I received my strength of body and from my mother, Eva of Grancy, whatever piety of soul I had. When I was twenty-five, I saw the Sepulcher of Christ and stood on Mount Calvary. That does something to a person, Your Excellency. Life looks a lot different after that. On my way back from the Holy Land I almost died of fever. I was cured by a relic of St. Ambrosian. And let me tell you, *that* does something to a person!

"You know, Your Excellency, we men of nobility and prowess at arms become very self-sufficient; we practically forget that we are dependent beings. A skirmish with death or a visit to the place where God died makes one think differently. Well, these two telling experiences had hardly settled in my soul when I married an angel, if ever earth held one. She taught me more practical piety than even my pilgrimage had. Alice of Montbar, my Lord, was a soul of burning Faith. She saw the world and all things in the world through eyes that you and I and the rest of us seldom use; she saw everything in the light of Faith, everything as part of God's plan. Nothing could disturb her, for every happening was somehow or other a 'coming of Christ' to her. Constant contact with such a person does much to a man. She made my life different. She made me different."

Tescelin paused in his talking, but not in his pacing. After making two turns of the room he resumed his narrative in a lower tone but one that had a more gripping ring to it. "She died young," he said. "Alice was only forty when she left us. That hurt, Your Excellency, hurt much; hurt deep in the dark of night and in the sunlit glory of day. It still hurts. They say, 'Time heals all wounds'; maybe they are right; but let me tell you that it takes a long, long time for some wounds. Understand me, my Lord, I'm talking about loneliness, not about lack of resignation. I know that it was God's will that she go when she did; I was resigned then, and have ever been. But resignation does not fill the void. No, indeed! And yet, God does balance things. I had a replica of Alice in Humbeline; she acted like her, looked like her, almost thought like her. Then a vision of a stirring old age was given me as I saw my older sons win knighthood. First Guy, then Gerard, and then young Andrew. I thought that my down-going years would be spent amidst the clatter of hoofs and the clash of armor as my lads did all that I had done and more. But you know what happened. Bernard took every one of them. Think of that, my Lord, every one of them! And I was left with a castle that was filled with empty echoes. Don't you think that that hurt?"

Again Tescelin stopped talking but kept pacing. Suddenly, however, he stopped short before the Duke's chair and said, "Now, Your Excellency, let me tell you something. I have had what many will call 'a blessed life.' And why? Because I was nobly born, given tremendous estates, won a lovely wife, have always been fortunate in battle, had the high favor of my liege Lord and a family that was a credit. But, Your Excellency, these people do not know the real blessings of my life. No! But I'll tell you, and 'I'll say that the greatest blessings that I ever received were those that most people would call sorrows! I can thank God for much, my Lord, but I can never thank Him enough for beating me to my knees, putting tears in my eyes and tears in my heart, and forcing me to say,

'Thou art the Lord God of all.' Your Excellency, there is nothing in the whole wide world that will make us realize what we are, that we are only tiny, dependent creatures of God—there is nothing, I say, like sorrow"; and with that he brought his fist down on the table before the Duke of Burgundy's face.

After a little pause he went on saying, "Five years have passed since Bernard and the boys went to Citeaux. They have been the longest and loneliest five years of my life; and yet, perhaps the most profitable. Ah, my Lord, there is nothing like solitude to mother thought. My huge, empty castle has been a solitude to me and the big thought that it has brought forth is this: Life is only to get close to God; nothing else matters!"

He paced the length of the room again, then said, "Well, to come to my point. You know that Bernard was at Fontaines a short while ago. You likewise know that he preached a very powerful sermon on hell. But what you don't know is that he and I had a long talk in which I told him much that I have just told you. His reply was that God was calling me to the cloister. I was not exactly startled, but I did object and objected on the very grounds you have objected this evening. 'What can a man of seventy do in the Abbey?' Do you know his answer?"

"What was it?"

"He answered with a single question. He looked at me and said, 'Can't you pray?'"

Tescelin let the three words have their effect on the Duke before he went on by saying, "Without waiting for reply he said, 'A child of seven can lift its heart and mind to God; I suppose a man of seventy can do the same. We have plenty of strong, young workers; we can make use of more old, ardent prayers. Martha got dinner for our Lord, but Mary chose the better part.' Then, my Lord, he said a thing that has given me food for thought ever since; it is the most helpful truth that I have meditated in months, aye, in years; it is the most inspiring fact that I have thought on all my life. He said, 'There is no such thing as a useless old man in God's wide world! God never does a useless thing. He does not give life to one who is useless; as long as man breathes, God has a special use for him!' Isn't that but common sense, my Lord? And yet, how often do we look upon people, especially old people, as useless! We're all wrong. God never gives life to one who is useless! So you see why I go to Clairvaux— I am not useless and I can pray."

The Duke was greatly impressed by Tescelin's manner and message. He watched his Counsellor's every move and grasped his every word. The last sentence struck him so forcefully that he started visibly. But before he could speak, Tescelin resumed his story with, "And now, Your Excellency, one last reason. All my life I have had a great concern for God's Church; and all my life my heart has ached because of what princes have done to that Church. Hence, it was like my own heart speaking when my boy said, 'Come to Clairvaux and pray for God's Church; come and weep for sinners.' There, my Lord, in very brief is why an old man of seventy goes to the Abbey to become a lay brother. It's not loneliness for my boys; it is love for my God. My arms are weak. My step is slow. But my heart and my mind can be lifted up to Him; and that is prayer. I will not be useless. I'll do penance and I'll pray. That will be giving glory to God, and to give Him glory is the only purpose for existing. Can a man of my years make any other answer to the sharp, short, inspiring question, 'Can't you pray?'"

The Duke's whole demeanor had changed as Tescelin spoke. He had never seen his Counsellor so animated or deeply serious before, nor had he ever heard him speak with such force and feeling. He arose at Tescelin's last question, put out his hand and said, "Give me your hand, Tawny, and let me say that I feel favored by God to have known you. Go, by all means, go! I'll take care of your estates as you have outlined and I'll look after Humbeline as if she were my own daughter. Go and serve me in a new way. Pray for me. And tell your boy, Bernard, that his question, 'Can't you pray?' and his remark that no creature is useless mean much to me. I shall never forget them." With that, two noblemen clasped hands and said more by the pressure of fingers and the light in their eyes than they had with their lips.

Death on the World's Most Bitter Battlefield

Just two years from the time Tescelin and Hugh of Burgundy parted, Gerard, the man of one idea, was found kneeling beside the heaped up mound of a freshly filled grave. Standing across from him and watching his every move was Geoffrey de la Roche, the Prior of Clairvaux. Gerard had been kneeling statue-like for some time; his eyes alone moved; they wandered from iron cross at the head of the grave to the dank dirt that formed the mound. Suddenly he flung himself full length on the grave, kissed the cross and the mound and broke into a heartbroken sob as he moaned, "Forgive me, Father, for ever thinking that you could be a coward." Tears flowed fast and the stern, ascetic monk was but a boy again. The Prior had been waiting for something like this. He moved now, bent down, put his hands on the shaking shoulders and said, "Come, Gerard, come to my room and tell me all about it."

Hardly had they entered the room when Gerard broke out again and sobbed, "I'm not crying in sorrow, Geoffrey; I'm crying in shame. It's not for my father I weep; it's for myself. Think of it! One time I said that he was a coward. Oh, what sort of a fool was I? He told me that I'd understand one day, and I'm telling you, this is the day!" Geoffrey wisely waited for the deeply moved man to tell his story in his own way. Gerard went on, "You've seen him for two full years, Geoffrey; he was regular, wasn't he?"

"Most regular," came the reply.

"Would anyone, who did not know, suspect that this aged lay brother known as Tescelin was the father of Clairvaux's Abbot and the father of five others in the community?"

"Never."

"Have you ever thought what that meant, Geoffrey? My father, who had commanded hundreds all his life, who was Counsellor and intimate friend of Burgundy's Duke, who was Lord of Fontaines and all its dependencies, took orders from his boys! Geoffrey, that calls for heroism. We can all get used to the demands of our vow of poverty, and find no great difficulty in observing our vow of chastity; but who is there, who calls himself a man and has had any experience, who will not admit that he feels an almost instinctive rebellion against obeying a fellow man?"

"It is the surging of our innate independence," agreed Geoffrey.

"Yes, and how it surges when the one who commands is in many respects your equal! What must it have cost my father, then, to have obeyed his boys? Geoffrey, it's miraculous."

"It is," put in the Prior, "and I say that, not because he is your father, but because I know something of his life before he came here. Contrast his last two years with any other years of his life and you'll have more reason to exclaim. Think of it, Gerard, your father rose at two A.M.—and why? Only to praise God. He worked on the farm and with the cattle for long hours at a stretch—and why? Why should he, who had been lord, knight and counsellor, soil his hands and weary his back at such menial labors? Why? Only to praise God. He kept silence almost the whole day through, was satisfied with the poorest of clothing and the plainest of food—and why?

"Why should Tescelin, Lord of Fontaines and favorite of the Duke, spend his old age doing the seemingly foolish thing of wearying his body with hard work and denying it all the niceties of life, resting it on a hard bed for only a few hours and refreshing it with only the plainest of plain vegetables? Why? Why? Why?—Only to praise God! What an inspiration he has been to all of us! Manuscripts and books are good to help us on to sanctity; the voice of the living teacher is better, but for real results give me the sight of an old warrior going through the routine of the day with the light of love in his eyes and a song in his heart, that is best of all! And that, Gerard, was your father."

"Thank you, Geoffrey," said Gerard as he wiped away the tears. "I am his son; naturally I would admire him, but to have you pay the tribute that I feel is his due, consoles me greatly. He was a warrior, every inch of him. And his last two years proved it more conclusively than his sixty-eight preceding. He died on what I am coming to consider the world's most bitter battlefield, where man must conquer not only the world and the devil, but also and especially himself. My father told me that there was a greater conquest than that of vanquishing a foe who comes at you from without, clad in armor and armed with steel. He proved that to me the past two years. But what I am ashamed of, Geoffrey, and what I will be eternally ashamed of is the fact that one day I thought him a coward. I was young then. I didn't know what bravery was. I have learned since, for I have learned what it takes to prove your love for God. My father has taught me well; I must live worthy of such a sire. He told me that he'd teach me a deeper loyalty and a greater love. He has. It is love for God that makes the life of a man great, and makes a man live greatly. My father had it."

There was a new light in Gerard's eyes as he said it and Geoffrey was glad that he had waited at the grave. This interview had made an admirer out of a grieving man. Gerard left then to seek out his brother Bernard; and as the door closed on his retreating form, Geoffrey said, "Yes, your father had it; and without any fear of error I say, 'like father, like son.'"

Can you blame the grateful and ever appreciative Order of Citeaux for calling this grand old warrior "Venerable"?

The Mother
Who Became a Saint

"Blood tells...."

Abbot Jarenton, seeing that the discussion was leading to no conclusion, decided to change the subject; but Abbot Frederic, who wanted finality to every discussion, decided that the subject should not be changed. And yet, since he was only a guest at St. Benignus de Dijon, and of no long acquaintance with Abbot Jarenton, he had to employ all his mastery in the art of conversation so that he might appear to be gracefully yielding to his host when in reality he was stubbornly maintaining his point. Frederic was adroit, but Jarenton had lived too long with men not to see through his maneuverings, and had too great a sense of humor not to lend himself to Frederic's game. So the discussion went on even though they talked of other matters.

It was amusing to one, engrossing to the other; no spider and fly, or cat and canary ever watched one another more carefully than did these two abbots as they talked about the weather, the crops, prelates, princes and the ruling powers, yet all the while discussed sanctity. Frederic had claimed that it was almost entirely the work of God; that the saints were His special favorites whom He deluged with such grace that they could hardly be other than what they were; while Jarenton insisted that every son of Adam and every daughter of Eve had it in them to be saints if they would only pay the price.

Frederic was German, physically and mentally; hence, with his painstaking, systematic, ponderous and almost plodding way of thinking and talking, he formed a sharp contrast to the vivacious, quick-brained and quick-tongued Frenchman, Jarenton. The discussion had filled the best part of the morning, and during it they had balanced scripture text with scripture text, saint with saint, and example with example. Frederic had no sooner triumphantly quoted, "For it is God who works in you both to will and to accomplish," than Jarenton good-naturedly countered with, "Yes, but don't forget the preceding verse and the one that follows; both are imperatives! And if I remember rightly the preceding one goes, 'Work out your salvation with fear and trembling,' and the succeeding one reads, 'Do all things without murmuring.'"

Frederic then tried to sum up his whole case in the single line of St. Paul, "I am what I am by the grace of God"; but Jarenton had asked him to recall the rest of that very verse, "and his grace in me has not been void, but I have labored more abundantly than all of them." The French abbot got great relish from that retort and laid a heavy accent on the words, "I have labored." Frederic let him have his enjoyment, but then paid him back in his own coin by asking, "And how does that verse end? Is it not something like, 'yet not I...' do you hear, my Lord Abbot? 'Yet not I...but the grace of God with me.'"

It was all done with charming gracefulness. Two keen minds were fencing; and it had been parry and thrust, thrust and parry, the whole morning through. Saint had been countered with saint; John the Baptist was leveled off by St. Peter, the Apostles who had answered the call by the rich young man who had walked away sad. As soon as Frederic would point out the Pelagian tendencies in Jarenton's tenets, the Frenchman would remind his guest of the Manicheans. When Frederic asked if man was to determine Almighty God, Jarenton asked if God was to destroy His creatures' free will. To end it all Jarenton said, "Come, let us go over to see the church." Frederic arose, but while heading for the door said, "The church where souls are sanctified by God through His sacraments."

"Yes," laughed Jarenton, "the church where souls sanctify themselves by receiving the sacraments and praising their God."

The discussion knew a little lull as the Abbot of St. Benignus pointed out the many beauties of his church. Perhaps it would have known an ending had they not happened upon two serfs who stood talking before six statues of stone. Jarenton motioned to his companion to be silent, then led him to a little nook whence they could see and hear without being seen or heard. "Now listen," whispered Jarenton, "this ought to be good."

They waited but a moment, then the high, clear voice of the first serf came to them: "This third statue represents Bernard. He was no great hand with the lance or the battle-axe; but he had brains. He is the one who led the whole family into the cloister."

Frederic raised his eyebrows in question, and Jarenton answered with a nod of his head that said, "That's a fact." The German abbot listened more intently then as the serf went on.

"He was a marvelous boy and is a still more marvelous man. He took the cream of our nobility, thirty of the finest men of the Duchy, and led them to the monastery in the swamp at Citeaux. That was only the beginning. A few years later he was made Abbot of Clairvaux and at this moment has a valley crowded with monks. He has his whole family there—all these statues," he said as he waved his hand toward the six stone figures; "he has many of his near relations there; a whole swarm of knights and nobles, and so many serfs you can't count them. Why, he even had his father there! Yes, Tescelin the Tawny, Lord of Fontaines died just a few years back as a lay brother in the community at Clairvaux."

"His father!" gasped the second serf. "You mean the Duke of Burgundy's Counsellor?"

"I mean the Duke of Burgundy's Counsellor," said the first serf with an air of condescension and great complacency. "Oh, the boy is a wonder! Now this next statue is young Andrew; and what a promising lad he was! Think of it! He was knighted before he was seventeen. What a warrior he would have been. But he went with Bernard and he stayed with Bernard. This is Bartholomew; as lovable a lad as you ever laid eyes on. He had the build of his father, but the disposition of his mother. Everybody loved him. This last is Nivard; and to him I give more credit than to all the rest."

"Why so?" asked the second serf.

"Because he had better prospects than the others and more time to realize what he was giving up. You see, when all his brothers left he was heir apparent to all of Fontaines. Just think what would have been his—that grand castle up yonder is the smallest part of it. He would have had more land than you can run through in two days, serfs enough to make a colony, the friendship and favor of the Duke—why, he would have had everything that a man hopes for, works for and prays for. And yet, he went. Just as soon as he was old enough, he went."

"Do you think he was old enough to know what he was doing?" asked the second serf.

"Absolutely," came the flat reply. "He had two years in which to think it over. He wasn't any child. He was going on sixteen; and no son of Tescelin the Tawny ever reached that age without knowing that two and two make four. He knew what he was doing all right; and knew it even better than the others; for he had time to look at both sides of the fence. You see, he used to visit his brothers at Citeaux and saw what it was like there; and from what some friends of mine tell me, when at home he had to fight down the opposition of his father, who was constantly pointing out all that was to be his. Naturally Tescelin wanted some son of his to carry on the family name and keep up the estate."

Frederic again looked at Jarenton with those eyebrows of his asking questions, and received the same confirmatory nod as answer. The German abbot was all interest now; he was standing on tiptoe and in his anxiety to catch every single word was leaning far forward. Jarenton smiled.

"Well, there you are," said the first serf, "and there you are not; for the good Abbot Jarenton hasn't completed his job as yet. Two more statues belong here: one of Tescelin himself and the other of Humbeline, the only girl in the family. A real queen if ever there was one. You'd love her. She married Guy of Marcy, and the whole countryside proclaimed it as fine a match as could be made. But do you know where the good lady is at this moment?"

"No. I don't," came the reply.

"She is in the convent at Jully."

"What!" exclaimed the second serf. "After being married?"

"After being married," proudly echoed the first serf. "Now what do you think? Isn't what I told you true: isn't Dijon's greatest glory outside Dijon? Isn't the family of Fontaines something to talk about? Did you ever hear the like?"

"No, I must say I didn't. But I'm puzzled and you must help me. Here are six statues representing the six boys; you say that there should be two more: one for the father and one for the sister. All right. They are all religious, so I suppose their statues have some place in church. But will you tell me what she is doing here?" and he pointed to the tomb of the mother. "She was the only one who wasn't a religious. What place has she got in this church?"

"What place has she got in this church?" repeated the first serf in an indignant tone; then grunted, "Humph! I can see now, my good friend Clontof, why you are no great success at raising cattle. No wonder your master sent you here to learn something. Didn't you ever hear the saying, 'Blood tells'?"

"I did," said Clontof in a slightly offended air, "but I'd like to know what raising cattle and blood have to do with my question."

"Sure, man, if you only knew, it is your answer."

"Don't joke, Durtal, on such a holy subject and in such a sacred place."

"Joke? Joke? I was never more serious in my life. Your question astounds me. You say they have a place here because they are religious, but she hasn't a place because she wasn't one. Ah, Clontof, that's too much. Will you tell me where they got their religion? Don't you know that not only blue eyes, light hair and fair skin, but also cleanness of heart, of mind and of conscience, honor, virtue and valor come from parents? Don't you know that not only beauty of body, but also beauty of soul is a question of breeding? Don't you know that blood tells in religious matters as well as in all others? 'What is she doing here?' Why, man alive, if it weren't for her, they wouldn't be here! She mothered those six boys and that one girl I told you about. She was Tescelin the Tawny's wife and had much to do in making him the man he was. And you ask, 'What is she doing here?' That is not the intelligent question to ask. No! But looking at the six statues, the real man who knows anything about heredity would immediately ask, 'Who was their mother?'

"Heredity does not end with flesh and blood and physical characteristics. Never. It goes down through the flesh and blood into the mind and will of the soul. Spiritual heredity is a fact, Clontof, every bit as real as physical heredity. Of course," added Durtal in a calmer tone, "it's a puzzling business all told. For just as in many a fine litter you often find a runt, so, too, in many a fine family you'll find a black sheep. But that does not change the fact of spiritual heredity any more than the presence of runts keeps us from mating blooded stock."

"Do you mean to say that holiness is simply a matter of our sires?" asked Clontof in a tone that spelled not only incredulity but belligerency.

Durtal looked at him musingly, then quietly said, "My friend, if I put the best seed on the continent into bad soil, I won't get a bumper crop; but if I have the best soil in the world and put bad seed into it, you know what kind of a crop I'll get! Well, it is something like that with men. Some who have the best of parents turn out badly because of environment, company or neglect; but it calls for a miracle of the first class to take a child of wantonness and make him a holy man. Much, Clontof, very much is in the blood! I don't say all, but I do say much. I can graft a wild growth onto a good tree and it will assume many of the characteristics of that tree, but I can always detect the dash of wildness in the fruit."

"Are you saying that we are just like trees and cattle?" said Clontof in anger.

"No," laughed Durtal, "but I'll be saying some people are, if you keep on misunderstanding me! Here, my good fellow, let me put it this way: Bernard was a very beautiful boy. He had large, blue eyes, golden hair and a soft, smooth complexion. Now, where did he get them?"

"From his parents, I suppose," came the gruff reply.

"Good!" exclaimed the good-natured Durtal. "For his father was known as Tescelin the Tawny. He had golden hair and a golden beard. While his mother, Alice of Montbar, had the most beautiful eyes I have ever seen in a human face. Now I am going to tell you that Bernard had one of the fiercest, boldest, most daring of spirits you'd care to meet, while at the same time he was one of the most considerate, gentle and generous men the serfs of the land have ever seen. How do you account for those characteristics?"

"I don't know." This, a trifle sullenly.

"Do it the same way that you did for the eyes, hair and skin," said Durtal with a chuckle. "Just say, 'His parents,' and you'll be perfectly right; for Burgundy boasts no braver knight than was Tescelin the Tawny, while not only Fontaines but even Dijon will sing the praises of Alice, the generous Alice, for years to come. So if you want to know why the mother of these six is buried in this church, the answer is, 'These six!' For as God is God I'm sure that their holiness was due in great part to her.

"Ah, Clontof, she was a mother, let me tell you! She nursed every one of them at her own breast; and that is something very few noble women of our day do! I'm positive these children drew more than mere physical sustenance from such nursing. As they grew, her knee was their only school house. Just as she had refused hired nurses for their suckling days, so did she refuse hired tutors for their early years. Only when they were strong physically, mentally and spiritually, did she allow them to fare forth; and even then she kept a watchful eye on them. In short, Clontof, Alice of Montbar was a mother who believed that mothering ended only with death; and the greatest monument to her great mothering is not these six statues. No! The greatest is the dedications that these children made of themselves to God.

"These statues are here not because of the holiness of the ones that they represent, but because of the holiness of the one who begot them. Abbot Jarenton did not have them made to honor the son; he did it to honor the mother; and in that he was most right. 'By their fruits you shall know them.' But come, I see that the words of an old man like me have little effect on you; come, we will ask Angela, the little widow, and Joan, the little orphan, why Alice of Montbar is buried in the church of St. Benignus de Dijon. Come."

They left then, and Abbot Frederic turned to Jarenton, his eyes alight with eagerness and his voice vibrant with enthusiasm as he said, "Let's follow them."

Jarenton laughed softly and asked, "Aren't you afraid that Durtal will upset your theory on sanctity? He seems to say that it is not a question of God or of man, but of our mothers. But no, Frederic, we do not have to follow them. You can hear what Angela and Joan have to say over in my study. So let us have a little dinner first. Come."

God's Will Be Done

After dinner Jarenton saw that his guest was comfortably seated before he opened a large book that rested on his desk. He flicked over a few pages, found the place he wanted, then turned his chair so that he could look at Frederic and also at the book. When he had settled himself squarely he began, "Abbot Frederic, I enjoyed our little discussion this morning immensely. I can and have argued both sides of that case many times; sometimes I argue as you did, saying that the saints are God's favorites who have been deluged with extraordinary graces. A strong case can be made out for that thesis both from Scripture and by examples; and yet, in my heart of hearts I feel that the side I defended today is the truer side.

"In my very bones I feel that all of us have sufficient grace to be great saints if we would only cooperate with it. In inviting us to follow Him, Christ obligated Himself to give us the necessary strength to follow, and to follow not as did the Apostles at the time of the Passion—from afar—but as close as did the Cyrenean. Or as Bernard of Fontaines puts it, 'Close enough to catch up with Him.' Bernard well says that it will do us little good to follow unless we do catch up! But let that be as it may, you heard something new in church today, didn't you? What do you think of the theory of the serf?"

"About spiritual heredity?" asked Frederic.

"Exactly," answered Jarenton.

"Well," said Frederic, "I'd like to mull the matter over before making any absolute statement on it, but offhand, I'd say right now that there is much plausibility for it. If I inherit my physical characteristics, why not my spiritual ones? Some may say because the body alone is generated by the parents while the soul is created directly by God. And that is true. But still the interaction of soul on body and body on soul is so intimate that the serf may be right. Then there is the very patent fact that the adage 'like father like son' has been borne out again and again in the moral order as well as the physical. Warrior sons from warrior sires and virtuous maidens from virtuous mothers. It is a notion worth considering. I shall study it out in my own abbey amongst my own men. But Durtal, as he was called, gave me more than a notion this morning; he has piqued my curiosity to the breaking point. I want to know all about this Alice of Montbar who could draw such a eulogy from such a man. I would love to hear what the widow and orphan might have to say."

"I promised that you'd hear them, didn't I? Well, you will. But before you listen to them, listen to me. Abbot Frederic, I have been in religion a good many years as you know, and yet I can safely say that I learned more religion from this woman, Alice of Montbar, than I ever learned from masters of novices, abbots, religious instructors or pious books."

"That's either a glowing eulogy of the woman or a sad confession of a deplorable situation."

"Take it as the former," said Jarenton, "and let me tell you that I learned my lessons not from her lips but from her ways. The first and grandest truth she taught me was that while 'charity begins at home,' it does not end there. And that is one Christlike lesson we followers of Christ often miss. Here was a noble lady with a fairly large family and tremendous estates. She had serfs enough to engage the attention of two ordinary persons, and yet she was found almost daily in the crude cabins of Dijon's poor and at the bedside of Dijon's sick. Now realize, Frederic, that Dijon is a good three miles from the castle of Fontaines. You heard Durtal speak of the widow Angela and the orphan Joan. They are Dijon people. They are my parishioners; and here," he said as he flicked the pages of the book, "are five full pages of other orphans, widows, poor and sick who belong to my parish; and practically every one of them could tell you of Lady Alice's kindness and Christlike charity."

"You mean she would send them things?" put in Frederic.

"I mean that she would come herself. Ah," sighed Jarenton, "if we only knew how to act the part of Christ as this woman did! No dramatics. No show. No posing or pretention. But with a naturalness, an ease and a grace that rendered her every gesture lovely. You know, Frederic, there is no one prouder than the poor. How they resent pity! How they will spurn anything given them by

one who does it simply out of pity. It is a pride that I
hesitate to condemn, for it has its foundation in a just
appraisal of their innate nobility. They realize that they
are persons; and while they may be poor in the goods of
the world, they are possessed of an immortal soul and
are in all essentials equal to lord, baron, count or king.

"Indeed I don't condemn the noble pride of the poor.
Rather I say, 'May heaven bless them for it!' For when
fully analyzed it is but a consciousness that they are children of God and brothers of Jesus Christ. And yet, that
very consciousness can make things very embarrassing
for one who wants to help them. I have found giving aid
to the poor one of the most delicate duties of the minis-
try. To give without offending them is an art; and one
that I haven't mastered as yet. But I did see the perfect
mastery of it in this woman from Fontaines. Frederic, she
gave and gave and gave to the poor, and by some magic
had them receiving it all with pleasure. They never resented her donations. She had most of them feeling that
they were the donors; that they were the ones conferring
the favor and that they were giving Alice of Montbar
great happiness in allowing her to help them.

"Now that is what I call the genius and the ingenuousness of Christ. You know your Gospel, Frederic; you
know how Christ gave and gave and gave. One day it
would be strength of body and soundness of limb to pal-
sied and paralytic; another day it would be a clear skin to
a hideous leper; the next day maybe the revelation of
sunlight to the blind or of melody to the deaf, or perhaps
He would loose the tongue of the mute to the wonder of
speech. In very truth, 'He went about doing good'; and
the only ones who resented it were those who could have
alleviated the suffering of the poor and the sick, and did
not. The proud Pharisees and the scornful Scribes resented Him and His every work of mercy; but the out-
casts of humanity, the unfavored and the unfortunate

whom He befriended by His miracles of mercy never felt that He was condescendingly pitying them. He had the art of giving to such a degree that the recipient never felt embarrassed.

"And isn't it true today? He still gives and gives and gives; why, He even gives Himself! And does it in such a way that neither I, nor you, nor any other mortal, feels awestruck or self-conscious. I call it the divine art, and I say that Alice, the Lady from Fontaines, had it to perfection. Angela the widow would tell you how happy she made Lady Alice by allowing her to share her bereavement. Joan the orphan would tell you that she made Lady Alice very happy just by allowing her to dress her up in warm, clean clothes and to play with her doll."

"Play with her doll?" said Frederic in unbelief.

"Yes," came the answer, "play with her doll. That was part of her magic; she could act as a little child without ever losing her dignity. She could put everyone at their ease, be it man, woman or child. Why, I have heard of her cleaning the body, the bed and the whole cabin of one poor old soul who was practically helpless because of rheumatism. And from what they tell me that cabin, the bed and the body needed cleaning."

"Was she just naturally generous and sympathetic?" asked Frederic. "Many women are, you know. It is an instinct with them."

"That is very true, Frederic. And it may have been the case with Lady Alice. God may have endowed her with one of those sensitive and sympathetic natures and given her a natural tendency toward kindness. But let me tell you that she supernaturalized that nature and supernaturalized that tendency so that it would be and was divine charity."

"How do you prove that, Jarenton? That is a large statement."

"Germans are scientific, aren't they, Frederic? They like to have proofs for everything," Jarenton said good-naturedly. "Very well, I'll let little Joan prove my large statement for me. Joan is a lovable little thing. In fact, all Dijon claims her for sweetheart. She has an imagination that is ever on the rove, and is more romantic than any love-sick adolescent. One day she asked Lady Alice why she always came alone on her visits. 'Why don't you come attended by some handsome squire?' she asked. 'Or accompanied by some bold knight? Great, beautiful ladies should have great, beautiful escorts.' The Lady Alice smiled, took the little one on her lap and said, 'Sweetheart mine, I am escorted by the grandest Knight in all the world; One that you must come to know and love.' 'Where is he?' gasped the child. 'Right in here,' whispered Lady Alice, and pointed to her heart. Then she went on by saying, 'Joan dear, I go with God to do the work of God. I want Him alone to see it.' Of course, the child did not grasp the full significance of such a saintly remark, but she did have keenness enough to ask, 'What is the work of God?' And Lady Alice said, 'You, my child; you are the work of God, for whatever I do to you, the least of His little ones, I do to Him.'"

"That is a fair proof and I admire the deep piety of the woman," said Frederic with a thoughtful look. "But, Jarenton, I hope you won't be offended when I tell you that the eulogy given by Durtal in the church this morning impressed me more than what you have just told me."

"Offended?" laughed Jarenton. "Offended? I should say not. I'm delighted. For while I see sanctity in her truly heroic deeds of charity, and while these five pages," said he, pointing to the book in front of him, "could tell you much the same as Angela and Joan have been telling you, I know that many will see very little more than deep piety. Many discerning men put little trust in external works."

"Well," countered Frederic, "it is not that I distrust them. No indeed. For, 'Faith without good works is dead'; but I like to be sure that the good works have been prompted by Faith. That's the essential point, for as you know better than I, substantives weigh little in God's balance, while adverbs and verbs tilt those scales surprisingly."

"Nicely phrased," complimented Jarenton. "It is not what we do, but why; not how much, but how well; not how energetically, but how lovingly; not the mountains that we move, but the motive that urged us to move them. That is all most true, Frederic; but let us remember that we have to move the mountains; good intentions alone will avail nothing."

"I see that I have struck a favorite theme of yours," remarked the visiting abbot with a smile.

"More than a theme, Frederic; a truth and a guiding principle. One that I tell myself and my monks day in and day out. It is not our labors that God wants, but the love with which those labors are done; and I accent both words 'love' and 'labors.' But I put most of the accent on the love, 'For if I speak with the tongue of men and angels and have not charity.... And if I should distribute all my goods to feed the poor, and deliver my body to be burned and have not charity...'"

"...it profiteth me nothing," finished Frederic.

"Absolutely nothing," said Jarenton with emphasis. "But I can assure you that whatever Lady Alice did—and she did much more than any one individual in Dijon even suspects—was done with charity. I am not telling you about a pious soul, Frederic; I am talking just now about a saintly one; and the distance between piety and sanctity is infinite!"

"The more you talk, Jarenton, the more I see that you are a man after my own heart. I, too, hold that the difference between piety and sanctity is essential. Many say that it is only a difference of degree; I say, and you seem to say, that it is one of kind. I find the religious world well stocked with pious souls; I find very few saints."

"Agreed! But to be true to your thesis of this morning you will have to blame God for that situation, won't you?"

"Yes," answered the honest Frederic, "and that is the weakness of my thesis. You can blame man, and say that it is his fault for not cooperating with God's grace."

"I say that we are not sensitive enough to God's grace," broke in the Frenchman. "I think that our wills are good, but our intellects are not delicately enough attuned to catch the whispers of divinity; they are not actually sensitized so as to catch every ray of heavenly light that God throws upon them. I have found that most monasteries are filled with good will; but they are not filled with keen perception. It is not sluggishness of will that keeps us from being saints so much as it is slowness of the mind. That is why I am often tempted to stop these preachers who shout at you, 'Be men of prayer! Love God! Love Jesus! Be saints!' until they are blue in the face, and say to them, 'That is all I want to be and to do. My heart is ready. My will is right. Your duty is to tell me *how* to be a man of prayer, *how* to be a saint, *how* to love God and His Christ.'"

The corners of Frederic's lips twitched at his host's vehemence. "I know what you mean, Jarenton; and I know how you feel. But how about Alice of Montbar; did she preach as you would like?"

"Absolutely," came the flat reply.

"She did?" exclaimed Frederic.

"Yes, she did; and without ever saying a word. Frederic, she showed me how to be a saint by being a perfect mother."

"What do you mean?" asked his guest.

"This: the key to heaven, or if you prefer, the secret of sanctity is not in prayers or pious practices. Never. It is in doing the will of God with a ready will. And that sums up Alice of Montbar completely. She was convinced that it was the will of God that she be the wife of Tescelin the Tawny and mother to six boys and one girl; and as long as she lived she was just that, a wife and a mother, a perfect wife and mother, and all because such was the will of God in her regard."

"That's simplifying sanctity," said Frederic.

"Yes, and that's sanctifying simplicity," added Jarenton. "Oh, if the world would only learn what Alice teaches! If an abbot would only realize that for him sanctity consists not in being an abbot, but in being an abbot because being an abbot is the will of God in his regard; if monks would only realize that all they have to do to become saints is to be monks because being monks is the will of God in their regard; if fathers and mothers would only be fathers and mothers, not because of nature but because of grace and the God of grace, what a different world this would be, and what a different place heaven! But no! We abbots think that we must build big monasteries, make large communities, perform extraordinary penances and be shining lights by our exterior deportment. Monks are worse; and the laity almost entirely forget the supernatural element in their natural roles in life. It is lack of simplicity that shortens the roll call of the saints and swells the army of the mediocre. The little mother that raised the family of Fontaines teaches us all a tremendous lesson. Equivalently she says, 'Be yourself! For such is the will of God.' But how many of us are satisfied with being just ourselves?"

"Few, very few. We are always dreaming or planning, or wishing or hoping or even daring to be something or someone else."

"Precisely," put in Jarenton, "and that is why we get nowhere in the spiritual life with surprising rapidity. If God wants me to be a plowman, I'll never become a saint by aspiring to be a poet; and if He wants me to be a poet, the only way I'll ever become a saint is by being the very best poet I possibly can be. That is the lesson of the parable of the talents. We must work with what God gives us. If he has only given me one talent I'll never be excluded from heaven for not having ten, but for not having two! If God wants me to be an Abbot I'll never get to Him by dropping the pastoral staff in false humility and seizing a swineherd's stick. No, I must use that staff as my key to heaven; no other crook or stick or staff will unlock that gate for me. That's what we've got to learn and remember. It's burying our talents that ruins our lives, and striving to be what we were never meant to be that ruins our loves. In short, it's not being ourselves that prevents us from being saints; for that is being unsatisfied with the will of God in our regard."

"That is a lesson we seldom learn thoroughly," said Frederic.

"And yet it is glaring at us from every page of the Gospel," went on Jarenton. "Peter would never have become St. Peter had he striven to be as mild as St. Bartholomew or as delicately loving as St. John. No. He had to be Peter, the bold, blustering, bragging Rock. He had to love with a man's love, for that was the mold in which God had cast him. No tender embraces for him; no laying his head on the bosom of the Lord. Never! But a defiant burst of Faith in, 'You are the Christ, the Son of the living God,' an eager, enthusiastic reckless abandon in, 'Though I should die with you...' and the humble, heartbroken,

'You know all things, Lord; you know that I love you,' had to be Peter's road and he could walk no other and arrive!

"It's being what God wants us to be that makes us saints; fitting into the hole that He has fitted us for; square pegs belong in square holes, and salvation is attained by taking satisfaction in being just a square peg and fitting into our little square hole."

Surrender

"I wound you up," laughed Frederic.

"No. Say rather that Lady Alice taught me truth. She gave me the best exegesis of Scripture that I have ever received by attaining her high sanctity just by being a mother because that was the will of God for her. Ah, Frederic, the lesson that we miss is that Christ won salvation not by dying on the cross but by dying on the cross because crucifixion was the will of God in His regard. Once again, it is not what He did but why He did it. Salvation was not won for us by suffering, but by subjection, or if you will, by surrender to the will of God."

"Well said. But now show me how this all applies to Alice."

Jarenton started. He had been deep in his theme; deeper even than Frederic realized. The mention of Alice upset him for a moment; then in a burst of laughter he said, "May heaven bless you Germans. You certainly can stick to a point; and this time you have caught me just at the right point. 'Surrender' was the last thought that seized my mind and I can say that Alice of Montbar started her real life by a surrender, a complete and unqualified surrender to God. And that surrender gave her life's only real victory—sanctity."

Jarenton paused, but Frederic was too interested to be patient. "Go on," he said, "go on; tell me about it."

His host smiled. He saw that Frederic was not only being entertained, he was being thrilled. "Well," he went on, "Alice of Montbar was destined for the convent by her parents. To that end they had her educated as very few young ladies are educated. They wanted her to be ready to take her place in the convent beside the most cultured. Alice was a docile girl. Alice was an intelligent girl. She made marked progress in her studies. Then, like a bolt from the blue, her father announced that Tescelin the Tawny, Lord of Fontaines and Counsellor for the Duke, had asked for her hand and that he had given it.

"Alice surrendered! Without a murmur she surrendered. When asked in later years how she felt when her father made the announcement, she said, 'Like one from whom God was taking the heart.' That surrender cost that girl tremendously. When asked why she had made it so quietly her only answer was a question. She asked, 'What is the Fourth Commandment?' Twenty-five years after the event she made the statement that she was glad to do what she did because she was convinced that that was the will of God for her."

Jarenton paused before he summarized his first point. Frederic was watching him closely. "As you see, Frederic, Alice of Montbar started while still young to lead a simple life, a life that looked steadily at her polar star, the will of God."

"That's a good initial step," admitted the German abbot, "but I want a lot more before I'll beatify her."

"That's good sense, Frederic; but after the premises that I have laid down, don't expect extraordinary works. You won't get them."

"I don't want them," came the quick reply, "but I do want more than a consent to marry after having been destined for the convent."

Jarenton looked at the serious face of his guest. He was tempted to joke but he caught himself in time to say, "Won't you rephrase that, my Lord Abbot; won't you say, 'A ready surrender to God's will, even though that destroyed the plans of a lifetime'? You see, Frederic, I'm building my thesis on that one point. Alice was a saint not because she was a mother, but because she was a mother according to the will of God."

"Consider it rephrased and push on with your proof," smiled his guest.

"I'll be as summary as possible," said Jarenton. "Alice of Montbar went down to the gates of death seven different times without a whimper."

"Others have done as much. Some have done more. I know women who have borne ten, twelve and fourteen children," said Frederic coldly.

"Did they do it because it was the will of God? Did they look upon it as their God-given task in life, or did they accept it merely as the course of nature? Not *what*, Frederic, but *why* counts. Alice of Montbar knew what childbearing meant. She knew that she was going to suffer, and suffer intensely; but she also knew that she was cooperating with God in one of His greatest acts. It was an act of religion to her, one that bound her closer to her Maker. Yes, and let me tell you something more, Frederic. If ever a woman came near to priestliness, the Lady of Fontaines is that woman; for as soon as her child came forth she pressed it to her bosom as any mother would, and said those meaningful, marvelous, motherly words, 'My child'; but then immediately, as if recollecting herself, she would hold the child up on the paten of her two hands and make offering of it to God saying those words of consecration, 'This is your child, God. To me You have entrusted it. For that trust I am grateful and to it, with Your help, I'll be faithful.' Then she would lower the

child again on her heart and enter as it were, a communion with it. In all truth, it reminded one very forcefully
of the Mass."

"That is something different," admitted Frederic
with a shake of his head. "That is truly religious."

"Yes, and she was faithful to her trust as you heard
from Durtal this morning. In fact, those six statues are
Alice of Montbar's life story in stone. The best eulogy of a
mother will ever be her children. Six sons at Clairvaux,
her only daughter at Jully, and her husband dead after
two years as a lay brother tell you what kind of a Catholic
mother the Lady of Fontaines was."

"Vocations come from God, Jarenton," said Frederic
with some severity.

"True; but if ears are not attuned to the whispers of
God, vocations will never be answered; and ears are attuned by mothers who tell their tiny tots where they
came from, why they are here and where they are to go,"
came Jarenton's rapid response. "Vocations come from
God, Frederic; but He often, yes, almost always, speaks
through others. Many a soul has heard God's call only
because it was echoed from the heart of a mother. Durtal
made a claim that was perhaps a bit exaggerated, or
rather, let me say it was inadequate. I believe that there is
such a thing as spiritual heredity; but man is not the
product of heredity alone. No. It is the combination of
heredity, environment and education that shapes the
soul. And Alice had her share in all three elements in the
shaping of the souls of her children. She did her duty
with a vengeance."

"But that is only soldierliness; I'm looking for saintliness," objected Frederic.

"Duty done makes the soldier, I admit," answered
Jarenton. "But duty done lovingly, duty done because
that duty is the will of God and done only to glorify God
is not soldierliness. And that is what Alice of Montbar

did. Ah, Frederic, there are millions of mothers who are only mothers but who could be saintly mothers if they would but supernaturalize the natural. They love their children and they do all that they can for them; but they do not do it all for the greater honor and glory of God. They prepare their children for life but not for the after-life! They fit them to take their rightful place in society and their position in the world, too often forgetting that they have a place in the society of the saints and a position to gain in the other world! But Alice of Montbar fitted her children for both worlds and both societies, and did it without preaching or pietism."

Jarenton was speaking more rapidly now. There was fire in his words and fire in his eyes. He was on a theme that was dear to his heart and Frederic answered his enthusiasm with keen interest. After his vigorous expression on pietism, the Frenchman bent forward and touched his guest on the knee as he said, "Frederic, do you recall that rule of rhetoric that says, 'If you wish me to weep, you must weep before me.'"

"*Si vis me flere, flendum est tibi primum*," answered the German.

"I thought you'd have it at your tongue's tip," laughed Jarenton. "Well, let me tell you that its paraphrase is perfectly applicable in the spiritual order. 'If you want me to be a saint, show me how by your example!' Or simply, 'be one yourself first!' There is the whole secret of Alice's success. She has raised up a saintly family. That is evident to all. But what very few know is the way she did it. She made the supernatural natural to her children because it was natural to herself. They talked of God as naturally as they did of the weather and they talked to God as easily and as intimately as they did to one another. Why? Because that was how their mother acted."

Frederic sat back and said in a sad tone, "That's an art that very few cultivate, Jarenton. Not enough of us make the natural supernatural. We go looking for the supernatural in the unnatural and the result is shriveled souls.

"Isn't it heartbreaking to see sour faces in religion! They claim to be serving the God of Love and yet look as if vinegar and not blood was in their veins. Well, that will never be said of any of Alice's children because they played more than they prayed; were more often on a horse's back than on their knees; and knew how to make a headlong charge with the spear as well as they knew how to go to church.

"Alice was a pious woman; she held that the trinity of health, happiness and holiness should be found in the unity of every single person. That is why Fontaines castle and courtyards were always ringing with healthy shouts and happy laughter. A natural life was led by all but was shot through and through with the supernatural. Alice realized what many a pious soul forgets; namely, that God the Creator and God the Redeemer are one and the same God; therefore nature must be good!"

"You seem to know the castle and its inmates very intimately, Your Lordship," said Frederic.

"Better than I know myself," came the quick reply, "for I studied Lady Alice in life and in death."

"In death?" echoed his guest. "Were you present?"

"Thank God I was; and I never expect to see a holier one or a happier one."

"Tell me about it," came the eager request.

Going to God

"Let me begin by saying that Alice did not die; she simply went to God. That was the last lesson she taught me in life; she showed me as I never saw it before that death is but a going to God. You see, Frederic, the family of Fontaines had an exceptionally deep devotion to St. Ambrosian. On his feast all the clergy of Dijon gathered at the castle to celebrate the day solemnly and socially. After the morning of prayer and devotions a modest banquet was served. Well, in 1110 we were invited as usual but none of us suspected that this was to be the birthday of another saint, for none of us had been told that Alice had made an announcement that on this day she would be going to God.

"She had made this announcement months before; but for one reason or another, I suspect her robust health was the greatest reason, Tescelin and the boys paid little attention to it. On the eve of the feast, however, she suddenly came down with a high fever. Tescelin wanted to postpone the festivities planned for the morrow but Alice would not hear of it. In the morning the fever was down somewhat, and yet Alice asked for Viaticum, not Communion. This request did impress Tescelin and the older boys, but appearances deceived them. The fever was not alarmingly high and Alice was as calm and unperturbed as ever. After receiving Viaticum, she asked for Extreme Unction. I hesitated; but only for a moment. The sickness did not prompt me to administer the sacrament, but Alice's sanity and saintliness did. I knew that she was never given to dramatics; hence, I concluded that there was some deep reason for the request.

"I anointed her. I never saw such recollection and fervor. After that she insisted that we all attend the devotions and the banquet. She got her way. We all left. Everything went normally until toward the end of the meal; then I noticed that Guy, the eldest son, was called away by one of the attendants. He came back just as the meal ended. Seldom have I seen such a combination of puzzlement, solemnity and seriousness on one face as I saw on that boy's as he whispered to his father. Tescelin then quietly asked us all to go to Lady Alice's room immediately. Few suspected what that request meant; but to me the last word sounded like the deep, dull toll of the death knell. We went in to a woman who held heaven in her eyes. There was a radiance, an effulgence to that face that made us all gasp; when she spoke, her voice held the lilt of a lover. 'Reverend Fathers,' she said, 'very soon I will be going to God. Won't you speed me on my way by reciting the litany of the Saints?'"

Jarenton paused. Perhaps he was hearing again the voice with the lover's lilt. Perhaps he was seeing again the face with the strange effulgence. But Frederic broke the momentary reverie with the command, "Go on. Go on. Tell me all about it."

The French abbot looked into the eyes of his guest with an earnestness that was disturbing, then in accents that were solemn said, "Frederic, I have been in sanctuaries all my life; but let me tell you that when that woman spoke, I knew that I was in the holy of holies. And every last man in the gathering felt the same. The supernatural atmosphere was overpowering. God was close. We got to our knees and prayed the litany as we had never prayed it before. The patriarchs and prophets became more than mere names, the apostles and evangelists were people to call upon, and the martyrs, confessors and virgins became our elder brothers and sisters, as we knelt and heard the sweet voice of that woman answer every invocation. On we went steadily, surely, evenly; across the room came every response warmly, earnestly, feelingly. Every eye was fixed on the face of Alice of Montbar and her eyes were fixed on heaven. We reached the cry, 'Through Thy Passion and Cross, O Lord, deliver us,' when Lady Alice suddenly sat up, made the sign of the cross with deep reverence, lifted her arms toward the heavens, then settled back into the long, quiet sleep of death. Her soul had gone to God! A holy hush seized all. Here was mystery. Here was the subtle chemistry of death. Here was God. Into that awe-filled silence came a sound that went down deep into the depths of every soul; it was the sound of a breaking heart—it was her boy, Bernard."

Jarenton again paused. This time Frederic did not interrupt but sat as one wrapt in profoundest thought. At last he stirred and said, "That, my good Jarenton, sounds like the death of a saint."

"That was the death of a saint," Jarenton shifted his position and took on a new tone of voice. "And, Frederic, the proof of that is the testimony of the people. The common people are not easily deceived. When it comes to adjudging sanctity they are never deceived. They have an intuition that enables them to discern the true from the false, to pierce sham and subterfuge and to recognize God's near ones. When they acclaim anyone a saint, you can accept their acclamation."

"I admit that. What did they do about Alice?"

"What did they do?" echoed Jarenton. "They made a revelation that surprised the whole neighborhood. To the side of Alice's body came the nobility, as was to be expected; but what was not expected was the way the whole body of serfdom, both from Fontaines and Dijon, came with tears in their eyes and the one sorrowful, sobbing, worshipful phrase on their lips—'our mother.' Even Tescelin was surprised at the number and the rank of those who called his little wife by that possessive title of 'mother.' But what confirmed me in my long held estimation of this woman was the way that these people came into her presence and knelt by her side. They showed more respect, reverence and genuine awe than they do in church.

"It was this that moved me to a determination that to many might seem daring. I came here to the abbey, assembled the monks and marched them the three miles to Fontaines. We entered praying. While the community knelt by the remains, I took Tescelin aside and said, 'My Lord, the body of your saintly wife should not be placed alongside the bodies of ordinary Christians. Allow me to place it where it belongs—in my church, amongst the honored and holy dead.' He hesitated. Tescelin never was a hasty man; moreover, he was always a humble one. I feared for my request. He seemed to be weighing the matter very carefully; finally he bowed his head in assent and my heart leaped with joy. My monks lifted the body on their shoulders. We intoned the 'Benedictus' and thus inaugurated a solemn procession from Fontaines to Dijon.

"As we neared the city we were met by the entire populace, who had come out with candles and crosses to meet the remains of one they were openly calling, 'Blessed.' We made our way to the church and laid her where you saw the serfs talking this morning. And let me tell you, Frederic, I felt that I was depositing sacred relics in a sacred place."

For a moment the German abbot did not move. His eyes were fixed in an unseeing stare. He was thinking. He was lost in his thoughts. Then suddenly he straightened up, looked at Jarenton and said, "Have you a small sheet of paper and a quill? I would take a few notes. You have told me the story of a great wife and mother. I would remember it."

"I have told you the story of a great saint." Jarenton reached paper and quill to his guest. "A great saint precisely because she was a great wife and mother. But I haven't finished yet."

"No?" queried Frederic. "Even though you have buried her?"

"No," answered Jarenton with a shake of his head, "for her mothering did not end with the grave, and that is proof positive of her sanctity."

Frederic eyed his host quizzically, then with abruptness said, "Give me that proof, Jarenton," and bent to his task of taking notes.

"I wouldn't omit it for the world," said the Frenchman, "for it shows that a mother's love is stronger than death and that love always finds a way."

Love Finds a Way

Jarenton waited until Frederic had adjusted his paper on the back of a small book before he said, "I have much more faith in post-mortems than in pre-natals, Frederic."

"Meaning what?" said the German looking up from his paper.

"Meaning that while the oak is contained in the acorn we do not build our walls or lay our solid floors with acorns. Meaning that while the boy may be father to the man, I'd rather look at the man and tell you what manner of boy he has been than look at the boy and guess what sort of a man he'll turn out. Meaning that what most of our chronicles of holy men and women say about the visions and the prophecies that were seen and heard concerning them before their birth may be perfectly true, but give me the miracles and visions after their death and I feel safer."

"A good point," smiled Frederic.

"A very good point," insisted Jarenton, "and one that is very much to our point. You say that I have told you the story of a great mother. I say that I have told you the story of a great saint, and now I prove it by showing you how she mothered her children even after her death."

"This promises to be interesting," said Frederic as he once again adjusted his paper. "Proceed."

"Bernard had been her favorite. She had been his love. In every great step he had ever taken he had depended on her for advice and direction. Two years after her death he was contemplating the greatest step of his life: he was thinking of going to Citeaux. But where was she? The world called and called; the flesh beckoned and rebelled. Bernard was torn as all great souls are torn and he needed a steadying hand. But where could he find one? His father and older brothers were at Grancy fighting for the Duke; he had only Humbeline and his younger brothers with him. He battled it out and when he thought he had made up his mind he started for Grancy to announce his decision. Halfway there he stopped. All the old doubts arose again; all the old difficulties loomed larger. He was not at all sure of his decision now. Then suddenly he saw before him the face of his mother, and Bernard's mind was made up forever! Despite the grave's width and depth, despite death's awful finality, a mother's love had found a way to mother her boy."

"A real vision?" questioned Frederic.

"Real enough to fix Bernard's will to the sticking point. But that was not the only one. No. For mother love never dies and it always finds a way. That is why Alice came back to Andrew when he needed her most."

"When was that?" asked Frederic.

"When Bernard was arguing with him and trying to persuade him to go along to Citeaux. Andrew ambitioned knighthood and the goal of his ambition was well within sight. The clang of armor and the glamor of fame had more appeal for the lad than Bernard's pictures of Citeaux. It looked as if Bernard was going to lose, until suddenly Andrew looked up and saw before him his mother. She came and embraced him as she had done a thousand times in childhood; then she pointed to Bernard. It was enough. Let knighthood go; let glory go; Andrew went seeking God. Love had leaped the grave; and Alice was still mothering her boys."

"That's enough," said Frederic with finality. "You win your point. I have here the record of a saint," and he held up the thin sheet of yellowish white paper.

"May I see that record?" asked Jarenton.

"Why, certainly," answered Frederic in a puzzled tone as he handed the paper to the French abbot.

Jarenton took the paper and saw in a small, neat, and firm hand these ten lines:

1070—born Alice of Montbar.
1085—married Tescelin the Tawny, Lord of Fontaines
1110—died on St. Ambrosian's day
        buried in church of St. Benignus de Dijon
        sons—six, all at Clairvaux
        daughter—one, at Jully, nun after marriage
        husband—died a lay brother at Clairvaux
        two appearances to boys after her death
        great wife—great mother—great saint
        supernaturalized the natural

He read them aloud, then laughed as he said, "Typically German, Frederic, typically German. The cold facts in their chronological order. Systematic. Scientific. Sober. Sound and very, very sane. Yes, indeed, that is typically German."

"Well, my good friend Jarenton," countered Frederic jokingly, "haven't you been telling me all day that there is only one way to sanctity, namely, by being yourself, being what God made you? I want to be a saint, so I've got to be typically German."

"Ah ha!" exclaimed the French abbot, "so you admit my argument at last. You confess that it is up to you; you've got to do it."

"Aren't you forgetting something?" smiled Frederic.

"What?" asked Jarenton.

"You seem to be forgetting who made me German. I think it was God!"

Jarenton laughed good naturedly as he said, "You're more than German, Frederic, you're incorrigible."

The body of Blessed Alice remained just where Jarenton had placed it until October 17, 1250, when a holy jealousy moved the monks of Clairvaux to obtain a brief from Pope Innocent IV enabling them to take the venerable remains to the monastery where her husband and her boys had lived. Finally on March 19, 1251, the body of this great mother was placed in a tomb facing the altar of our Savior in the Abbatial Church of Clairvaux. It was the last touch to the naturalness of her supernaturality and the supernaturality of her motherliness.

Part 2

THE ELDER
MEMBERS

Bernard's Big Brother

"Are you serious?"

"Something is very wrong with this situation," said Tescelin looking down on his laughing wife as she cuddled her first grandchild to her heart.

"The trouble must be with you, then, old Tawny beard, for baby and I are in heaven. Aren't we, Adeline?" cooed Lady Alice into the unheeding ears of a pudgy bit of humanity hardly a month old.

"No," smiled Tescelin, "the trouble is not with me. It is entirely with you, my dear. You're altogether too young to be so old."

"Old? Old? Who's old? I feel like a girl of twenty."

"And look like one," he said happily, "and that is just the trouble. The title, 'Grandma' will never fit you, Alice. We'll have to find something more expressive of truth."

"Go away with your compliments. I'm old enough to love this angel-child; and that's all that matters. Call me anything you like," and with that she bent all her attention on the babe in her arms.

"I'm not complimenting you; I'm condemning this son of ours for making you so old when you are actually so young."

Guy, who had been standing behind his mother, his eyes sparkling with pride, possessiveness and real delight as he saw her grow young again while fondling his first child, looked up at his father and said, "You sound like His Lordship, Father. No one ever knows whether our Duke is complimenting handsomely or only preparing a call down."

His father walked to the table and placed his gloves upon it. "Well, boy, it was His Lordship who gave me the idea. He's worried about you, so he finds fault with me."

"That's like him," put in Guy. "Always doing things by indirection. What's worrying him just now?"

"Oh, he's not really worried. What he was trying to do was to compliment Alice, Elizabeth, you and myself; so he had to be gruff and grouchy and fault-finding. That is how Hugh always does things; not so much by indirection as by opposites."

"What did he have to say?" questioned Guy.

"Well, he greeted me with, 'And how is the old man this morning?' I answered, 'Oh, not so very old. Just one day older than yesterday.' 'No, you're not,' said he in that gruff voice of his, 'you're one title older.' That puzzled me. It could mean many things. As you know, our Duke is fond of dubbing people with meaningful titles that are often caustic and cutting; he also gives rewards. I did not want to be caught in any trap so I said with feigned formality, 'What does it please Your Excellency to call me this morning?' 'Grandpa,' he growled."

All laughed at the way Tescelin said it. It was a growl, and in its gruffness it held all the disgust a man can manifest with a tone. "Now, Elizabeth," said Guy to his wife, "do you see all the trouble you got my father into?"

"Oh no!" cut in Tescelin. "She got me into no trouble, for I turned it all on the Duke. First I told him that age was in the bones, not in babies; and then, that if he

was going to get disgusted with anyone because of my
new title, he'd have to get disgusted with himself. That
made him curious; so he asked, 'How so?'

"'If you hadn't made my oldest boy a man before he
had left his "teens," I wouldn't be a grandfather now,' I
said."

"'Who made him a man?' growled His Excellency.
'You did,' said I, 'when you laid the flat of a sword on his
back and dubbed a mere stripling, knight.' 'Well,' he said
with less of a growl, 'I only wish that I had more backs
like that of your boy to lay the sword on.' 'Uh huh,' said
I, 'but don't you see how attractive you made a youngster
to every girl in the Duchy?'"

"Aren't you men vain!" exclaimed Elizabeth de
Forez, Guy's young, beautiful and vivacious wife. "My
father told me that Guy had asked for my hand; you talk
as if I had asked for his."

"That does it! I'd rather match wits with His Excellency than with Your Ladyship, Elizabeth. You're much
too quick for me."

"Maybe you are getting old," came from Lady Alice,
as she momentarily looked up from the babe she was
fondling. "To insinuate that the well-bred daughters of
counts cast eyes at mere tyros who happen to have been
knighted makes me suspect that the Duke was right."

"It looks as if I made a faux pas, Guy," said Tescelin.
"The ladies are incensed. That's why I love to talk to the
gruff and grouchy Duke. Men are so understanding...."

"...of one another," competed Elizabeth. "'Deep
calls to deep'—the depths of vanity to the depths of con-
ceit."

"Just at present," said Guy as he smiled at his wife,
"I'm in the depths of curiosity. I'd like to know what the
Duke said."

"Well," resumed Tescelin, "he paid you a compliment when I spoke about knighthood...."

"Yes," said Guy with a blush. "I caught it; but I hoped that you would pass it over."

"He paid a greater compliment to Elizabeth when I spoke of the girls of the Duchy."

Elizabeth colored visibly and long, dark lashes were lowered over brilliant eyes. Tescelin looked on the very self-conscious young mother and exclaimed, "By heavens, the Duke is right. Elizabeth, my dear, you make me proud to be your father-in-law."

Elizabeth flashed a glance at Tescelin and blushed more violently. Guy saw the embarrassment of his wife, so he walked over behind her chair saying, "What did His Gruffness have to say about my little girl?"

"He said that if he had won for you the admiration of all the ladies by giving you knighthood, I had won for you the envy of all the men by allowing you to marry the most beautiful daughter any count ever raised."

"Oh, you men make me tired," exclaimed Elizabeth as a rich red mounted to her very forehead and so set off her brilliant eyes that they gleamed like sapphires.

"And you make us men gasp," said Tescelin as he walked over and laid his hand on her head as if he were imparting a benediction. Then looking up into the eyes of his oldest boy who stood behind his blushing wife, he said, "Guy, our little Elizabeth has become even more beautiful since becoming a mother. I congratulate you."

Lady Alice watched the effect her husband's words had on her young daughter-in-law, and the effect her daughter-in-law's evident beauty had on her husband. She thrilled to the modesty of Elizabeth and to the gallantry of her lord. She would have liked to prolong the interchange, but sympathy for the young mother moved her to distract the little group by saying, "And baby Adeline, just like her mother, says that you men make her tired. Come, Elizabeth, take your angel. These men have made her weary. She would go to sleep."

Elizabeth was only too glad to move. She was across the room in a glide, and taking the baby from Lady Alice, stood cooing those pretty nothings which only a mother can coo into the face of her child. She made a striking picture as she stood there in the full bloom of her first motherhood, unconscious of everyone but the tiny girl in her arms.

Tescelin and Guy looked their admiration while Lady Alice glowed with love. The Lord of Fontaines bent toward his son and whispered, "The beauteous Madonna." Guy smiled his appreciation of the tribute, then said, "Come, thou cause of envy, let's put our child to bed."

When they had retired, Tescelin turned to Lady Alice and said, "Yes, my love, you are far too young to be so old; the title of 'Grandma' will never fit you."

Alice smiled up at him and said, "Your eye seems especially keen this evening for youth and beauty, and your tongue exceptionally ready with compliments. What is it—the fresh bloom of fair Elizabeth?"

"She is stunning tonight, isn't she? I never noticed it before, but she is a remarkably beautiful girl. What has heightened her looks—is it motherhood?"

"Tescelin," sighed Alice, "you're like a child in some things. Of course it is motherhood. It has filled out her form and given her a new dignity and assurance."

"Oh, it's not that, my dear," replied Tescelin. "It's the light in her eyes; it's the radiance on her face; it's the glow, the flush, the glory that envelops her whole being. She's a different person."

His wife, wise in his ways, knew that despite his flood of words, he was still groping for an explanation; so she quietly asked, "What happens to young men who associate with noble knights?"

"Why, they take on their ways," said Tescelin with a hesitancy that showed he was puzzled.

"And what happens to young women who come in close contact with the Duchess, countess or the Queen?"

"The same thing," replied the still baffled lord.

"Well then, why should you marvel at the new beauty of your daughter-in-law? For almost a year she has been in the closest contact with the Author of Life and the God of Beauty. Mothers, you know, work hand in hand with God that inhabitants for heaven may see light on this earth. You're right, my dear, Elizabeth has a new and a dazzling radiance about her. It is the glow of the Godhead. She has been cooperating with the Creator of men. Now aren't you sorry that you were made a man and not a woman?"

Tescelin looked long at his wife and love shone from his eyes. Then he gently and somewhat solemnly said, "Thank you, my dear, for a true and lovely explanation; and thank God for you!"

Are You Serious?

Some five years later Guy had reason to recall the remark of his father about the quick wit and the quick tongue of his wife. It was autumn of 1111 and he had come home sitting on his horse like a conqueror, for he was conscious that he had made a mighty resolve and was about to enter on a great adventure. Elizabeth had greeted him effusively. Exclamations at his early return, questions as to his well-being, ejaculations of joy toppled over one another as he bent down to lift his two little girls to be kissed. Life seemed very lovable to Guy as he listened to the excited greetings of his charming wife and looked into the dancing eyes of his two laughing daughters. He felt his pulse quicken as he said, "No," he had not been wounded; and "No," Grancy had not been taken; for he knew that the next question would be, "What brought you home, then?"

It came, and he had answered that he had come home to say good-bye; for he was going to become a monk in the monastery at Citeaux. At first Elizabeth laughed and asked what they had mixed with the wine at Grancy; but when Guy went on and said that his uncle Gaudry, his brother Andrew and several other knights were going with Bernard, she stopped laughing. "Are you serious?" she asked, and received the reply that he was most serious. Guy then went on to relate how Bernard had come to Grancy and spoken of living for God with such force and fire that Gaudry had laid down his arms and joined his younger nephew, then Andrew had followed suit, and finally he himself had determined to do the same if she would but give her consent.

Then it came! A veritable tirade. Guy had never seen a passionate woman aroused before and the fury of his wife's onslaught frightened him more than any headlong charge of steel-clad foeman ever had. He found himself stepping backwards as his wife advanced with flaming eyes and wildly gesturing arms.

The suddenness and fierceness of her attack so upset him that he did not catch her every word, but he caught enough to know that in her eyes he had made a fool of himself by listening to his younger brother and a bigger fool by even dreaming that she would give her consent. "Get on your horse," she had said, "and like a man ride back to Grancy where your sanity may be found again. And don't let me see your face until you are ready to crawl on your knees and beg the pardon of these two little ones for your momentary madness." The last words that Guy heard were, "Get out!"

He got on his horse, but he did not ride to Grancy; he rode to Fontaines instead to seek out Bernard and break the news to him. He found his younger brother in his room drawing up a list of names. As soon as he entered, Bernard greeted him with, "I'm glad you've come, Guy, you can help me draw up this list. I have here a number of relatives and friends whom I would like to enlist in our enterprise. Look! I've got a dozen already. There's Uncle Gaudry, young Bartholomew and Andrew; Gerard will come in time, then there's Hugh of Macon, Geoffrey de la Roche, young cousin Robert, yourself...."

"Company, halt!" cried Guy with what he meant to be a cheerful smile.

"Huh?" gasped Bernard as he looked up from his list.

"You'll have to strike that last name off, Bernard."

"Why?" asked the younger brother with a show of resistance.

"Because of three women," replied Guy with a smile.

"What three women?" angrily asked Bernard.

"Elizabeth de Forez and her two charming daughters," said Guy pleasantly. "I'm sorry, Bernard; but Elizabeth would not consent; and, of course, without her consent I cannot go." Guy's smile vanished and a deep seriousness shaded his whole face as he said, "I was not very diplomatic in my approach. I broke the news too abruptly and sent my good wife almost into hysterics."

"Didn't you argue with her?" exclaimed Bernard in impatience. "Didn't you tell her how much God expects of us? Didn't you show her that this is the noblest enterprise that can engage the mind, heart and being of man? Didn't you...what did you tell her anyhow?"

Seeing that Bernard was growing excited, Guy assumed his "big brother" air as he said, "My good fellow, you do not know women or you'd never talk like that. No, Bernard, one does not argue with a woman who is aroused, and under no pretext with one who is on the verge of hysterics; and my Elizabeth was on the very verge when I left her."

"I'll argue with her," said Bernard in a blustering tone, "and I'll convince her."

"Don't be foolish, Bernard. Listen to an older and a wiser man. Elizabeth has justice on her side. I'm her husband. I'm the father of her two children. I'm bound to her and to them for life."

"Oh," said Bernard in disgust, "we thrashed that all out days ago. She can go to a convent. The children can go to her father or come here. Humbeline would love to have them."

"That's right, Bernard," said Guy with utter calm and perfect control, "they could; but they will not. This has got to be a matter of purely voluntary consent all around. I'm sorry that my wife retains hers; for you have persuaded me that I should give God more than I have been giving Him, and I'd love to give Him all, as you plan. But you know the old saying: 'Charity,' which is love for God, 'begins at home.' I'll have to stay behind. But I have a plan of my own."

"What is it?" snapped Bernard.

"I'm going to live differently. I'm going to serve God in the world as husband and father. I'll give up the pursuit of empty fame; I'll refuse all honors from the Duke; I'll give my surplus wealth to the poor; I'll be as much of a monk as it is possible for a man to be without being in a monastery. That is the thought with which God inspired me as I rode from home."

"God never inspires compromise," broke in Bernard, "and heroic though your resolution is, to me it is nothing but compromise."

"But what else can I do? I'm a married man."

"So is Uncle Gaudry; yet he's not backing water."

"But he got his wife's permission."

"Yes, and we'll get yours...."

"Don't talk foolishly. I know Elizabeth de Forez. Her mind is made up and no man in the world will change it."

"But, Guy, you've got to come! I've got to have you in my band or all is lost," said Bernard; then changing his tone of voice, he went on, "You're our big brother. All our lives we've looked up to you. Whatever you did was the right thing to do; whatever you said was law. Don't you see what it will mean to the others if you back out now?"

"But, Bernard, I'm not backing out. I want to go. But there is my wife and my children...."

Bernard got up from his table, took his hat from a hook, snatched up his quirt and started for the door.

"Where are you going?" asked Guy.

"I'm going to see your wife," came the determined reply as Bernard strode from the room.

"Not without me," shouted Guy as he hurried after the flying feet of his younger brother.

They had a fast ride to Guy's mansion that day. Not a word passed between them, but thoughts were racing through their minds faster than the hurried beat of their horses' hooves. Guy was worried both for Bernard and his wife. He could see that his younger brother was too ardent and too absorbed in his project to talk calmly, while he knew that his wife would be merciless once she laid her tongue on Bernard. All told, Guy had a very unhappy gallop home; and fast though he had been, Bernard was out of the saddle and at the door before him. Then came a series of surprises.

Bernard greeted Elizabeth with a laugh and a compliment. "Roses would blush with envy if they could see the bloom on your cheeks, Elizabeth," he said, "and your daughters," he continued as he bent down to lift little Adeline in his arms, "are their mother in miniature."

Elizabeth was a woman, and although she had not fully recovered from her fit of angry indignation, as could be seen from the way she eyed her husband, yet Bernard's greeting and manner mollified her sufficiently to have her say in a fairly friendly tone, "And what does my handsome brother-in-law want for his gracious compliments?"

Guy was speechless. This was the direct opposite to what he had expected and feared. Bernard went on laughing as he set little Adeline down and said, "Be as beautiful as your mother, Adeline, but don't ever acquire her suspicious mind."

Elizabeth echoed his laugh in a higher octave and said, "Be as wise as your mother, Adeline, and know that every flatterer is a beggar, no matter how handsome he may be or facile with speech. What's on your mind, Bernard?"

"There it is again, Adeline," said Bernard, still addressing the five-year-old miniature of Elizabeth, "drop in for a friendly visit and you are under suspicion from the start."

"I know that you didn't come here to see the roses in my cheeks or the stars in my daughters' eyes," said Elizabeth. "I also know that your presence with this madman husband of mine," she went on with a scorn-filled toss of her head in Guy's direction, "means an argument. I'm ready. Let's have it."

"Did you hear that, Adeline?" said Bernard as he bent down and looked his niece squarely in the eyes. "Your Mamma is calling your Daddy naughty names. I think you and sister had better go out in the garden and gather the beautiful gold and yellow and reddish brown leaves that autumn has showered so gorgeously and generously."

"Oh, if that's all you want," said Elizabeth, "consider it done." Then in a commanding tone she cried, "Jeannine!" A servant appeared immediately. "Take the children into the garden. We would be alone for a while."

Jeannine smiled at the two little girls who seemed delighted with the prospect of gathering the multi-colored, scattered wealth of October. As soon as they had left, Elizabeth sat down very composedly, and gracefully gesturing toward a chair said, "Won't you be seated?"

"I'll stand, if you don't mind," said Bernard, "for I mean to be brief."

"I'll sit," said Guy, "for I know this won't be brief."

"Oh! You have a tongue," said Elizabeth turning toward her husband. "I thought you had lost that along with your good sense; you've been so dumb since you came in."

"Please, Elizabeth!" put in Bernard in very smooth tones. "Let's be sensible about this thing."

"Sensible? Sensible?" cried Elizabeth. "That's all I'm praying for! But when one of Burgundy's most promising knights leaves the siege of Grancy in order to ride home and tell his worried wife and two little daughters that he is going to become a monk, it's time to pray harder."

"But, Elizabeth, have you given this matter any consideration at all?" asked Bernard in the same smooth, sweet tone.

"Consideration?" cried Elizabeth and stopped. Then in a voice that dripped derision she very calmly said, "Poor boy! You're handsome. They tell me you're clever. But I am glad that your mother is not alive to see you in this state. You should ride home quietly, Bernard dear, have someone call a doctor and you go straight to bed; for," and here her voice came up shrill and her eyes blazed as she said, "you're mad!"

"I know it," calmly answered Bernard, "and so would you be if you saw people whom you loved, thwarting the designs of God. Do you realize that your husband wants to serve God Almighty?"

"Isn't that lovely!" answered Elizabeth. "And whom do you think married people serve—the devil?"

"No, no," quickly replied Bernard, "but this is different. Guy wants to swear away his life to God alone."

"How many lives has he got?" asked Elizabeth with a disdainful glance in Guy's direction. "I think he has sworn one away already. Didn't you say something about 'till death do us part' the day we were married, dear?" The last word reeked with sarcasm and set Guy sitting on the edge of his chair."

"Yes, Elizabeth, I did; and I mean to live by it unless you are willing to do something nobler. I didn't want Bernard to come here. I...."

"But Bernard came," broke in his younger brother, "and he came to see if the noble daughter of Count de Forez won't do the noble thing for God. Think of it, Elizabeth! A chance to make a sacrifice for God Almighty, a chance to prove your love for One who has loved you to death, a chance to be worthy of your noble blood, both that which you inherited from your truly noble father, and that which you inherited from Jesus Christ. Won't you be noble?"

Elizabeth had placed her hands in her lap, sat very erect in her chair and watched every movement that Bernard made. As he climaxed his appeal with the question, she sat back and very leisurely said, "I see that they teach rhetoric and the art of declamation at St. Vorles School at Chatillon sur Seine. Isn't it too bad that they don't teach logic? Bernard dear, didn't any of the priests ever tell you that the marriage bond is indissoluble? I know that that is a very big word for little boys, but it means that once a man and woman have been made husband and wife by God's great sacrament, they stay husband and wife until death; and that, by God's law. Do you understand?" Here her voice rose and all leisureliness of manner left her as she leaned forward and asked, "How, then, can God be calling Guy to the cloister, when six long years ago He called him to be my husband? Does God contradict Himself? Or do they teach some new theology at Chatillon?"

"No," replied Bernard very thoughtfully, "not a new theology, Elizabeth, but the old theology very thoroughly. Don't you ever remember having heard the words, 'Friend, come up higher'?"

"I do," replied Elizabeth in a voice that bespoke no love for Bernard, "but I do not remember ever hearing them applied to a husband with the connotation that his wife should go down lower. Just what am I supposed to do when Guy goes to be your little playmate at Citeaux? Am I to stay here and knit socks and mittens for the pair of you? And what of Adeline and her sister? Shall I say: 'Now you two little darlings run right along and get married immediately so that Papa can go with Bernard to the lovely swamps at Citeaux'? Bernard, act your age and use your logic."

"That's what I'm trying to do," answered Bernard with growing force and fire, "but the environment is against me. But no! Excuse me, Elizabeth, let us not argue in such a strain; let us discuss this matter as coolly as possible."

"Coolly? Coolly?" exclaimed Elizabeth; then shrugging her shoulders as if to keep warm, she said, "Not coolly, Bernard, but coldly. Now listen. I took Guy 'for better and for worse'; this is the worst yet, but he's mine still, signed by the sacred sign of God's great sacrament. We vowed a vow that day which I mean to keep. I am his and he is mine, 'til death do us part.'"

"Yes, Elizabeth, what you say is absolutely true; but did that vow necessarily mean that you have to live together? Can't you two be one soul as well as one flesh? Can't Guy be your inspiration and love as a monk who is dedicated to God, and you be Guy's great inspiration and love as a nun...?"

"As a what?" Elizabeth almost screamed.

"A nun," said Bernard with burning force, "a woman who loves God more than herself; a woman who knows what this world is worth and what this life is for; a woman who can and does see farther than her nose and has ambitions higher than a name, a home and a place in society; a woman who longs to win a real name, a heavenly mansion, and a place among the saints; a woman...."

"...who has never been married and has not begotten two children for God," blazed back Elizabeth.

Bernard paused. Walking over to Guy who sat a disconsolate audience to this passionate clash of minds and hearts he said, "Hasn't your wife ever heard of married women going to the convent? Doesn't she know the discipline of God's Church on the matter?"

Guy looked up and with pain in his eyes and pain in his voice said, "It's no use, lad. Elizabeth is right in her view. You are right in yours. But you two are looking at the same thing from vastly different angles."

"I'm looking at it from God's angle," said Bernard.

"And I?" questioned Elizabeth. "From whose angle am I viewing it, pray tell me. Can it be from the devil's?"

"No, Elizabeth, I didn't say that, nor insinuate it. But I do say that you have an opportunity of doing something great for God and you are missing it. You have a chance of being really noble, of sacrificing something near and dear, of being God's heroine...."

"Oh, stop the rhetoric!" broke in Elizabeth. "It wearies me. Guy can become a monk after I am dead." With that she arose and made as if she would leave the room, but Bernard, whose face was flushed now, stood squarely before her and in a voice choked with repressed emotion said, "Elizabeth de Forez, let me tell you with all the earnestness of my soul that your husband will be a monk, and that with your permission; either the one you have just now given, namely, your death, or one given more in accord with the nobility of your person."

"Are you trying to intimidate me?" asked Elizabeth very haughtily.

"No. Just predicting. Remember my words: Before Easter, freed either by your permission or your death!" With that Bernard bowed to his sister-in-law, nodded to Guy and flung himself from the room.

Elizabeth stood where he had stopped her; her eyes were on the door through which Bernard had passed. The rapid rise and fall of her bosom told of her agitated soul. Her voice was steady, but the pallor of her countenance belied the words she addressed to her very uneasy husband, "Tell that baby brother of yours," she said, "that I do not scare easily." Then she walked from the room like a queen.

Strange Ways

The gold and brown leaves that Adeline and her little sister had gathered that memorable October day were lying beneath winter's first snow when Bernard was again riding the road from Fontaines. This time, however, he had been sent for by his sister-in-law and was welcomed into a house that was filled with the fearful hush of a dread sickness. He was ushered into Elizabeth's room where he found Guy anxiously bending over his very pallid wife.

As soon as Bernard entered, Elizabeth sat up and held out her two thin arms to him saying, "Oh, I'm so glad that you have come! So glad." When Bernard had kissed her hands, she sank back on the pillows and smoothed a place on the counterpane for him to sit. He demurred and made a gesture toward a chair; but she shook her head and patted the coverlet as she said, "No, right here, by me." Bernard sat. Guy was on the opposite side of the bed holding his wife's right hand.

Elizabeth stretched out her left hand to Bernard; when he took it she closed her eyes and sighed deeply. For a moment all was still. Then without opening her eyes and in a rather thin voice Elizabeth said, "It is not Easter yet, is it Bernard?"

"No," came the whispered reply.

"And yet, I am sick; very sick; sick unto death."

"Don't say that, Elizabeth," put in Guy in a broken voice.

"I will say it," answered Elizabeth, "and I will ask you both to listen to me. I'm very tired and can speak only a little."

"We are listening," said Bernard softly after a noticeable pause during which Elizabeth's sighs sounded strangely like smothered sobs.

"My eyes have been opened," said the sick woman. "I see as I never saw before. The last time we met, Bernard, I thought you were mad, and that your parting words were mere anger. I see now that I was the one who was mad and that your words were prophecy." She paused for breath. Guy's and Bernard's eyes met across the counterpane.

"God's ways are strange ways," came the voice of the sick woman. "I don't claim to understand them; but I do see that God wants Guy." There was another pause; then in a little firmer voice she said, "And I want to give him to God." With that she seemed to faint. Bernard and

Guy quickly looked at one another, then at the white face on the pillow. Bernard placed a hand on her forehead and Elizabeth opened her eyes. As she did so, two crystal tears welled up and spilled down her pallid cheeks. Lifting her swimming eyes to Bernard she said, "God's ways are strange, aren't they?" Then turning to Guy she shook her head slightly and whispered, "'Til death do us part'—but God is calling you higher and I must let you go." She closed her eyes a moment, then into the hush of the room came this prayer, "Oh, dear God, he is yours. You could have taken him to you by the spear, the battle-axe or accident, and I would have had no say. I have one now, and I say: 'Take him! Take him while living, and love him in life and in death!'" She opened her eyes again and the tears fell fast. She loosened her hand from Bernard's clasp and stretching her arms out to her husband said, "Kiss me, Guy dear, and seal this sacrament as we sealed the other." Guy bent reverently, and his tears mingled with the salty ones on Elizabeth's cheeks as they kissed one another with a solemnity that was sacred.

Loosening her arm from around Guy's shoulder, she held her hand out to Bernard saying, "And you, prophet of God, will you witness my act of renouncement with a brotherly kiss?"

Bernard bent forward and just before his lips touched Elizabeth's he said, "Elizabeth dear, this sickness is not to the death. God has other work for you to do. I know that you will do it nobly."

When Bernard straightened back after his kiss, Elizabeth let her hands lie one in Guy's hand and the other in that of his younger brother. For a moment or two she rested thus, then smiled slowly and a bit sadly as she said, "I'm happier, much happier. I would rest now. You two may go."

The two brothers tiptoed from the sick room. When they had reached the main hall Bernard turned to his older brother and said, "God's ways are sure ways! You are free at last."

Guy's face did not reflect Bernard's enthusiasm. He was quite evidently distressed. "Do you think she'll recover?" he asked.

"Recover? Recover? She's as good as well now, Guy. I mean it. This is God's hand pointing your path for you."

"I wish I had your faith, Bernard. Just at present all that I can see is a very sick wife who is perhaps a little bit superstitious."

Bernard started at the word. He looked at Guy with a flash of anger blazing from his eyes and said, "And you're my big brother! Shame! What do you want God to do—appear in person and speak to us? Your wife refused. She fell sick. She grants leave now. She'll get well. And you speak of superstition! Better go to confession and accuse yourself of presumption! I'll be expecting you to join us within the month. You'll find us at Chatillon sur Seine. Come prepared to give your all to God." With that Bernard shook his brother's hand, vaulted into the saddle, turned his horse's head, and snow was seen to fly from speeding hooves.

The "Big Brother" Complex

In 1122, just a little over ten years since Bernard had recommended that he accuse himself of presumption, Guy was walking the path that wound its way in and out among the trees of Clairvaux's valley with William of St. Thierry, Abbot of the Cluniac foundation in that town, by his side. It was spring; crocuses were peaking through the blackened leaves that had been last summer's glory; shy anemones lifted their five-petalled heads timidly, looking with wonder and surprise on this strange world of shadow and sunshine; here and there, in the deeply shaded hollows, patches of yet unmelted snow told that King Winter had but recently beat his hurried retreat. The Cluniac Abbot had eyes for all these traces that told so vividly of life and death, but Guy was blind to nature. He plodded along with head bent and eyes unseeing; his mind a prey to anxious concern.

William allowed him his preoccupation for a goodly stretch of the woods, then stirred up a sudden flutter of wings with a sudden silvery ripple of laughter and said, "Your trouble, Guy, is that you were born before Bernard. Your hair would not be sprinkled with so much grey, nor would that forehead of yours be so often furrowed had you been born with him or after him. You're suffering from what I call 'big-brotherliness.'"

"Is that a disease?" came the almost gruff rejoinder.

"Yes," laughed Abbot William, "and an incurable one. I have heard old men of eighty speak worriedly about 'that young brother of mine'; and then found out that the young brother was only seventy-six. Just why should you be so upset about Bernard? He's a little over twenty-one, I think; and furthermore, he's your Abbot."

"I know that," came the quick reply, "and as my Abbot I respect, honor, and obey him; but never forget that he is my younger brother and as such I have a care for him."

"There you are!" exclaimed William. "Just as I told you. You're sick with 'big-brotherliness.'"

"Well, you'd be sick with it, too, if you had seen what I have seen in the past year...," replied Guy.

"For instance...," said the Abbot.

"For instance, I was walking with Bernard through the township of Chateau-Laudon when a lad suddenly accosts us, and showing us his frightful fistula, begs Bernard to cure him. Not to pray for him, mind you, not to bless him, but to cure him. And what does my humble brother do? He who is always preaching so much humility to us. What does he do? Without a moment's hesitation he raises his hand and makes the sign of the cross over the fellow's foot. Now that is what I call, not imprudence, but rank presumption."

"Uh-huh," grunted William. "What happened to the foot?"

Guy looked at him very cautiously from out the corner of his eye and answered, "It was cured."

William's delighted laugh again rang out in the quiet of the empty wood, this time setting a chipmunk, who had been bravely sunning himself in the early spring sunshine, scuttling to his hole.

"What are you laughing at?" asked Guy.

"At the rank presumption that works miracles," replied William.

"Miracles? Humbug!" growled Guy. "I tell you that such an action is tempting God."

"But God responded to the tempting, didn't He?" asked William with a smile.

"Yes, but that doesn't give my brother any right to the liberties he's been taking. Why look! You've heard of Josbert, haven't you, the Viscount of Dijon?"

"I should say I have," answered William. "A hard man if ever there was one."

"I know," said Guy, "he's a relative of ours. Early last fall he was struck with paralysis. The family immediately sent for Bernard and myself. We went, taking along with us our uncle Gaudry. When we reached the house we found Josbert unable to speak. The family was terribly upset, for Josbert had not been to the sacraments in a long, long time and this stroke looked very serious. They begged Bernard to do all in his power to help him. And do you know what my humble brother does?"

"I don't," said William repressing a smile at Guy's distress.

"He says, 'This man has offended God grievously. He has been tyrannical toward the poor and high-handed in his dealing with the Church and her properties. Promise to make restitution to all he has wronged and guarantee to put an end to all his unjust exactions and I will promise that he will have an opportunity to confess. I promise it in the name of the Lord.' Did you ever hear such presumption?" asked Guy. "'I promise it in the name of the Lord.'"

"Well, what happened?" asked Abbot William.

"Oh, they promised readily enough, and though Gaudry and I told Bernard that he was being rash, imprudent, presumptuous and flying in the face of God, he simply smiles and whispers, 'Have confidence. What you find so difficult to believe, God can do with ease.' That's his new name for presumption," snorted Guy. "Confidence!"

"I caught it," said William, "but go on with the story."

"Well," said Guy rather reluctantly, "we went to a nearby church and Bernard celebrated Mass for the sick man. He had just finished when Josbert's eldest son came rushing into the sacristy crying, 'My father is able to speak. He is calling for a confessor. Come.'"

"So presumption worked another miracle."

"Miracle? Miracle? Nonsense!" exclaimed Guy in disgust. "It was the Mass that did it."

"I see," said William. "Now, Guy, tell me: what do you think of all these stories that are circulating about your brother being a wonder-worker? There is the one about the boy with the fistula, another about an old lady with paralysis, another about...."

"Fables!" broke in Guy. "All fables!"

"All?" queried the Abbot.

"Well," said Guy with hesitancy, "I don't know about all. But, look here, Lord Abbot, let us not talk about things that no one can ever be sure about. I don't know whether all these stories are true or false, but I wish that they would stop. They can't help my brother any. He's liable to get some false notions. I know he's holy, very holy, and I can tell you that he receives many revelations during prayer. But let us stop there. I distrust the extraordinary."

"Guy," said Abbot William, "everyone simply has to love you, you are so blessedly honest. It is your outstanding virtue. As for myself, you win my affection because of your disease. You have a highly active case of incurable 'big-brotherliness.' Now be honest enough to answer me this: Is this Cistercian life difficult?"

As soon as his companion switched the conversation away from Bernard and his miracles, Guy's whole attitude changed; his step became more sprightly, his head lifted higher, and even his voice lost its gruffness. He became the Guy of old again—the soldier.

"That's a large question, Your Lordship," he said. "For some people this life would be impossible; for others, easy; for all those in between these extremes, it would be fairly hard."

"Well, how have you found it for yourself?" came the quick interrogation.

Guy stooped and picked an anemone that seemed to shiver in the shade of an oak; he twisted it in his fingers for a moment, then looked at William and said, "For me, in the beginning, this life was all but impossible."

"What do you mean?" asked the Abbot.

"Just what I say," answered Guy. "In the beginning this life was all but impossible. You must remember, my good Abbot, that I was knighted before I was nineteen, married before I was twenty and a father before I was legally a man. You must also remember that I spent most of my days and many of my nights with men who lived life at a high tempo. Action, energy, excitement, were in the air we breathed. I clashed with many a worthy foeman while doing service for the Duke; and I knew the intoxication brought on by the heady wine of victory. My life was one rollicking round of camp, battle, home and camp again. Never a dull moment. Then came Citeaux! What a change! Instead of boisterous, swaggering, hard-fighting, lovable comrades-in-arms I had the company of silent ascetics. Instead of the clash of arms and the spine-tingling tilt with death, instead of moments charged and surcharged with excitement, I had the hush of the swampland, the daily, deadening routine of psalm-singing, tilling the ground and psalm-singing again. I tell you, Abbot, those first few months were almost maddening."

William of St. Thierry was taken by complete surprise. He had never heard anything so nakedly honest in his life; nor had he ever expected anything so red-bloodedly human from a monk of Citeaux. All he could do was breathe a "Yes, the contrast was sharp," and "You must have longed for battle and its blood-rousing clash of arms. How did you manage to hold on?"

Guy tossed away the anemone he had crushed, then smiled a little sheepishly as he answered, "I guess the fundamental reason was that disease you spoke about. I really think my 'big-brotherliness,' as you call it, kept me in the ranks with my face to the foe those first awful months. You see, I had Bernard and Gerard, Bartholomew and Andrew to think of. I couldn't let them down. I was their older brother. If I retreated, they might have lost courage."

"That's a human motive," commented the Abbot and smiled as he added, "that disease can be salutary, can't it, Guy?"

"It certainly was in those days, and I look upon it as a gift from God, a great gift; even though you call it a disease. I wonder, my good Abbot, if our Lord Jesus Christ, didn't feel some such thing as this 'big-brotherliness' that you talk about when he knelt in the Garden of Gethsemene that first Holy Thursday night and looked death full in the face. I wonder if He didn't feel that steadying call, 'You must not let your younger brothers down.' I like to think it was that which spurred Him on to say, 'Not my will, but yours be done.' I may be wrong; but it is just my way of supernaturalizing the natural."

"A beautiful thought, Guy," complimented the Abbot, "and one that brings Jesus so much nearer to us than thinking of Him only as Lord and God. Did you have such thoughts in your early days?"

"I hardly think so," answered Guy honestly, "at least not in all its clarity. Undoubtedly God was near, and deep down in the very center of my being must have been that unshakable determination to be loyal to God in this Cistercian living. You see, I have not the fancy or imagination of Bernard. I am older and cannot respond to some of his catch phrases and rallying cries. He was and still is quite romantic about it all. But let me tell you, Abbot William, it wasn't the echo of battle or the memory of men who had fought by my side that pained me the most. No. It was the echo of a baby's laugh and a little girl's joyous prattle; it was the memory of a whisper from her whom I had wooed and won that was the hardest of all to bear." He paused, then added, "We are our own worst enemy and memory is our cruellest torturer."

"I can well imagine that," agreed William. "But, Guy, you must get marvelous consolation from the realization of where she is now and what she is doing."

"I do," answered Guy thoughtfully. "God humbles me more and more with His mercies. He also gives me more intentions for which to pray. Did you hear that my good Elizabeth has been elected Superior of Jully?"

"Not only that," replied William, "but I have also heard that she is a real mother and model to all. I look for great things from Jully, Guy; for, as you know, the spirituality of a house depends almost entirely on the sanctity of the superior. Little Adeline is with her mother, isn't she?"

"Yes, she has a disease like my 'big-brotherliness,'" laughed Guy, "only I suppose that we will have to call her sickness 'little-daughterliness.' She wanted to be near her mother."

"It looks as if God were using the natural again to bring about great supernaturalness, doesn't it? But tell me more about yourself and this Cistercian life."

"Oh," said Guy, "the first year was the worst. It is not the physical austerities of this life that hurt, Abbot William. The body can get accustomed to almost anything. The food is simple and sparse. The beds are hard. The hours in choir and the fields are long. But I often experienced longer hours, harder beds and worse food while fighting for His Excellency, the Duke. No, these are not so awfully difficult. But the mental sufferings—ah, that is a different matter."

"How so?" asked the Abbot.

"Well, you see, Stephen Harding was a sympathetic and very understanding Abbot. He knew what would bother us most, so he very wisely filled our days to the brim. Hardly a minute was allowed for our own personal disposal during those first months of novitiate. He kept us so busy that we did not have time to think of what we had left behind. The days passed quickly, but the nights—oh! Those nights when sleep was banished by the echoes of the past. Ah, but you're not interested in my nightmares of the years that are gone."

"I think I understand fully; but what I want to know is how soon did all difficulty end for you."

"All difficulty," echoed Guy; and he accented the "all." "Why, my good Abbot, all difficulty will end only when I am dead. Each stage of life has its own difficulties. Those of my novitiate were the cruellest, because the temptation was to go back. But as soon as we left Cîteaux, we found a whole new crop of different difficulties awaiting us here at Clairvaux. Our first few years were awful. There was extreme poverty. We did not have food enough, nor clothing enough. To make matters worse, Bernard was at his ascetical worst. He wanted more than perfection! But just as soon as he came to his senses and the extreme poverty was lifted, I found myself with new difficulties. I am what they call the 'sub-cellarer' of this monastery. My brother, Gerard, is the 'cellarer.' That means that Gerard and I have to take care of all the temporalities connected with this ever-growing community and this wide and deep valley. Sometimes I wonder just what I am: monk, farmer, woodsman, herdsman, builder, stonemason, or what. Don't talk about all difficulties vanishing...."

"I see," interrupted the Abbot with a smile. "But, Guy, about the life itself—the silence, the cloister, the fasts, the labor—is it all so awfully difficult?"

Guy turned in the path and faced back toward the monastery before answering. Only after he had stepped across a little brook that was noisy with the splash of many waters did he venture to say, "The Cistercian mode of living is impossible, unless one has seen the Christ of Calvary. Everything about it is a bit exaggerated, isn't it Abbot William?"

"Comparatively speaking, yes," answered the Abbot. "You do more in the penitential line than any Order in the Church today."

"Well, that exaggeration needs some justification," resumed Guy. "And there is only one. It is, as Bernard says, that invitation which lovers accept as a command; it is the, 'Come, follow me,' of Jesus Christ." He stopped and laid his hand on a towering oak. He seemed to be studying the bark. After a moment's pause, he turned to the Abbot who had stopped with him, and said, "Your Lordship, the only reason I can give for kissing two little girls a last good-bye and saying a final farewell to the woman I promised to have and to hold 'till death do us part' is the exaggeration that wrought redemption; that awful exaggeration of a God nailed to a tree. I am trying to catch up with Jesus Christ, as Bernard so often exhorts us to do. Now to anyone who grasps that concept, to anyone who has caught the truth of Calvary, this Cistercian life is a delight, even though it pinches, pains and wearies."

"Then it is not entirely a question of 'big-brotherliness,' is it?" said William as they made the last turn in the path and came in sight of the monastery buildings.

"Well, I hope you won't mind my contradicting Your Lordship, but I really think that that is all that it is—the 'big-brotherliness' of Jesus Christ stimulating us, His younger brothers, to hurry on and catch up."

"And you tell me that you're not as romantic as Bernard...."

"That's not romanticism, that is realism," answered Guy. "Jesus is 'the first-born of many brethren.'"

"Enough!" cried the Abbot. "Bernard is giving all of you his art of quoting Scripture. There he is now. I must see him. Thank you, Guy, for your honesty and inspiration."

"My what?" gasped Guy, but William had gone.

My Big Brother Can Help Us Now

Guy had been right when he summed up his life as a succession of new difficulties. The year of novitiate had been hard; the first year at Clairvaux harder, and this, the twenty-first year there, was actually the hardest of all. But Guy did not mind it, for William of St. Thierry had been right when he said that Guy was afflicted with incurable 'big-brotherliness.'

Of course, he contracted that malady back in the castle of Fontaines some forty-five years before, when his mother first gave him the care of little Gerard. Guy became the 'big brother' that day and as Gerard was followed by Bernard, Humbeline, Andrew, Bartholomew and Nivard, he had little chance of losing his title. The first-born in any large family knows responsibility from childhood, and never lays aside his charge even in old age. So it was with Guy. He worried about Bernard. He worried about Gerard. He worried about Andrew, Bartholomew and Nivard. And that, in spite of the fact that Bernard was his Abbot, Gerard his superior in the cellarer's office, and all the rest at least his equal in the community. He was concerned about their physical well-being, and, as we have seen, deeply concerned about their spiritual health. It had ever been. It would ever be. He could not help it. It was all because he had been born first. To many this 'big-brotherliness' was amusing; to the brothers it was often annoying; but to all it was really admirable. For, next to the inexpressible love and care of a mother, there is in God's wide world no greater love perhaps than that of and for 'the big brother.'

In midsummer of 1135, when Clairvaux lay panting under a merciless hot spell, Bernard sent for Guy, and did it with a scowl on his forehead and a trace of irritation in his voice. The 'big brother' complex was not all one-sided. Bernard and the others relied on Guy in more ways than one. The habit of youth had matured into manhood's true appreciation, and Guy was called on to counsel, guide and help. Bernard had made him sub-cellarer not so much because of his position in the family as for his prudence and practicality. And hence, though he was spiritual father to Guy, Bernard still found himself dependent on one he had always looked up to.

Some such thought was worming its way to the surface of Bernard's mind when a footfall he immediately recognized as Guy's was heard outside his door. Then came the well-known knock. Bernard gave the signal to enter with a tone that bespoke determination. Guy entered. He was soaked with perspiration. The dampness stood out on his white habit; his face was a lurid red over which streams of perspiration poured. Guy was hot, very hot; and he looked tired. He knelt, received his brother's blessing, then said, "Something on your mind, my Reverend Father?"

"Very much," came the quick reply. "What is this I hear about the monk who died in Normandy? Is it true that you gave orders to have him buried there?"

"It is," came the quiet but very firm reply from Guy.

"Why?" snapped Bernard.

"I thought it the prudent and practical thing to do. We're busy with the building of the monastery. We need every hand we have. I also thought poverty demanded it. Normandy is a goodly distance from here. We have no horses that could make the journey. We would have had to hire relays."

"Hmm," mused Bernard. "So it was a question of horses and money, was it?"

"Not to mention men. We've got a gigantic task in this new building. We cannot afford to spare a single soul. Furthermore," added Guy, "isn't it only common sense? What difference does it make where we lay his body as long as his soul has gone to God?"

"But he requested that he sleep here at Clairvaux, among his brethren," answered Bernard.

"Sentimentality!"

"What?" questioned Bernard quickly.

"I said, 'sentimentality,'" replied Guy, "and you know that it is nothing else. How often have I heard you tell postulants to leave their bodies at the door, that they would find room only for their souls here? And you are right! Then why grow maudlin over a corpse? He was a good monk. His soul is safe."

"So that's how you look at it, is it? Well, let me tell you something. You, too, will lack the very satisfaction this brother craved. You will not be buried here at Clairvaux."

Guy looked at his brother very studyingly and found him most determined. His eyes held fire and his eyebrows pulled his forehead down in a frown. Guy wiped the perspiration from his brow and managed a smile as he said, "I like not that tone of voice, Reverend Father...."

"Oh, call me Bernard," broke in his brother. "There is no need for formality between us."

"I see, Reverend Father," answered Guy. "As I was saying, your tone of voice takes me back twenty-three years. It was in that very tone of voice that you predicted my wife's capitulation or death. Are you prophesying now, or is it just the heat?"

"It is not the heat," came the speedy reply. Then Bernard smiled. The whole atmosphere of the room changed with that smile. He did not look like the same person who had spoken two seconds before. There was a mellowness, a charm, a radiant serenity to his countenance that called forth an answering smile from Guy, who said, "That's better. That's much better!"

"It is a trifle warm, isn't it, Guy? But why do you have to make things warmer by your stinginess? Oh, Guy, poverty never calls for a sparing hand where your brothers are concerned. Never! Economy and parsimony are not even distant relations to religious poverty. But it's done now. Let it go."

"I'm sorry to have disappointed you, Bernard," said Guy, "but that's what you get for making a dolt sub-cellarer. I belong far back in the ranks...."

"You belong just where you're put," broke in his younger brother. "And now give me your advice. What would you think of sending young Nivard to Brittany? A Duke Conon has given us a site for a monastery at de Buzay. I was seriously thinking of taking Nivard from Vaucelles and sending him to de Buzay as Prior. What do you say?"

"This is the first time that you have thought of making any of the family a first superior."

"I know it," answered Bernard. "I hate nepotism!"

"Well," said Guy after some thought, "the lad has done a fine job at Vaucelles...."

"Yes," put in Bernard, "everyone has been enthusiastic about the way he has trained the novices. Many call him the perfect novice master."

"Then why not leave well enough alone?"

"Because I think well enough can always be bettered," returned Bernard. "I think Nivard is a real leader. He has had a few years' experience molding novices; I believe he will be a success with monks. What do you say?"

"I know he will do his best. He's a conscientious little tyke. He has a way with him, too. Everybody likes him. He'll give them your doctrine on love for God. He'll..."

"My doctrine?" broke in Bernard. "You mean God's doctrine. I only preach the first commandment."

"I know," said Guy. "So, as I was saying, he'll give them God's first commandment in Bernard's fashion. My only reason for hesitating is that he happens to be our youngest brother. Will small minds cry 'family favoritism'?"

"I don't think so," said Bernard musingly. "I haven't heard the semblance of an accusation in twenty-one years...."

"Yes, but you've given us only positions that were burdensome. Gerard, cellarer; myself, sub-cellarer; Andrew, gatekeeper; Bartholomew, sacristan; Nivard, master of novices. There was no brilliance connected with any of these offices! That's why you've heard nothing. But to make Nivard Prior...and yet, why not? He has every qualification as far as I can see."

"That's exactly what I've been thinking," said Bernard. "And I think I'll follow my old principle of the right man in the right place regardless of kinship, affection or criticism."

"Humph," snorted Guy. "So that's your principle is it? Then I can conclude that Gerard and I are just good workhorses, can I?"

Bernard looked at his older brother and a twinkle of merriment stole into his truly beautiful eyes as he said, "Gerard is good, but you must remember that you are only *sub*-cellarer." Then after sharing a glance of complete understanding with Guy, he said, "In all seriousness, Guy, I'd send you to Brittany, but I'd be lost without my big brother!"

"Stop!" exclaimed Guy as he held up his hand. "You almost complimented me then. If you ever did that I'd know for certain that either the heat at Clairvaux or your work in Italy on that awful schism had affected you. Tell me, did you manage to pick up any news of Humbeline in your travels?"

"Not directly," answered Bernard, "but I have news from Jully. As I was coming back from Italy I heard that the community at Jully is very interestedly watching what they call 'a race to overtake Christ.' Elizabeth, Humbeline and Adeline seem to be rivaling one another in their efforts to become saints. And from one report, Adeline seems to be in the lead."

Guy's eyes sparkled. His whole countenance glowed as he breathed, "God's strange, but marvelous ways! Oh, Bernard, do we thank Him enough? Think of it! My wife, my daughter and my sister serving Him and Him alone in the one convent. It's breath-taking. It's humiliating. It's inspiring! I'm glad they've caught your spark and are hurrying after Christ."

"My spark!" smiled Bernard. "My spark? Didn't I hear you say something about *your* wife and *your* daughter and *your* sister? Guy, *you're* amusing. But before you go into any more rhapsodies or ecstacies, run along and let me do some work, and please pray for the termination of this awful schism."

That summer fled into autumn, and autumn died into winter without any change in the schism caused by Peter de Leone as anti-pope. During these months Bernard began his sermons on the Canticle of Canticles and had Guy worried lest he prove impractical as he opened his heart and let his community gaze on depths some of them never dreamed existed.

It was a trying time for Bernard and for Guy. The schism weighed heavily on Bernard's mind, and anything that worried Bernard worried Guy; then the new monastery was being built, one that was destined to house seven hundred monks; finally princes and prelates kept clamoring for colonies from Clairvaux to found new monasteries in their domains. Each new foundation meant new work and worry for Guy, for he had to prepare the monks for the journey.

In 1136, he thought he had too much work and worry at Clairvaux itself, but Bernard thought differently, so he called his oldest brother to his room and said, "Guy, I want you to go to the diocese of Bourges. Take charge of the building of the new monastery there. See that it is well built and according to Cistercian traditions. Sorry to be so abrupt, but you will have to hurry if you would accompany the donor." That was all. It startled Guy a little, but he was used to Bernard's hurried commands, so he was off in a moment.

By the time that late October's winds were stripping the trees of their yellow and scarlet leaves, Guy had the monastery at Bourges under roof, so he felt that he could return to Clairvaux and his brothers. He started back, but on the eve of All Saints' Day, he turned his horse's head toward the monastery of Pontigny, for a fever was racing through his veins and pounding at his temples making the world swim before him and his seat in the saddle very uncertain.

At the gate of the monastery he slumped forward, fell on his horse's neck, then slipped from the saddle just as the gatekeeper arrived. A very sick man was carried to the infirmary and put to bed. All the resources of the monastery were quickly called into play, for this was the Abbot of Clairvaux's big brother. But work as they would, the fever would not abate. At the hour of Compline Guy looked up from eyes that were clouded with pain and managed a smile as he said, "God is coming. Sudden as a thief; but not so stealthily. My lamp is burning. I am ready for the Bridegroom."

At that very moment, over one hundred miles to the east, the community of Clairvaux was assembled in their chapter room. Bernard looked down the four parallel lines of hooded monks and lay brothers and with a choke in his voice said, "Pray with me the prayers for the dying. Our big brother Guy is in his last agony."

The prayers were started and the fervor in Bernard's voice caused many a breath to be caught in a sudden gasp. On they went, earnestly, beseechingly, solemnly. Men were pulling at the heartstrings of God with piteous pleas. To those in the chapter room it seemed that heaven was just above them and that God was bending down to catch every syllable they uttered. On and on went that warm, soul-stirring voice of Bernard's. It seemed almost tremulous with tears as petition after petition rose from his lips. Then suddenly he stopped. A startled hush gripped the room. A gasp was heard here and there as surprised men caught their breath. Then came the well-known triumphant tone of their Abbot, "My brethren," he said, "let us change our prayer. Let us now ask Guy to intercede with God for us! Yes, for our big brother is now in a place where he can do so effectively."

The community looked at one another. They did not immediately catch the full import of Bernard's words. Only the keenest realized that in one little sentence their Abbot had announced Guy's death and beatitude. Gradually, like a flame licking its way along the leaves in a furrow, the realization passed from monk to monk. Then faces brightened, and eyes brimmed with tears, tears of joy and gratitude, as they looked up to stars, and the sigh, "Thank God," was almost audible.

Guy was buried at Pontigny, far from his beloved Clairvaux. Bernard had uttered prophecy that hot summer's morn in 1135. But I don't think his big brother's happiness in heaven was greatly disturbed by the lack of a grave in the Valley of Light.

Some sixteen years after, Bernard lay ill at Clairvaux and many of the numerous community thought that his end was near. One of them suddenly caught sight of four men whom he recognized as Geoffrey of Langres, Humbert of Igny, and Bernard's two brothers Guy and Gerard. These four embraced the sick man and held converse with him for some time. Then they started to withdraw. "Going without me?" queried Bernard. "This time, yes," came the reply, "but after the season of the new crops our desire and yours will be satisfied." Guy was still playing the big brother. He must prepare Bernard for death. They had a reunion in heaven the following August.

Can This Be Madness?

Most of us will understand and agree with the words Elizabeth de Forez addressed to Bernard in the autumn of 1111. To request that a young, beautiful and vivacious wife, who is the mother of two winsome little daughters, should grant her knighted husband permission to become a monk while she betakes herself to a convent seems to demand the reply, "You're mad!" That answer will find ready echo in the sympathetic minds and hearts of most of us.

Not so many of us will understand and agree with the permission she gave some weeks later. And only the very few will either agree or understand her own action years after. Some of us will be tempted to say, "She was mad." But listen to what history relates:

Not many years after Guy had gone to Citeaux, Elizabeth de Forez entered the Benedictine convent at Jully. Her piety and zeal were such that not long after her profession she was elected Superior and won for herself the eulogy, "A woman of uncommon virtue, the mother of many virgins." That line won for her ultimately the title "Blessed Elizabeth," a title which means that her life was crowned with the only success worth striving for—sanctity!

Her little Adeline followed her to Jully and was trained in the religious life by her. On her death the daughter went to the convent at Poulangy which adopted the reform of Citeaux. In time she became the Abbess of this convent, and under her rule Poulangy became noted for its holiness. Today Adeline holds the same title as her mother and her father; she is called "Blessed Adeline."

Now if Elizabeth de Forez had insisted that Guy stay by her side and Bernard go about his business, she would never have been known beyond the tiny circle of illiterate serfs, who lived on that speck of the earth that is called Fontaines, in the few years during those ages history has dubbed "Dark." Today, what a contrast!

Undoubtedly God's ways are strange ways, very strange ways. But isn't it a glorious strangeness? Unquestionably Bernard's request sounded mad. It was mad. But it made three "Blesseds" for heaven. While of Adeline's little sister, history does not even give her name. We only know that she married someone.

It makes one think, doesn't it?

The Man of One Idea

"We have to be exaggerated."

Gerard tested the last link of his steel corslet. It was a task that he insisted on doing himself; for he claimed that the one heart he had was too precious a treasure to be entrusted to the careless fingers of some serf. He had found no flaw in the armor, and yet he frowned, and frowned deeply, as he pulled on the last link.

"Something loose, Gerard? If so, there is an armorer working down in the hollow."

Gerard dropped the corslet on the stump of a tree that he was making serve as a bench and said, "No, Dennis, there is nothing wrong with the mail. But there are some links loose around here; links that the armorer down in the hollow can't fix."

"What are you talking about? It's David himself who is working down there. And there is no better smith in the country."

"I know," answered Gerard. "But David never worked on the links I have reference to. Have you seen my uncle Gaudry around?"

"No, not today."

"He's one link. Have you seen my brother Andrew or Guy around?"

"No, not lately."

"They're two more links."

"What do you mean, Gerard? What's wrong with you anyhow? You don't act like yourself. You don't talk like yourself. Why, you don't even look like yourself. Cheer up, man! This siege won't last long. We'll take Grancy before the snow flies. Come now, give us your smile."

"Dennis," said Gerard, "you've been in this army longer than I; so, tell me: Can men be sane who ride away from a siege in order to become monks?"

Dennis pushed Gerard's corslet aside as he sat down on the tree stump and said, "You're liable to see anything in this army, Gerard. But I would say that real men never ride away from a siege at all. But why the question? And why the solemn face? Smile, man; it won't hurt you."

"No, it won't hurt me," said Gerard. "It will kill me! Now to wipe that smile off your face, let me tell you that Gaudry and my two brothers have ridden away from this siege for the sole purpose of becoming monks, and Cistercian monks at that!"

"What?" exclaimed Dennis leaping to his feet and seizing Gerard by the two arms. "Say that again. Say it again and say it slowly."

Gerard scowled in impatience as he pushed Dennis from him saying, "Be quiet or you'll arouse the whole camp. Sit down again and do some thinking with me."

Dennis protested, but Gerard backed him up to the tree stump and sat him on it. Dennis was one of those little, fiery men, keen, quick, supple and as durable as steel. Gerard with his youth, his robust frame, and his obvious strength, made quite a contrast to his little companion. When he succeeded in sitting the sputtering Dennis down, Gerard stood over him and said, "They call me 'one-idea Gerard,' don't they, Dennis?" The little one shook his head as he grunted, "Uh-huh." "Well," went on Gerard, "I'm glad they do; and I'm glad it's true.

I had one idea as a boy, and now that I am a man, I have the same one idea. It is to be a man, a real man, a knight as noble, as brave, as fearless as my father. Is there anything wrong in that?"

"Of course not," snapped Dennis with a disgusted shake of his head. "But what has that got to do with Gaudry, Guy and Andrew?"

"They're not men of one idea," replied Gerard. "And I'm beginning to wonder if they are men at all."

"Back up, there!" exclaimed Dennis starting up from his seat and holding out a hand in protest. "You're talking about two real veterans and a youngster who promises well."

"I know. I know," answered Gerard hurriedly as he pushed the protesting Dennis back on the tree stump, "and that's what puzzles me. What has come over them? If they had left to become 'Hospitallers' I could understand their move. For then all they would have to do would be to put a black mantle with its red Maltese cross over their shoulders, keep their suits of armor, their battle-axes and their steeds; keep all the skill that they have won by years at war and use it for the glory of God. But no! They've gone to become marsh-dwellers. They've gone to lay aside their arms and armor. They've gone to take the cowl of the Cistercians and become plowboys and cowherds and...."

"Gerard, what are you talking about? Do you mean to tell me that Gaudry, Lord of Tuillon, has gone to become a monk? Why, he's a married man! He's one of the highest ranking officers in the army. He's.... Oh, you must be mistaken."

"You're right, Dennis. I must be greatly mistaken. You're very right; either I am crazy or they are. But I am telling you that my brother Bernard came into this camp three days back and talked like a fanatic. He was all afire about serving God as a Cistercian monk and he won Gaudry, Lord of Tuillon, married man and ranking officer though he is; he won Guy, my oldest brother, heir apparent to Fontaines and married man too; he won young Andrew, the boy who promised to be Burgundy's proudest knight; and today, Bernard was back again trying to win me. Now I want to know who is the fool...."

"But I don't understand," broke in Dennis. "You mean to say that these three are going to give up the army forever? That they are going to become monks?"

Gerard put his hands on his hips, hung his head on one side and looked exasperatedly at his little comrade as he asked, "Dennis, how often do you have to be told a thing? Three times already I've said that these three have left the army. They are no longer here. They've gone to become monks! Now what I want to know is who is insane, they or I?"

"I'm insane!" said Dennis jumping up from his stump and rapidly pacing the length of the shelter. "Yes, I'm insane. All I can hear is nonsense from your lips; and you never speak nonsense."

"Sit down and talk sense," commanded Gerard with a gesture toward the stump.

"No," said Dennis. "I'll be like Godfrey de Bouillon. I'll sit on the earth, and may three or five or even ten emirs walk in on me."

"What are you talking about?—Godfrey de Bouillon—emirs—and sitting on the ground. Stand up!"

"Didn't you ever hear that story?" asked Dennis without stirring from his seat on the ground. "You see, several emirs came down from their mountains in Samaria to pay homage and present gifts to the new King of Jerusalem. They found him seated just as I am now, but without a raving soldier like you in front of him. They were amazed to find the King unattended and remarked on His Majesty's place of rest. Godfrey, in true oriental fashion, calmly asked, 'Why should not the earth, from which we are sprung and to which we must return after death, serve us as a seat while we live?' The emirs went away marveling at his wisdom. So now, my young friend, I'm on the ground; marvel at my wisdom and show a little yourself. Give me the whole story."

Gerard gave vent to a sigh of helplessness and sat down on the stump facing the squatting Dennis and began by saying, "My brother Bernard...."

"That's the slight one, isn't it? Fair hair like your father's, fair skin like your mother's, a fine-looking lad?"

"That's Bernard," said Gerard, "Well, three days back he came into camp...."

"All afire," supplied Dennis. "I know that; but what did he say? How did he get Gaudry to consider his proposition? What were his arguments?"

"Oh, I don't know all of them," answered Gerard in disgust. "Bernard can talk like a dervish dances. It is not what he says, but how he says it. It is not only his mouth that speaks but his eyes, his head, his hands, his whole body and being. It was a lot about being men and heroes and generous and grateful and giving our all to God, our knightly selves and our knightly service. He was here again today with the same...."

Just then a voice was heard saying, "Is he in there now? Well, I'm going to see him."

Dennis and Gerard looked at the opening of the rude shelter in time to see Bernard hand his reins to a groom and stride toward them with determination evident in his every move. With a mere hurried nod to the squatting Dennis he walked to Gerard and abruptly asked, "Are you coming?"

Gerard arose slowly, put his two hands on his brother's shoulders and said, "Bernard, if you were asking me to join the Knights of the Holy Sepulcher, organized last year by Baldwin, King of Jerusalem, I might consider your request. If you were asking me to ride to Germany and do all in my power to smash that sacrilegious Henry V, I'd more than consider your request. But when you say, 'Citeaux'—pardon my smiling. I'm a man, a knight, a warrior; and that I intend to stay. Do you hear me? That I intend to stay! So, run along now and don't waste any more of your time or mine. It's too precious."

"The man of one idea talking, eh?" said Bernard as he glared at his brother.

"That's right, Bernard, the man of one big idea; and it's not to become a monk in the swamps. Incidentally, lad, do you see that town over there with its battlemented castles? Well, that's Grancy. Do you see all these warriors around here? Well, they're the Duke of Burgundy's men, and they are laying siege to that town. So you see this is no place for nice little boys who want to become monks. So run along."

"I shall, Gerard," said Bernard with blazing eyes, "but before I do, I want you to hear this. Obviously nothing but some real suffering will shake that one idea of yours out of your head. Well and good." Then taking a step nearer his brother, he went on, "Very soon this side of yours will be opened. A lance will do it. And through that opening," said Bernard as he placed his hand just below the ribs on Gerard's right side, "your heart will be reached and your hard head."

Gerard gave a soft, low laugh. "I'll remember the exact spot, Bernard," he said as he brushed his brother's hand from his side. "But now, be a good little brother and run along. I've got to fix up this shelter."

Bernard wheeled around and his back was positively eloquent as he strode to his waiting horse. When the hoof beats had fully died away, Dennis made his first move since Bernard's appearance. Getting up from the ground he picked up Gerard's steel corslet and while examining it closely he said, "Be sure that this is in good condition, Gerard. Be sure that it is in very good condition. I didn't like the way that brother of yours spoke. What a firebrand! So that's Bernard, is it? I see now why Guy and Gaudry and Andrew left the siege. Young Bernard has more fire than any ten of us. Whew! What a man! You're right when you say that his mouth alone does not speak, it's his whole being. I feel as if I had just seen a thunderbolt. I'm glad he didn't speak to me."

"I suppose you'd go with him," said Gerard in scorn.

"I'm not saying I would and I'm not saying I wouldn't," replied the little warrior shaking his head, "but I have my own ideas on the subject."

"So have I," replied Gerard, "and you've just heard them. So let's forget Bernard and fix this place up more comfortably. We may be here for weeks."

With that they set to work, but while Dennis' hands and feet moved here and there, moving this and that, his mind was occupied with a study in character contrasts. He had caught his first flash of Bernard, and found it an illuminating one. He could only marvel at the concentrated power in the one slight frame. Then he had to smile as he looked at Gerard and realized how perfectly he had been named when they dubbed him 'one idea.' For this last encounter showed him Gerard as a hardheaded man, a balky man, one who would never move until proof positive had been given that motion is an absolute necessity.

Dennis nodded his head in assent as he reflected that there was much in favor of such minds and such men. They are slow to start he admitted, but once in motion, they gather such momentum that they become practically irresistible forces. If Gerard had not been so intent on his work, he would have seen laughter dancing in Dennis' eyes as the little man studied his face. Dennis finally told himself that men of Gerard's type suffer not from slow thought processes but from deep-seated prejudices. One idea grips them, goes into a persuasion, then mounts to a complete obsession. When he reached this stage of his analysis Dennis chuckled audibly and startled Gerard into asking, "What are you laughing at?"

"Oh, I was just thinking," answered the little man, "thinking how it takes heaven and earth to shake some men loose from their fixed ideas."

"Meaning me?" questioned Gerard.

"You and all others like you," laughed Dennis. "All I've got to say before leaving you, Sir Knight, is that your attitude of mind is as dangerous as it is beneficial. It will lead you to sanctity or suicide. Adieu!" And with that he bowed and bowed as he gracefully backed out òf the rude shelter and left Gerard in a quandary whether to laugh at the comic exit or to storm at the character sketch. He finally laughed.

Dennis had been right in his summation and his observation. Gerard was one of those individuals who have only one end, one aim, one ambition; and such individuals do become either saints or suicides. Gerard almost became both.

Time for Thought

Bernard had a very disconsolate ride back to Fontaines that bright October afternoon in 1111, for he had set his heart on winning this favorite brother of his to join him in the great adventure of becoming a Cistercian monk. Gerard was the second oldest of the family and easily the most loved and most lovable of the boys. "Good-natured Gerard," was the way most people spoke of him, for cheerfulness was always twinkling in his eyes, and joy radiating from his person. He was not the fiery leader that Bernard was, nor the composed and commanding character that Guy became, but with his quiet simplicity and natural sociability, he was found to be the most popular of Tescelin's sons. Bernard loved him with that undemonstrative but fiercely burning love that can exist only between two brothers of almost the same age and of contrasting characteristics.

As Bernard breasted the last rise on his long ride home the sun was silhouetting the castle of Fontaines on a background of crimson and flame. It was a thrilling sight and had Bernard sitting straighter in his saddle as his heart lifted and his spirits swelled. Even his horse was affected and tossed his head and set his black manè flying as he spiritedly single-footed towards his journey's end. A breath of evening breeze touched a tall maple that stood hard by the road and sent leafy flakes, engoldened by glad October's hand, fluttering on Bernard and his mount. Bernard looked up to the leafy shower of gold and laughed aloud as he said, "Yes, and I know that the Spirit of God will breathe on Gerard and shake him loose even as these leaves; shake him completely loose from that one idea of his. The big, lovable, hard-headed lout!"

At about the same moment that Bernard spoke his eulogy to the wind, little Dennis looked in on the object of the praise and asked, "Will you join the boys in my tent, Gerard? We're going to have a little game by candle-light."

"Not tonight, Dennis. I'm not in the mood. I'm going to turn in before the stars come out. Who knows but what we may have to turn out before they go in?"

"Huh," snorted Dennis. "Not from that sleepy town. They prefer the stout walls of castles to the open plain. They'll never bother us. Take my word for it." Then changing his tone, he said, "Well, if you won't join us, you won't. I know you. So, sleep tight. Happy dreams!" And Dennis was away.

Gerard did not have very happy dreams that night despite Dennis' good wish, for Bernard, Gaudry and Guy with emirs from Samaria and monks from Citeaux and men from Grancy passed and repassed in impossible combinations. But it was the last which awoke him, and awoke him with a suddenness that shocked. He faintly heard his name called in high excitement, "Gerard! Gerard! Gerard!" Struggling with his sleep, he flung himself off his couch and became wide awake as he saw a small group of mail-clad warriors bearing in on him. He made one darting motion toward his battle-axe and then came blackness.

Two hours later Gerard was lying in one of Grancy's prisons, shackled hand and foot, with two attendants sitting by. "That boy has a bad wound," said the elder of the two as he looked again at the dressing he had made.

"Well, fix it up right," snapped the other. "That boy has got to live. He'll bring a fat ransom."

"Who is he?" came the first.

"I don't know," came the gruff reply. "I heard him called 'Gerard,' but judging from his quarters and his arms he must be some high noble."

The other bent to Gerard's right side and felt the bandage he had placed there. He gave a grunt of satisfaction and said, "Right below the ribs, and by a lance head, too. He's a lucky boy it didn't go any further. Who captured him?"

"I did," snarled the other, "for I wounded him. I was in his shelter before the others and had just stepped to one side out of the light of the entrance when he awoke. He was off his couch in a bound and like lightning his right arm shot out toward a battle-axe that looked brutal. I saw my opening and shot my lance up under his outstretched arm, and there is your man."

Just then a groan from the shackled prisoner stopped their talk. Gerard stirred, mumbled brokenly and opened his eyes. He shook his head, looked around in bewildered fright and shouted, "Oh! Oh! I'm a monk, a Cistercian monk." The guards looked at one another. Then the younger broke into a hard, harsh laugh. "Ha!" he said, "the joke's on me. I thought that I had captured a noble, one that would bring a mighty ransom. Now I learn that I have wounded only a monk. You can have him, Pierre. Teach him your art of binding up wounds. I'm going to bed. It's been a miserable night."

Gerard listened as well as he could and the mists of bewilderment gradually lifted from his mind. Trying to move he found that he was shackled hand and foot, but more! He found a burning stab of pain in his right side and yes! It was just below the ribs, exactly where Bernard's hand had rested. Gerard closed his eyes then and as the door banged behind his disgruntled assailant he said to himself, "I wish I were a Cistercian monk!"

The weeks passed and Gerard's side healed perfectly, but his head and his heart hurt much. He did not like the exact way that Bernard's prediction had been fulfilled. He wanted to call it just a strange coincidence, and forget the prediction even as he was forgetting the wound. He would not call it a prophecy, for that would mean that he would have to give up the one idea of his life, that of being a famous knight. But as the days went into weeks and the weeks into months and Gerard had only the four walls of his prison to look at, he began slowly, oh, so slowly to admit the possibility of another life than that of man-at-arms. He hadn't really admitted it as yet. No, it would take more than a prophecy from Bernard to make him do that; but Gerard did make some faint mental gestures toward admitting it. He conceded that possibly Bernard's prediction was more than mere prediction, and that life in a swamp couldn't be any worse than life in a cell.

Snow had flown and flown many times since Dennis had said that Grancy would be taken; and Grancy was not taken. In fact, the snows of 1111 were melting beneath the warm breath of March in 1112 when news came to Gerard, not that Grancy had fallen, but that Bernard and thirty nobles were setting out for Citeaux. He could not believe his ears. Despite his shackles he paced his cell torn between admiration and exasperation, muttering to himself, "Thirty? Thirty? But no, it can't be. Yet Bernard does not lie. Thirty. I wonder who they can be. It's wonderful. Yes, and it's awful! That's why Grancy has not been taken! That fanatic brother of mine has upset the whole army. Thirty. How did he ever get thirty? Was that a prophecy about me? Or was it only accident that I got hit exactly where his hand had rested? Thirty? And Bernard sends word that I am to trust in God and that all will be well. Huh! How easily said. And yet..." Gerard felt his side and the scar tissue where the lance had pierced.

Five months in a cell can seem like an eternity; and that is just what it seemed like to the shackled Gerard. He grew restless under the restraint, angry at the army for not taking the town and puzzled by the lack of ransom. Naturally Bernard and his project of Citeaux entered his thoughts often and colored most of his moods. He tried to picture warriors like Gaudry and Guy going through the routine of a monastic day. He laughed to himself often and pitied them much; but by trying to fathom the motive that had urged them on, Gerard gradually developed a God-consciousness that had him in awe. His mother had taught him well and his father had given him the best of example; but it took five months in a prison cell to give birth to an awareness of God that he felt to the very marrow of his bones. As this grew he often nodded and told the four walls and the little window of his cell that knights could become monks and serve God loyally. But he wondered if it should not be in Jerusalem as a Hospitaller or a Guardian of the Holy Sepulcher rather than at Citeaux. These newly founded military Orders appealed greatly to Gerard and never more so than as his God-consciousness developed in a Grancy prison and he realized that he ought to be giving something back to God for all that God had given him.

At the twilight hour one morning in mid-March, just before the last silver-petalled flower withered in the heaven's whitening blue, Gerard, while tossing on his hard bed, dreamed that he heard a voice saying, "This day you shall be freed." With the dawn he awoke and spent a wearying day wondering what the dream could have meant. As evening came on he stood at his little window watching the early chill stars come out and cling to the edge of some frosty clouds. Inadvertently, he touched the manacles of his wrists and was startled to wide-awake alertness by the sound of snapping iron. He jumped as they clanged on the floor of his cell. Anxiously he looked to the door but nobody came. Bending down he touched the iron anklets and they, too, fell away. He was in no reverie now!

"This day you shall be freed" rang in his ears. He dared not believe it, even as he hoped that it was true. Cautiously he crept to the door and gasped when he found it unlocked and the corridor empty. With every sense at nervous attention he felt his way along the wall and stole on tiptoe to the castle courtyard. This too was empty, but Gerard's heart failed him as he looked at the massive gate. "This day you shall be freed," again rang in his ears. Trembling with fright and shaking with anxiety he approached the forbidding barrier. He put his hand on it timidly, then jumped back in terror; for it had yielded to his slightest pressure. With wildly beating heart he pushed it just wide enough for him to squeeze through. But as the gate closed behind him Gerard knew panic for he found himself standing on what looked to him like the most thickly populated street imaginable. All Grancy seemed to be out, and it all seemed to be on that particular street at that precise moment. Many were hurrying toward the church and these gave Gerard a desperate idea. If he could only reach that church he would be safe, for the right of asylum would never be violated. He felt frozen to the spot but instinct urged him to move, so taking a deep breath he started to walk toward the church. He felt that everyone was staring at him but since nobody stopped him he marched on. Fifty yards, forty yards, thirty, twenty, now only ten yards away was the church door; but right here Gerard stood stock-still, for there in front of him was the jailor's brother.

Flight or fight? Gerard felt impelled to both; but before he had decided which, his breath was taken from him by the greeting, "You'd better hurry or you'll miss the sermon." Gerard waited for no more. He hurried to that sermon as he had never hurried to any other sermon in his whole life. He reached the door, took one mighty step inside, and as his two feet came together he heaved one of the most grateful sighs of his twenty-five years. He was safe, absolutely safe; a miracle had done it!

Gerard heard very little of the sermon that night, for his mind was fully occupied reviewing the events of the past five months; and even to his hard head it was all too clear God was calling! That's all that Bernard's prophecy and its exact fulfillment could mean. That's all his dream of the morning and his astounding escape this evening said. Yes, God was calling. It was true. He must answer. He had to do it. He simply had to give up the one idea of his life and shake himself loose from his heart-deep ideal. It would not be knighthood and fame, it would have to be—Citeaux. The man of one idea shook himself, got to his knees and as an act of thanksgiving said bluntly, "Yes, Lord, I'll go."

Dennis Visits Citeaux

Some fourteen months after that heroic act of thanks-giving, which did not have a single word about thanks in it, little Dennis made his way through the swampy woods of Citeaux to the clearing where the monastery stood. After a short chat with the smiling Stephen Harding, the Abbot of the house, Dennis was allowed to see his former comrade-in-arms. Gerard was delighted with the permission. He came in on Dennis with all the zest of old, held out his two arms and hugged the little man until he struggled in protest.

"Easy! Easy, Gerard. I'm only a creature of clay. I'll break."

Gerard's laugh rang out with all its golden good nature and boyish delight as he set Dennis down and said, "That's my gentle way of saying 'You're welcome, little pygmy!' You see, we don't speak here; we use sign language. That's my sign for 'I'm glad to see you.' Now tell me: how are you?"

"It's my place to ask you that," said Dennis. "You look as if you've been through a hard campaign. What's wrong? As I look at you all I can think of is—long siege and short rations. Don't they feed you?"

"Of course they feed us. I'm just keeping in fighting trim. Not one ounce of excess baggage. Look at those hands. Never in better shape. Hard, calloused, a grip of iron." So saying, he gripped Dennis' arm and led him to a bench.

"Ow!" exclaimed the little knight, "it feels like wrought iron," and he pulled his arm away from Gerard as he sat down. When Gerard had drawn up a stool to the opposite side of the table, Dennis looked at him and smiled as he said, "Well, man of one idea, Bernard was right, wasn't he? You were wounded. You were captured. You capitulated."

"Uh-huh," answered Gerard. "Thank God he was right. I think I'll have him talk to you."

"Oh, no! No!" cried the little one in a hurry. "I don't want even to see Bernard. He might prophesy about me. I came here to see you and only you. Tell me, Gerard, what have you been doing with yourself?"

"Killing myself," said Gerard with a laugh.

"You look it," asserted Dennis seriously. "You've lost weight."

"Oh, I don't mean that, Dennis. Anyone can kill the body. It's the old man that I'm trying to kill. The self that wants to be great, to be looked up to. You know, the urge to be a 'somebody.' That's the old Gerard that I've been trying to kill. And let me tell you, little man, he's the toughest foe I've ever met. He simply won't die."

Dennis looked at the laughing Gerard and frowned as he asked, "What are you talking about? Speak my language, will you? I want to know what you've been doing the past year. What is this life like?"

"Like a tournament, Dennis. Never a dull moment. Adversaries on every side and it's fight! fight! fight! You ought to join. It's glorious."

"Mmmm-m," said Dennis. "I ought to. But tell me: do you fight in those clothes?"

"Fight in them, work in them, sleep in them, eat in them, read in them. It's a campaign that allows no leisure, Dennis. You'd love it."

"I suppose I would," said the little knight with a look that added the unsaid negative. "I'm not here to enlist. I'm here to learn what you've been doing with yourself. Tell me in plain terms, won't you?"

"Such unaccustomed seriousness, Dennis! What's gotten into you?" asked Gerard as he placed his forearms on the plain rough board that served as a table and leaned toward his little companion.

"You! I haven't been able to get you out of my mind for over a year. I heard about your capture and escape. I heard about your hurrying here, and for fourteen months I've been looking for you to come back. When your father told me that you had taken your vows I knew that the die was cast. You've never broken your word in your life. So I had to come and find out what had happened to your one idea."

"I've still got it," said Gerard with a smile.

"You what?" exclaimed Dennis. "Why, you always wanted to be the most famous knight in the army...."

"That's right," cut in Gerard, "and I still want to be that."

"Then why did you take your vows?"

"Just to become the bravest knight," answered Gerard.

"Gerard, talk sense!" said Dennis in disgust.

"I am, Dennis, but you're not hearing sensibly," countered Gerard. "There's more than one army in the world and more than one sovereign. You think that I'm talking about the Duke of Burgundy and his warriors. No, Dennis, I'm talking about the militia of the King of kings."

"Oh, I see. Gone allegorical, have you? Well, tell me all about it," begged the little man.

"There isn't much to tell..." began Gerard.

"Is it true that you get up at two o'clock?" asked Dennis.

"Partly true," answered Gerard, "only partly. For on Sundays it is half past one; and on holydays, one o'clock."

"But why? Where is the sense in turning things upside down? God made the night for rest. Why disturb it with your psalm-singing? Those are the things that I want to know. I've been thinking it all over for a year or more. They say that you spend seven hours of the day in church, almost as many in the fields working like serfs, that you eat only one meal a day and that nothing but a mess of herbs with watered wine and black bread. Now all that sounds a bit nonsensical to me. It's inhuman. How do you defend it? Why not be like other people?..."

"I suppose one of the reasons is that most other people are not like what they should be," broke in Gerard with a laugh. Then he went on, "You've asked a lot of questions, Dennis. They show that you have been thinking about us. But no, would you be surprised to learn that they are the very questions that I've asked myself, not once, but a thousand times since I last saw you at Grancy? Yes, I've wondered why these Cistercians turned things upside down, as you say. When other people are sleeping, we are wide awake and singing. While all other people try to rise above their station in life, seeking ever to go higher and higher, we bend our every effort in going down. While serfs want to become nobles, and nobles long to be sovereigns, we, who were nobles, become like and lower than the serfs. While most men seek freedom from menial manual labor with cattle, corn and the stubborn soil, we monks of Citeaux work at nothing else. People are social and seek ever greater sociability; we are silent. People pamper the body, serving it good food and better drink, while we take only the plainest, commonest and coarsest. As you say we have turned things upside down."

"That's it," put in Dennis, "just upside down. Now, why?"

"Perhaps, Dennis, it is because most people have things inside out and bottom side up. Tell me, how often did you or I ever think of becoming like unto God as we laid siege to this town or attacked that castle? How often did we strive to do something for the King of kings as we served Burgundy's Duke?"

"Why, we always did our duty. We never stole, never wronged the defeated, never injured the weak or defenseless. I'd say that Burgundy's men have always been upright, noble and justly proud. *'Noblesse oblige'* means much to us," answered the little fellow with real warmth.

"I know it does," said Gerard, "but you haven't told me what it means to God. Don't you see, Dennis, that most people are serving self; not the Duke, the Duchy or God. Let us face facts. It wasn't the Duke or his cause that fired us to brave doing and even braver daring. It was only a chance for glory. Why, Dennis, had you and I been born in Normandy, we most likely would be Englishmen now."

"What do you mean?"

"I mean that every soldier is a soldier of fortune," replied Gerard.

"You've gone cynical," snorted Dennis.

"No, just honest! Look! If we had been born in Normandy, our attention would naturally have gone to England where our great Duke, William the Conqueror, became king, wouldn't it?"

"I suppose it would," growled Dennis.

"And being what we were," continued Gerard, "men who loved a fight, isn't it to be expected that we would have crossed the Channel to a land that promised fight?"

"Maybe we would," admitted the still upset Dennis.

"Then don't you see," asked Gerard, "that we would have been like any vagabond men-at-arms, just soldiers of fortune, seeking a fight and fame, even though we would call ourselves 'men devoted to their sovereign'?"

"Well, what has all this got to do with Citeaux and Cistercian monks?" demanded the slightly angry Dennis.

"It is its reason for existence! Most people, Dennis, are seeking self and only self; Cistercian monks slay self. Most people are seeking fame and fortune and personal satisfaction; Cistercian monks seek only the glory of God. Too many people are making a god out of themselves; we strive to make ourselves like unto God. Now tell me who have things most upside down, the people or the monks?"

"When you put it as baldly as that, only one reply can be made. But, Gerard, don't you exaggerate? There are plenty of good people in the world; plenty of them! And doesn't your monastery exaggerate? There are plenty of other monks who do not eat as you do, sleep as you do, work as you do, sing as you do. Tell me, is your life as awful as people say it is?"

"From the outside looking in, Dennis, it appears awful; from the inside looking out, it's just a bit of heaven."

"Honestly?" asked Dennis and the nod of his head and the light in his eyes were bigger question marks than the lift of his voice.

Gerard was serious now. The smile had gone from his lips and the lines of his face showed him gaunt. He was not the Gerard of Grancy. Fourteen months of vigils and vegetable diet had changed the robust and rugged warrior to the lean and emaciated monk. He glanced sharply at his little comrade and said, "Looking at the husk, Dennis, you can never tell what the kernel is like. I've said that Citeaux from the inside is a little bit of heaven; but I must add that before one gets it in proper perspective it can be a big bit of hell."

Dennis straightened in his seat. This was the Gerard of old talking now. He placed both elbows on the table and leaned toward the young monk into whose eyes had come the stare of one who looks long distances and sees fierce shadows. "Someone has summed up the year of novitiate in a single short line, Dennis, saying it is:

'The world forgetting, by the world forgot.'

"It is not a bad summary. He has hit on a happy choice of words and a much happier choice of tenses. That 'forgot' is priceless. Had he said 'forgotten,' it would take us longer to read than the worldly world remembered; for if the world has a memory at all, it is as long as a gasp. We created quite a stir in our little circle of friends when we came here, I know; but I also know that by most, in fact, by all except the most intimate, we were 'forgot' and promptly 'forgot.' By some in twelve hours; by others in twelve days; by the rest in twelve weeks. It doesn't matter. But it does open one's eyes to what really counts! It does show one the changeless Friend."

Gerard was musing aloud now rather than talking to Dennis. His gaze was out the window and his eyes were fixed in an unseeing stare. Suddenly he turned to his little comrade and said, "But, 'the world forgetting'—Ah! that's a different proposition. It takes more than twelve days or twelve weeks. Perhaps it may take more than twelve years. Some memories are surprisingly long, Dennis. It is hard to forget your friends of childhood; harder still, those of later years. I've seen you often in my mind's eye as I plowed, dug the earth or felled trees. I've seen George and Maurice and Charles and those others who stood with us stirrup to stirrup and then charged into battle's crash. Yes, some things are not easily forgotten.

"Do you remember.... But, no! We must not begin! Just let me say that the thrill that surged in our veins when a field was won was intoxicating; and one often longs for that intoxication. Let me say that I remember the home I had and the one I might have had; that I remember the dream that led me through youth and changed into a burning ideal as I entered manhood. Let me say that I haven't forgotten what I was and what I wanted to be. No. Some things will not leave the soul."

Gerard paused. Dennis did not dare to move. His eyes were fixed on the young monk's face noting every light and shadow that touched it. He was now hearing what he had come to hear; but hearing it as he never expected to hear it! Gerard's sincere soul was articulate, and Dennis was absorbed in its story.

The young monk looked up quickly from a study of his hands and said, "I suppose you are wondering why I stay, since I cannot completely forget."

"Right," snapped Dennis. "Not only I, but a goodly number of other knights who haven't forgotten as quickly as you think."

"Dennis, I've told you as much as I've told my Abbot. Some days in the past fourteen months have been gray, some blue and some a deep, deep black. But I've learned something of the 'upside-downwardness' of the world and men; I've relearned what my mother taught me; I am learning to believe what you and I and all the rest of us have always *professed* to believe; I am trying to live the 'Credo' we so often merely said."

"Meaning what?" asked Dennis.

"Meaning that I'm trying to live for God alone; trying to catch up to Jesus Christ. God made me for Himself. He made me to know Him, love Him and serve Him. This is one place I can do all three. They tell me that the angels of heaven spend their lives in one long act of adoration. I'm trying to rival them; and that is why I say that Citeaux is just a little bit of heaven. From the outside of the wall all you can see is the austerity; I've just given you a glimpse from the inside of the awe of it all. The husk is forbidding, I admit; but when the kernel is reached..." and Gerard gave a sigh.

Dennis stirred in his seat. "You talk as if you loved it, Gerard."

"I'm trying to love *Him*, Dennis; and since this is one sure way, I do love it."

The little knight arose on that and started to walk around the table. "So you've got to go through hell before you reach heaven, eh?" he said.

"Something like that," smiled Gerard, "but to take it out of the parlance of the camp, we say that Calvary is the price one must pay for the glory of the Resurrection."

"But, Gerard, why be extreme? Why the exaggeration? Why all the penance? This monastery stands out like a lighthouse."

"I know it," laughed Gerard, "and I hope that it will serve as one! Dennis, you haven't caught the secret yet. We are the balancers of the world. We have to be exaggerated."

"What do you mean—the balancers of the world?" asked the little man with a frown.

Gerard held out his two hands and said, "There are exaggerated sinners in the world, aren't there?" When the little knight nodded his head, Gerard went on, "Well, then there must be exaggerated penitents to even things up. We are the exaggerated ones. We mean to balance the exaggerated sinners."

"Oh, I see," said Dennis in a tone of voice that told he was pondering something. He took a step or two toward the door, then flashed around on Gerard with, "Wait a second! A little while ago you said you were rivaling the angels; that your one work was to adore God. You said you were living for God alone. Now you say that you live for the world, the wayward world; and that you aim to outbalance the sinners. Those two aims seem to cancel one another, and instead of balancers of the world, you people may well be the world's greatest contradiction. Better make up your mind, Gerard. You used to be a man of one idea, but now—well, I don't know."

"How many persons are there in Christ?" asked Gerard as he levelled a finger at the perplexed Dennis.

"One," came the answer in a tone that told of puzzlement.

"How many natures?" came the next question.

"Two," answered Dennis.

"Any contradiction?"

"No," admitted Dennis, "but what has that to do with you?"

"I'll show you in a moment but just now I must lay my foundation well. Two things can be in the one without a contradiction, can't they? Now answer me this: who made you?"

"God."

"And who redeemed you?"

"God."

"And how many Gods are there?"

"One."

"So creation and redemption, two distinct actions can be performed by the one same God without contradiction?"

"I admit that," granted Dennis, "but again I must ask you what in the world has it to do with you?"

"You'll see in a second," replied Gerard, "but before you do let me ask you if you know St. Benedict's motto. We are Benedictines, you know."

"Yes, you are...," exclaimed Dennis, and added a most emphatic, "not! Cluny is Benedictine, and you are as much like Cluny as night is like day."

"Let that pass for the moment and tell me St. Benedict's motto," urged Gerard.

"*Ora et labora*—Pray and work," translated the energetic Dennis.

"Two things by one monk, and no contradiction," said Gerard with feeling. "Now, Dennis, let me tell you that prayer can be work, and hard work at times; while work should always be a prayer. And certainly, there is no need to tell an old reprobate like you that prayer is often given as a penance. So you see, *'ora et labora'* means prayer and penance, the two works that make up our one life. They are interchangeable and are often interchanged. But the point that you've missed so far is that the end and aim of both is the same. We pray to God to have mercy on sinners and do penance for sinners to appease an outraged God; and though it sounds as if we had two ends in view, our only aim is to give glory to Him who made us for that one purpose. Do you see?"

Dennis shook his head so Gerard went on, "Our lives are one long act of adoration and reparation. Our reparation is our grandest act of adoration and our adoration the most satisfying reparation. We are striving to do more than rival the angels. We have the sublime effrontery to dedicate our lives to the one purpose of being like unto Jesus Christ. His life was adoration and perfect reparation. But who can tell with absolute certainty whether His primary purpose was to glorify the Father or to satisfy for man? I like to think that they are practically identical; and I know my only reason for dressing in this uniform and fighting under His standard in this swampland of Citeaux is to do what He did. So you see, Dennis, I've still got my one idea. I'm still striving to be the greatest knight of them all; or perhaps I should say *'like'* the greatest Knight of them all who ever battled for the salvation of the world and the glory of God."

"Whew!" whistled Dennis as he blinked, rubbed his eyes and asked, "Am I listening to Gerard of Fontaines? Do they teach you all those things here? You look like a fighter, you sound like a fighter...."

"And I am a fighter," finished Gerard as he pounded the table. "I've changed arms, army and sovereign, Dennis. That's all. I've still got my one idea and ideal; only it's been heightened. You know enough Latin to catch the bugle blast in this trumpet-tongued call to arms, *'Domino Christo vero Regi militaturus,'* don't you?"

"To do battle for Christ the true King," translated Dennis.

"Well, that's the invitation that St. Benedict extends to all who live under his Rule. I love that word, *'militaturus.'* In it I hear the jangle of spurs, the clatter of armor and the importunate pawing and neighing of horses. I smell battle when I hear it."

"By heavens! You haven't changed, Gerard. You're still human. Ah, it sounds good to hear you talk that way!" said Dennis with relish.

"I know what you've been thinking, Dennis. You've seen some emasculated models in monkish robes and suspected that they were the real thing. No! They are only the caricature. A monk is a follower of Jesus Christ. Therefore, he's got to be human, for his King and Leader was the world's greatest Man! But come, let me show you the grounds and the monks at work."

Dennis started for the door with Gerard at his side, but just before he opened it he stopped and put his hand on Gerard's arm saying, "Promise that Bernard will not speak to me."

"Neither Bernard nor any other one of the monks will say as much as a single word to you. It is the Rule. Besides," Gerard said banteringly, "I don't think that you're big enough to be a world balancer; we only take heavy weights here." With that they left the room.

One Alone

Two years later Gerard was at Clairvaux and looking very worried. The trees on the hillsides were bare except for a few withered and yellowed leaves that rattled in a wind that was sharp and had in it the scent of snow. Gerard had reason to look worried, for he had just come from a storeroom that was full of emptiness and winter was coming on. The year before, Stephen Harding had sent him with his brothers to found this new monastery of which Bernard had been made Abbot, and Bernard had appointed Gerard cellarer.

It was not long before Gerard realized that cellarer is synonymous with worry and work; for he is the one who has charge of all the temporalities of the monastery from the farm, the buildings and the cattle down to and including the kitchen kindling. It is his duty to see to it that the storeroom is filled with edible herbs, the wine barrel with at least a watered wine, and the oven with a dough that will make coarse bread. Gerard grew his first gray hairs during this first year at Clairvaux, and even now in the late fall of 1115 his forehead was furrowed. Though he hated to do it, he had to knock on Bernard's door and say, "Reverend Father, we are in desperate straits."

"Pshaw!" said Bernard with a smile, "I thought you were bringing me news."

"But I mean it, Bernard," said Gerard who would not respond to his brother's smile. "The cellar is practically empty and the sky holds snow."

"Behold the lilies of the field..." began Bernard still smiling.

"Oh, I know," broke in Gerard, "and 'the birds of the air.' But I don't see any lilies in the field right now and the birds have all gone south! Let's be practical."

"Let's be prayerful," replied Bernard as he broadened his smile. "How much will take you over the winter?"

Gerard started. "That's a sudden question, Reverend Father. I don't know exactly; but I think that if I had ten or twelve livres right now I could face the snow with a smile."

"I haven't a sou," said Bernard, "but I have trust in God. You go back to work. I'll do the worrying. I'll worry God with prayers."

Gerard left the Abbot's room and made his way out to the woods where the others were working, but as he neared them he said softly, "Trust in God, sailor, but row for shore. Ah, well, perhaps I don't pray enough."

One hour later as he was tussling with a man-sized log a voice asked, "Are you cellarer of this monastery?" Gerard jumped, let the log fall and looked up into the smiling face of his brother and Abbot, Bernard.

"*Benedicite*, Reverend Father," gasped Gerard.

"*Dominus*," said Bernard.

"Gosh! you took the breath from me," went on Gerard. Then as he mounted the bank on which Bernard stood he said, "Yes, I'm cellarer of this monastery because a brother of mine had to appoint someone and I was the only one around. Why do you ask?"

"Can you count?" said Bernard.

"I used to be able to," came the reply.

"Then, count this," said Bernard as he handed him a purse.

Gerard opened it, sat on a log and began to count some coins. When he had finished he looked at Bernard in awe and asked, "Where did you get these?"

"How many livres are there?" was Bernard's only answer.

"Just twelve!" exclaimed Gerard with warmth.

"How many did you say you needed to make you smile at snow?"

"Just twelve!" came the reply in the same tone.

"So what?"

"*So* tell me where you got them," urged Gerard.

"No, that's not the answer," said Bernard, "*So* trust God always, and instead of worrying, worry Him with prayers. Gerard, I had no sooner knelt in the Oratory to tell our King of our predicament than Andrew came and told me that there was a strange lady at the gatehouse wishing to see me. I went and saw a woman who looked anxious and even scared. She simply said, 'Father Abbot, will you please pray for my husband? He is very ill.' 'Gladly,' I replied, and before I could say any more she pressed that purse into my hand saying, 'Please accept this little offering. I hope it will be of some use.' And with that she was gone. I didn't open the purse, Gerard; but I felt sure that it held the provisions for the winter."

Gerard struck his breast and said, "I don't pray enough. I don't trust God enough. I don't..."

"You don't do a lot of things. You're a terrible sinner," cut in his brother. But even this pleasantry failed to take the look of sorrow from Gerard's eyes. Bernard noticed it, so he immediately sat on the log next to his brother and said, "Gerard, can you give me a few ideas for tomorrow's talk in chapter? I feel sterile. Give me something that will appeal to all from old Gaudry and Guy down to young cousin Robert. Give me something virile; something that appeals to you."

"Tell them what just happened, and tell them not to be like me. I don't trust enough," replied Gerard.

"I know you don't. You told me that before. I believed you the first time. But now tell me what is your ideal; what thought spurs you on most; what is your sheet anchor when things get stormy?"

Gerard put the purse of coins into his pocket, straightened out his robe and answered, "You can ask the most unexpected questions at the most unusual times, Bernard. You almost embarrass me. However, the thought that appeals most to me is the thought of Jesus Christ."

"Too vague, Gerard; too general," commented Bernard.

"Not to me," replied his brother. "Look! Most people view this life as *something*, don't they? They look at the choir, the cloister, the diet, the dormitory and the manual labor and see only the choir, cloister, diet, dormitory and manual labor. Now such a view can be not only discouraging but actually disgusting. I look at it all as *Someone*. My choir is singing with, in, through and for Jesus Christ. My cellarer's job with all its work and worry is nothing but an appointment from Jesus Christ to be fulfilled for Jesus Christ. My Abbot is my brother, yes, my brother Bernard, and my Brother, Jesus Christ! Don't you see then, how that view changes everything? I know that I'm expressing myself poorly; but you can catch the idea, can't you?"

"Yes, I catch the idea and I appreciate your view; but that can only be seen in the light of faith," said his Abbot brother.

"Ah, Bernard," replied Gerard, "there is no other light in which to look at this life. Look at it in the light of unaided reason, and it is insanity! But look at it as the answer to the 'Come, follow me' of Christ, then and only then is it the most sublime wisdom. It is Someone or it is a slow, stupid suicide."

"Huh," grunted Bernard, "you can be blunt about it, can't you?" and he crushed two dried leaves in his hand.

"Say 'honest' rather than 'blunt,' Bernard," countered Gerard. "If we look on this existence of ours as a *living*, we're crazy; but when we look upon it as a *loving*, a loving of God and a living in Him, with Him and for Him—ah! then I can work and worry, then I can be hungry and cold, then I can sing and even starve if need be with a laugh on my lips and a song in my heart; for then it is Someone and not something."

"That's enough," said Bernard as he arose. "If I can tell them all that you have told me and tell them in the way that you have just told me there will be no sleeping in the chapter room tomorrow morning. Go back to your work now, and don't lose that money." With that he smiled, made the sign of the cross over Gerard and left.

Gerard watched him as he made his way through the trees and just as he vanished from sight exclaimed, "Humph! Asking me for ideas when he's full of them himself," and with a look toward the skies that was an act of thanksgiving he went down to tussle with the log again.

Gerard Visits the Grange

Those twelve livres stocked the cellars sufficiently to carry the little community through the snows, and with the spring and the growing popularity of Bernard, Gerard's frowns were fewer, but his work increased. Clairvaux was becoming Clairvaux. A vineyard showed its orderly rows on one slope while in the cleared ground of the opposite slope grain could be seen waving in the sun. Behind the abbey itself, a young orchard stood in stately array, and just beyond it the gardens stretched, cut into squares by silver channels of crystal clear water which came from the Aube, whose glistening flow could be seen at the end of the valley. Gerard had been woodsman, herdsman, farmer and even fisherman. He had constructed canals, pools and breakwaters, making the Aube serve in the capacity of fish preserve, irrigation master and driver of the wheels of the mills. Gerard wanted manpower, horsepower and waterpower in the Valley of Light, so he harnessed the fair flowing Aube and made it do a hundred and one different tasks; then he sent it back to its bed with a satisfaction of service well rendered.

But the immediate vicinity of the Abbey was not the only scene of the cellarer's activity. For up the slopes sheep grazed and down in the lowlands cattle rested in the shade of oak, ash and lime trees or slowly munched the dark emerald of the meadow. Gerard was responsible for all these. As the years went on the Abbey's land extended and granges had to be constructed in those fields that were too far from the house to allow the tillers of the soil or the keepers of the cattle to return every day. Gerard had to visit these granges to see if the brethren were all well and the work progressing. It was while looking after this, that and the other thing, that Gerard smiled to himself and asked, "Where in the world did they ever get the effrontery to speak of the 'lazy monks'?"

One day about 1125 he said, "Brother Conrad, I'm making a visit to the most distant grange tomorrow. I want you to come along." The brother bowed. Early next morning he was seen in earnest conversation with the Prior of the monastery, Geoffrey de la Roche, a relative of the family of Fontaines. The Prior pointed to his room and shook his head. They then entered the building. A few minutes later the brother came out with a package carefully concealed beneath his cloak. Not long after, Gerard met him and asked, "Are you ready?" The brother nodded. "What have you there?" said Gerard pointing to a bundle at the brother's feet.

"A few provisions for the grange. The Prior suggested that I bring them along," answered the brother.

"How heavy is it?" asked Gerard as he bent to lift it. "The grange is a long way off and it's going to be a hot day. Oh!" he said as he raised it a few feet, "that's not too bad. We'll swap off every little while. I want you to enjoy this outing, Brother. It's work for me, but not for you. You're to be companion and observer. I want you to look at the ground on the grange." The brother smiled his thanks and prepared to follow. People always smiled at Gerard. They could not help it. He had a freshness and a buoyancy about him that simply compelled a smile.

Gerard had been right in both of his statements. It *was* a long walk and it *was* a hot day. During it he had managed to take the bundle from the brother more often than the brother liked, for Gerard was his superior. But what could he do with a man who always smiled and said something pleasant as he took the burden out of his hands? As they toiled up the last slope and came out on the level of the open fields, the brother patted the package he had just received from Gerard and said, "We'll fix him yet, won't we?" and there was a twinkle of satisfaction in his eye.

They were not expected at the grange; hence, only the lay brother cook was there to greet them. He was delighted to see Gerard and showed it by embracing him in real French fashion. Then he showed Conrad how to tend the steaming kettles and hurried from the little house, whistled sweetly and a horse came trotting across the field to him. With one spring he was on his back and away toward the woods. Twenty minutes later he was back with four other lay brothers who greeted Gerard in the same effusive fashion as had the cook.

Brother Conrad had kept in the background during all this and it was not until the table was laid for the seven of them and each was at his place that he undid the package he and Gerard had so carefully carried. From the midst of an assortment of provisions he triumphantly drew a bottle of Clairvaux's choicest wine. With something of a flourish he placed it before Gerard and said, "Father Prior sends you this as a surprise."

Gerard looked at the bottle, then at the brother. "All for me?" he asked; and when Conrad had said, "Every last drop," Gerard smiled his thanks. Then rising he drew the cork with a resounding "plop." Two of the brothers of the grange were seen to lick their lips. Gerard smiled more broadly and walking to the container from which they drew water for the meal, lifted the lid and poured every drop of Clairvaux's choicest wine into it. Then taking the brothers' six cups he filled them from the container and said, "Father Prior sends you this through me as a big surprise. Enjoy it!" Then with his broadest smile he resumed his seat. The brothers swore that it was the best water they had ever tasted.

Conrad saw the ground that day and gave his expert opinion on it. He said it was good but needed liming. Gerard saw much more than the ground; he saw the brothers, their quarters, their horses, their equipment, and all the possibilities that lay in the field, the forest and the sparkling cascade that made liquid melody as it leaped over rocks and swirled in small hollows.

It had been a long afternoon and a profitable one. As they were preparing to leave the grange the oldest of the brothers came up to Gerard. He was stoop shouldered and his head hung low, but when he looked up from under his whitened eyebrows a gleam was seen in his eyes that spoke of peace and purity and the presence of God. His voice was weak and just the tiniest bit cracked, yet when he spoke one heard a softness and a melody that comes only from those who have matured, grown old and mellowed in the close companionship of Jesus Christ. Just now he quietly asked, "May I have a word with you?"

"Why certainly, Hugo," replied Gerard in a voice that held not the slightest trace of weariness, "but I hope you have more than one word for me, for the sight of you spells Fontaines to me and the sound of your voice conjures up my father, my mother and my former home."

"That's what I wanted to tell you about, Gerard," said the gentle old man softly. "I served your father and the family the best part of my life. When he came to Clairvaux I had to come too. He meant life to me. I suppose many a serf finds his heart thus wound round his master. I loved your father, Gerard. He was my pride, my ideal. If I loved him as knight, I almost adored him as monk; and all I want to say now is that that action of yours in giving us the wine so generously, so gracefully, so good-naturedly took me back about thirty years. You did that just as your father would have done it. You grow to look more like him day by day, Gerard, and I have reason to think that the resemblance does not stop with the physical. I hope you won't think me bold if I tell you that I pray that you become exactly like him. He was a saint."

Gerard's eyes filled as the old man went on softly speaking and the only answer he could make now was to place his two hands on the bent shoulders, smile through tears and kiss the withered cheeks of the humble, holy lay brother who had one time been his serf.

Bernard Bargains with God

Brother Hugo would have had more reason to say, "How like your father!" had he seen Gerard at Viterbo in March of 1137, for he was handling a motley crowd of people with all the ease and charm of a trained diplomat. The mere curiosity seekers were soon sifted out and sent away with a pleasant word of explanation; the sincere souls and those in distress, either mental or physical, he separated to one side, while those who had immediate business he allowed into the little room where Bernard sat. He was expert at handling crowds, for that is what he had been doing in every big city of France and Italy where Bernard stopped. His brother did not always preach to the people, but as soon as word was passed that the Abbot of Clairvaux, the champion of Pope Innocent II, was in town, a crowd gathered round the house in which he stayed, and people clamored for an audience. Gerard was Bernard's buffer and took the shock of the crowd so fully that Bernard felt next to nothing.

This morning at Viterbo, Gerard was seated at a small table making notes of the applicants. It had been a hard morning and our buffer was tired. He had just dismissed a very talkative woman and was hurriedly making a note on her when the last of a large throng stood before him. Without looking up Gerard very pleasantly said, "Yes, and what is your wish this morning?"

"I want to know if I am heavy enough to balance the world," came the startling reply. "Look at me," continued the applicant as he held out his arms and turned around so that Gerard, looking up, saw only the back of a rather short man wearing a pilgrim's cloak. Gerard was startled by the question and puzzled by the man's voice, for there was a certain familiar ring to it that started echoes in his memory. He knew that he had heard the voice before but he could not definitely say where. On top of this disturbing element the question, "Is this a religious fanatic or an insane man before me?" suddenly shot into his mind to dispute place with his struggle to locate the echoes that were ringing in his memory. Gerard stared at the back for a moment or two, then slowly said, "Balance the world, eh? I don't know. That's a fairly heavy substance, you must remember."

"I know it is," replied the pilgrim; "heavier than any of us realize. And yet, I know some men in a swamp who tried it."

Gerard was now convinced that he was dealing with a crazy man. Not wishing any scene he decided to humor him, so he asked, "Did they have any success?"

"Some," came the surprising reply. "At least they sent one sinner from France to Jerusalem," and with that he turned around.

Gerard jumped to his feet, threw out both arms, and walking toward the pilgrim cried, "Dennis! Dennis! Dennis!" in a voice that rang with bewilderment, delight and warm affection. He held him in his embrace and pounded his back saying, "You old war horse, what are you doing in Viterbo?"

"Getting pounded by a mad monk who doesn't know his own strength," came the gasping response.

The people on either side of the room were smiling at the reunion of the friends. They were all Latins and used to effusiveness, but the manly vigor and radiant warmth shown by both Gerard and Dennis affected even the Latins. Gerard had presence of mind enough to ask a general pardon as he pulled the little pilgrim out of the room after him. When he had closed the door of a little side chamber behind him, Gerard thumped the shoulders of his former comrade-in-arms and said, "You don't know how glad I am to see you, Dennis; but why the cloak?"

"It's a long story, Gerard; too long for this morning. All I'll say now is that your family robbed the Duke of Burgundy of one fine little fighter and sent him over mountains and across seas to see the places where Christ lived and died. It took a lot to convert me. You didn't do it. Young Nivard didn't do it. Even your father didn't do it. But each of you contributed something. I kept pondering on why you became a monk; why your youngest brother should join you; why your noble father should die among you. But what finally made me lay aside my suit of armor and don this pilgrim's cloak was your sister Humbeline's entrance at Jully. When she gave up all that was hers, I said to myself, 'Dennis, it's time for you to travel.' So here I am, but the rest must wait until tomorrow, if I can see you then."

"Certainly, you can," said Gerard. "Come right after Mass. But..."

"No buts," broke in Dennis. "I'll be here right after Mass. Now tell me a little about yourself. Are you well?"

"I don't know," laughed Gerard, "and I haven't time to find out. Bernard calls himself 'the chimera of the age,' saying he is neither a monk nor a layman. He has reason to say, for he is forever on the go. But since he makes me his constant companion I lay claim to the title of the world's greatest chameleon."

Dennis laughed and asked, "Why the fancy title?"

"Look, Dennis," said Gerard hurriedly, "the last time I saw you I was striving to become a cloistered contemplative. To do that I had to change plenty of color, didn't I?"

"I'll say you did! The red of the warrior to the white of the peaceful monk."

"Something like that," said Gerard. "Well, I hadn't become anything like I wanted to become when I was sent to Clairvaux. Once there Bernard appointed me cellarer. More color changes! I had to be Martha and Mary at once. All right. I had just about accomplished that when my brother goes ahead and becomes 'The Voice of the Century' and he makes me his plenipotentiary guardian of the portals. I've seen every big city in France, Germany and Italy, it seems; and I'm as much like a cloistered contemplative as you are!"

Dennis laughed at Gerard's facial expressions as much as at his hurried summary of the past twenty years. "I don't know about being a chameleon, Gerard," he said, "but I must say that if you can change colors as fast as you change your facial expression, you most certainly are the world's greatest."

"Ah," exclaimed Gerard, "I was afraid that it was contagious."

"What are you talking about?" gasped Dennis.

"Facial animation," smiled Gerard. "I suppose I'm becoming like these Italians, I see so many of them. You don't have to know their language well, Dennis; just watch their faces! They talk more with their eyes and their eyebrows, their mobile mouths and flashing

teeth than they do with their tongues. It has always fascinated me to watch them. I suppose I've become like
them."

"Gerard," said Dennis, "I know you're busy and I
want tomorrow for ourselves, but before I leave tell me—
is Bernard all that people say he is?"

"I don't know," replied Gerard laughingly. "What do
they say?"

"In the Orient he is called the 'Thaumaturgus of the
West.' They say that he works miracles daily, almost
hourly."

"Big words, Dennis, and big wonders! No, I
wouldn't say that he worked miracles hourly, or even
daily. But I wouldn't want to be asked to state just how
many miracles he has worked."

"So it is true, then?"

"Oh, yes. It's absolutely true. Bernard is a close
friend of God. Of that I am positive."

"Then what in the world are you complaining about?
Calling yourself a chameleon!" said Dennis with much of
his old fire.

"I'm not complaining," laughed Gerard. "I was just
explaining. I'm delighted to be with him just to ward off
such vagrants as yourself from his person."

"How's your heart, Gerard?" asked Dennis very seriously.

"I don't know. I think it's still stout and strong,"
came the answer.

"That being the case," went on Dennis, "I can tell
you without fear."

"Tell me what?"

"Tell you that I'm not going to be warded off from
Bernard. I want to see him."

"You want to see him!" exclaimed Gerard, then
stopped and in a quiet, sorrowful voice said, "I lose
again."

Dennis looked at Gerard's long face and frowned as he asked, "You lose what?"

"My title. My hard won title," came the lament, "I'm not the world's greatest chameleon, Dennis—you are!"

At that they both laughed happily and as Dennis opened the door he said, "Yes, I've changed mightily. I admit it. But it is all because of that family of Fontaines! Until tomorrow then, Gerard, and don't forget to reserve me a good half hour with Bernard."

"I don't think I could promise that to Pope Innocent himself, Dennis; but I'll see what I can do for a chameleon like you. Till tomorrow then, God be with you," and he clapped the little pilgrim on the shoulder.

Shortly after Mass the next morning, Dennis made his way to the same abode and gained immediate entrance; but instead of Gerard he faced none other than Bernard, the Abbot of Clairvaux. Dennis told some friends afterwards that Bernard had looked right through him, then said, "You're Dennis, former knight, present pilgrim and future monk. Gerard was raving about you all night."

"Raving?" said Dennis, then started as the smile left Bernard's face and a look of anxiety came into his eyes.

"Yes, Dennis," he replied, "Gerard was raving last night. Some sort of sudden fever took him yesterday afternoon and no one could do anything with it."

"How is he now? May I see him?" asked the little man quickly.

"No, Dennis, you may not see him this morning," smiled Bernard. "But tomorrow is another day. Gerard will be well enough then to see the little man he talked so much about."

"Are you sure?" asked Dennis in great anxiety.

"Yes," said Bernard, "I'm positive." And he stressed the last word noticeably.

"But you said that nobody could do anything with..." and then Dennis stopped, got to his knees and said, "Reverend Father Bernard, you must pardon my insistence. But, you see, I have always loved Gerard...."

"Arise, Dennis," interrupted Bernard as he blessed the kneeling man. "You have not been insistent. I understand perfectly. But to put you at your ease I'll tell you that I bargained with God last night. I told Him that I needed Gerard on this journey. I told Him that if He would spare him to me now, He could take him any other time and in any other manner. I know that Gerard will be well tonight."

The little pilgrim had arisen at Bernard's word of command, but as he listened to the Abbot's declaration of his dealing with God, Dennis' eyes and mouth opened wide and stayed that way. He had never heard anyone speak with such reverence, love and assurance. It frightened him. He said afterwards that it was the same holy awe that he had felt when he stood for the first time on Mt. Calvary. He knew he was in the presence of a man of God.

Bernard sensed his bewilderment and eased the situation by smiling again and saying, "Gerard will be glad to see you tomorrow, Dennis; and I'll be glad to see you at Clairvaux. But tell me: why didn't a warrior like you join the Templars when you were in the Holy Land?"

"I was tempted to, Reverend Father, very much tempted to. But I couldn't get Gerard and you and the whole family out of my mind. Then I was afraid that I'd be more warrior than monk even though I did put a white mantle with its red cross over my suit of mail. As I knelt at the shrine of the Incarnation I said, 'If Citeaux enabled that family of warriors to become Knights of Jesus Christ, it will do the same for me.' So back I came, and as soon as I straighten out my affairs I'll beg you to receive me."

"No you won't," said Bernard quickly. "You'll beg nothing from me. You'll do me the favor of being Gerard's comrade-in-arms again."

Dennis smiled his thanks and the Abbot showed him to the door with the words, "Till tomorrow." Then he blessed him.

Meeting Death With a Song

Just one year later Dennis presented himself at Clairvaux ready to beg, as he had phrased it, or to do Bernard a favor, as the Abbot had rephrased it. At any rate, he was ready to become a monk. He waited in the little gatehouse while Andrew, who had recognized and warmly welcomed the former knight, went to tell Bernard of his arrival. The Abbot came down and surprised the little man with a strong, brotherly embrace. "Dennis! Dennis! I'm delighted to see you," said Bernard; and when he leaned back from his embrace Dennis was surprised to see tears in the Abbot's eyes. "Come, little man; over to my room we go. This is no place for intimates to talk."

Dennis followed him across the garden, up the flight of stairs and into the little room with the sloping roof. When he had closed the door and seated his little guest, Bernard sat down, leaned forward, placing his forearms on the small desk before him and said, "God kept His part of the bargain, Dennis. I'll have to give you a double welcome, one for Gerard and one for myself."

"Is Gerard away?" asked the little knight who had not caught the full force of Bernard's words.

"Yes, he's away; far away. And yet, as I look at you I feel him very near. Gerard is dead, Dennis."

"Dead!" exclaimed the little man as he sat bolt upright in his chair.

"Yes, dead," answered Bernard. "God is a strict bargainer. Don't you remember Viterbo? I told God that He could have Gerard any time if He but spared him to me for that journey."

"I remember now," said Dennis softly.

"Well, we weren't back long when God took him. Ah! but it was beautiful, Dennis, just beautiful!"

"Tell me about it," begged the little one.

"It was something that you have to see to appreciate fully," said Bernard, "but I love to talk about it. It brings him so near.

"You see," began the Abbot as he settled himself in his chair, "we came back from Italy and plunged into work here. Much had accumulated for both of us while we were away. Perhaps it was the absorption in this that made me forget my bargain. Perhaps it was just God's kind way in having me forget. At any rate, I had forgotten. Then one night they startled me with the news that Gerard was dying. Our infirmarian is not an alarmist, and he has attended enough of the brethren to know when death is near. So I knew that the summons was important. I hurried as best as I could and as I hastened down the stairs talking to God I suddenly recalled the bargain we had made at Viterbo. I had made the terms. He had accepted. I now had to stand by them. It all came in a flash, but as I flew across the garden I did ask God to allow me a few last words with him.

"I mounted the stairs quickly, but there at the top I came to a full stop, for I could hear Gerard—singing! Singing, mind you, Dennis; singing as death approached! I thought it might be delirium; but no! As soon as I entered I saw his eyes. They were clear, radiant, joy-filled. He was singing the one hundred and forty-eighth psalm. I can hear him now," said Bernard, and as he paused his own eyes became clear, radiant and joy-filled. "'Praise the Lord from the heavens; O praise Him from the heights,'" he sang in a soft, clear voice. "That's the song our Gerard sang as he died, Dennis; and he sang it to the end. When he had finished he looked at me, smiled and said, 'It is the end, Bernard.' Then borrowing our Lord's own words he softly breathed, 'Father, into Your hands I commend my spirit.'

"I then anointed him. Oh, Dennis, the words of that sacrament are beautiful. They burned their way right into my soul that night as I traced the cross on my brother's five senses. When I finished I bent down and whispered, 'Gerard.' He opened his eyes, closed them again and kept murmuring, 'My Father. My Father. My Father.' It was labored. It was low. But it was full of love and wonder and holy awe. I called him again. 'Gerard!' I said. He turned to me then and in a last swell of wonderment he exclaimed, 'Oh Bernard, how—good—God is—to us—to be—our FATHER!' Then he fell back—dead."

With the last word Bernard's two hands fell on the desk and he sat staring into space. Dennis knew that he was seeing the face of Gerard and hesitated to break the spell; but finally he murmured, "A beautiful death."

Bernard shook his head and echoed the little knight saying, "Yes, a beautiful death. But let me tell you, Dennis, it was such only because his had been a beautiful life. He was ever a man of one idea. For years he thought of Christ only as his King and Captain and himself a soldier; but as the years mounted he became more and more the child and God became his Father. To me his death seemed very much like the falling asleep of a very tired boy who loves and trusts his father completely. Ah, the supernatural is so natural, Dennis; and Gerard had caught the secret." Again the Abbot paused; as he did so Dennis rose, straightened to his full height and shut his teeth tightly. Looking up Bernard saw a deeply touched warrior. "Going?" he asked in surprise.

"If you please, Reverend Father. I'd like to be alone a little while."

Bernard understood. The clenched teeth and the firmly set lips told their story, and the wise Abbot very kindly said, "Go, talk to Andrew if you wish. He'll show you the monastery and the grounds." Dennis bowed his thanks and left.

He went down the steps much more slowly than he had mounted them, and a great loneliness gripped his heart as he thought how often Gerard had mounted those same stairs thinking of God, his King and his Father. For a little while he paced the garden but soon realized that he had to talk to someone and talk about Gerard, so he headed for the gatehouse and Andrew. He found him poring over some notes. "What have you there, Andrew?" he called out in as cheery a voice as he could muster, and when the gatekeeper looked up in surprise he added, "Bernard sent me to have a talk with you and have you show me my future home."

"You're going to stay?" exclaimed Andrew.

"Yes, any objection?" replied Dennis.

"Not a one," came the happy response, "except perhaps that you'll remind Bernard of someone he loved very much."

"You mean Gerard," said Dennis. "Bernard did love him, didn't he?"

"More than anyone ever guessed," said Andrew. "I was just looking over the eulogy he preached in the chapter. One of the monks took it down. It is the overflow of a passionately loving heart. Here, read it while I see what these people want," and Andrew handed a closely written page to the newest postulant. Dennis took the chair that Andrew had just vacated and eagerly read:

"How long shall I dissemble? How long shall I conceal within my breast the fire that consumes my broken heart?... What have I to do with the canticle of love when I am submerged in an ocean of grief? ...I have done violence to my feelings until now; I have striven to conceal my sorrow lest it might seem that faith had succumbed to natural affection. Therefore, while all others wept, I alone was tearless. With tearless eyes I followed the cruel bier; with tearless eyes I stood at the grave until the last sad rite was accomplished. With my own lips I pronounced the usual prayers over the corpse. With my own hands I sprinkled the clay over the body of my beloved Gerard so soon to turn to clay. They who watched me were weeping and wondering why I did not weep.... I tried to resist my sorrow with all the force I could gather from faith,...but, my brethren, I have to acknowledge myself vanquished. Now I must give vent to my intense pain....

"You know, O my children, how reasonable is my sorrow, how worthy of tears is the loss I have sustained; for you know how faithful a friend has been taken from my side.... He was my brother by blood, but much more by religious profession. Oh, pity my lot, you to whom all this is known! I was weak in body, and he supported me. I was cowardly, and he encouraged me. I was slothful and negligent, and he spurred me on. I was forgetful and improvident, and he acted as my monitor. Oh, whither have you been taken from me? Why have you been torn from my arms? We have loved each other in life, why then should we be parted in death? Oh, most cruel divorce, which only death could have the power to cause! ...Why have we been so united in brotherly affection? Or, so united, why so parted? O most mournful lot! But it is my plight that is pitiable, not his. For you, dear brother of mine, if separated from some dear ones, are now united to others still more dear; but what consolation is mine who has lost you, my only comfort?...

"Oh! Who will grant me soon to die and follow you? To die instead of you, I should not ask; for that would be to wrong you by delaying your entrance into glory. But to survive you—what is it but labor and pain? So long as I live I shall live in bitterness. I shall live in sadness.

"Gush forth now, my tears; for he is gone who by his presence prevented your flowing by excluding the cause. Open, you fountains of my unhappy head, and pour yourselves out in rivers of water, if perchance you may thus suffice to wash away the soil of my sins, whereby I have called down upon me the just wrath of heaven.... Wherefore, be indulgent to me all you that are holy.... I grieve and lament Gerard. The cause of my tears is Gerard. My soul cleaved to his. We two were made one less by the ties of flesh and blood than by the sameness of sentiments, conformity of minds and harmony of wills. And shall anyone forbid me to lament his loss?

"My very vitals have been torn out and shall it be said to me: 'Do not feel.' But I do feel. Oh yes! I feel. Because my strength is not the strength of stones, nor is my flesh brass. I most assuredly feel, and am in pain and my sorrow is continually before me.... I have confessed my sorrow and have not denied it. You may call it carnal. I do not deny it is human any more than I deny that I am a man.... I am not insensible to pain; and the thought of death coming to me or mine makes me shudder with horror. And Gerard was mine, surely mine....

"I grieve for you, my best-beloved Gerard, not as if your lot was pitiable, but because you are with me no more.... Would to God that I were certain that you were not lost to me forever, but only gone on before! Would to God that I had assurance that, even though late, yet at length I should follow you whither you have gone!

"Let no man tell me I should not allow myself to be overcome by natural grief. For the kind-hearted Samuel was allowed to indulge his sorrow over the reprobate King Saul, and the pious David over the treacherous Absalom...and behold a greater than Absalom is here! The Savior Himself, looking on Jerusalem, foreseeing its future fate, wept over it. And shall I not be suffered to feel my own desolation which is not future, but actually present?... Must I remain insensible to my fresh and grievous wound? Surely I may weep from pain since Jesus wept from compassion. For at the grave of Lazarus He certainly did not reprove the mourners, but, on the contrary, united His own tears with theirs. 'And Jesus wept,' writes the Evangelist. Those tears of His most assuredly betrayed no lack of confidence, but only testified to the reality of His human nature; for He immediately called the dead man back to life.... So neither is my weeping a sign of weak faith, but only of the weakness of my condition. From the fact that I cry out with pain on being smitten, do not suppose that I blame Him who smites. No! I only appeal to His compassion and endeavor to soften His severity. Hence, though my words are full of grief, they are free from the slightest taint of complaint. 'You are just, O Lord, and Your judgment right.' Gerard You gave; Gerard You have taken away; and if we lament his removal, we do not forget that he was only a loan.... But now my tears force me to finish."

Andrew came back just as Dennis finished the last line. He looked at the bent back of the former knight and said, "Well...," but as Dennis' head came up and Andrew saw tears in his eyes his voice changed in tone as he questioned, "What's the matter?"

"Nothing," choked out Dennis, "but I've just been looking at a brother's broken heart. If ever again I hear anyone say that Bernard of Clairvaux is a hard, feelingless man, I'll kill him!" And fire flashed through the tears that trembled on the eyelids of a deeply moved man.

"I understand," said Andrew. "But let me tell you, Dennis, that we mourn more than the death of a brother; we mourn the death of a saint. If the Gospel is true, then Gerard can demand from a just Judge the crown of glory. He didn't have any ecstasies as St. Paul did. He didn't work any miracles as did St. Peter and the rest. But he most certainly walked the way that Jesus traced—the ordinary way."

"What do you mean—the ordinary way?"

"I mean the way of Nazareth," came the forceful reply. "The way that Joseph walked all his life; the way that Mary walked practically all her life; and the way that Jesus walked for thirty long years. Ordinary, ordinary, everything was ordinary. Why, when Jesus began to preach, the Nazarenes looked at one another in bewilderment. They had known Jesus all His life, and He had been so ordinary that they summed Him up in the phrase: 'The son of the carpenter.' Ah, that is the revelation that gives meaning to this life of ours. Gerard was as hidden as was Jesus; yet he could say as did Jesus, 'I do always the things that please Him.' It was the way my mother and father taught us to walk. It was the way all my brothers have walked. It is the way you will walk if you stay here at Clairvaux."

"Oh, I'll stay!" said Dennis with vehemence. "To be like Gerard, if I dare not be like Jesus."

On July 1, 1702, the Congregation of Rites approved an Office in honor of this man of one idea and the lessons for its matins are taken verbatim from Bernard's eulogy. In 1871, Pius IX approved a beautiful Mass to be celebrated on January 30 in Gerard's honor; its opening prayer seems a combination of Bernard's brotherly love, Dennis' loving determination and the concept of Gerard's character as that of the man of one idea, for it prays to God that, "we may serve You on earth with an *absolute singleness of purpose* and merit to find in You *our only* joy in heaven."

Part 3

BERNARD

The Man Who Fell
in Love With God

"...It profits a man little to follow Christ if he fails to overtake him."

"Don't fear the face of the scorpion, Humbeline; its sting is in its tail."

"Which one of my admirers are you talking about now, big eyes?"

"Oh, just generalizing, just generalizing. But do remember that every flatterer is a beggar, even though he beg for nothing by word of mouth."

"You're trying to tell me something, Bernard; but I am not hearing very well. Just what are you trying to say?"

"Just this, little sister: Hold that love in suspicion which seems to find its support in the hope of gain."

"But, Bernard, every love seeks gain, and every lover seeks a beloved. Absolutely disinterested love is like Platonic friendship and altruism—words for the dictionary, not actualities of life."

"You talk like a philosopher, Humbeline; and a pessimistic one at that."

"I talk like a woman, little man; and an optimistic one as always. Love wants to have and to hold, and don't you forget it. Look. Do you see who is riding up that avenue of sunlight, sitting his horse like another Godfrey de Boullion, and undoubtedly feeling ten times more noble and a hundred times more proud? He is an example of a lover who wanted to gain something; and he gained it!"

Bernard looked, and down an avenue of sunlight formed by the slanting rays of the setting sun as they broke through the tops of the timber on the nearest hill, he saw a horse, which had evidently caught the spirit of his rider, stepping toward the main gate of the castle with head held high, neck proudly arched and mane flying. "Why, it's Andrew," said Bernard, "the newly knighted Andrew. He certainly does ride conscious of his dignity, doesn't he? Did a peacock ever display his feathers more archly?"

"Bernard, I sometimes wonder how anyone can love you with that tongue of yours and your mean imagination. Why wouldn't the boy be proud? How many other men in Burgundy, famed though she is for her hardy race of sturdy fighters, how many, I ask, have been knighted before they were seventeen? Why, the very sight of him stirs my blood and deepens my breathing. I'm proud of my little brother who is already so big a man."

"Humbeline," said Bernard, "you should have been a boy."

"Sometimes," she laughed, "I feel that I am. But why wouldn't I when all my life I've had only men to play with and talk to? Let me tell you, Bernard, to be the only girl in a family of seven is humiliating."

"Yes, it is!" he exclaimed. "Humiliating for us. Father has always made us treat you as queen; and as for Mother—ah, dear, loving Mother...."

There was a pause. Brother and sister looked out from the castle tower on a scene that would thrill the soul of an artist. But neither noticed the glory of the golden slope that the world calls Cote d'Or, for both were think-ing of their gentle mother whom they had laid to rest only a few months before.

"You miss her much, don't you, Bernard?" said Humbeline in a tone that was a caress.

"More than I can tell you, my sweet; even though you have always been my favorite brother."

"I know what you mean, Bernard; and I can say the same for you. Because of your surprising sympathy you have been a sister to me. Guy lost interest in me when he fell in love; Gerard has always been a man of one idea, and I have never been his big idea; as for Andrew, Bartholomew and Nivard, they were too young to under-stand me and my ways. But you and mother..."

"Come here, Humbeline," said Bernard as he put his arm around her and drew her down to a seat beside him, "sit close to me. I have something to tell you. I had to bring you up to the tower room, for this is my trysting place. When I get up here and am able to look across those long stretches of the plain to that dim, distant, blue line of the Jura and those magical subalpine marshes, I can think more clearly and I feel much nearer to God.

"It seems as if I must get above the clatter of the courtyard and the noises of the castle before I can confide anything. I used to sit here with Mother often. We would look straight across at the rival hill village of Talent and talk of peace; or glance sideways down upon the city of Dijon and talk of the City of God. Sometimes we would gaze at the vineyards just here at our feet, rooted in that rich soil that becomes so orange-brown from the sun, and talk of Him who said: 'I am the Vine, you the branches.'"

Bernard sprang to the window, his face lit with ea-gerness. "Oh, the beautiful Cote d'Or! Truly it is a golden slope, isn't it? When I look at those grapes and grasses and follow the rise to that tableland shadowed with trees, I am affected as you were a little while ago by the sight of

Andrew riding up that avenue of sunlight. Burgundy, proud Burgundy! The land of good men and good wine. My homeland! Where everyone is called brother or cousin, and bonhomie is in the very air. The duchy that is seldom at peace but always in prosperity. The home of chivalry and charity! Castle-crowned buffer land, standing bravely between France and the Empire and stirring only strong men and noble women!"

Humbeline took in the whole panorama: vineyards, orchards, rising hills topped by turreted castles, the whole golden slope and off there in the distance the blue blur that was the Jura mountains. The setting sun was gilding it all to a glory. She took it all in breathlessly and then said, "You love it, don't you, Bernard?"

"Yes, Humbeline, I love it; and I must leave it."

"What?"

"You saw Andrew ride in didn't you? He came from Grancy where the men of Burgundy are encamped preparing for battle. I ride to Grancy tomorrow to tell Father, Uncle Gaudry, Guy and Gerard that I am not going to the schools of Germany but am going to the monastery of Citeaux instead."

"But, Bernard, how often do you argue a thing? Didn't Guy and Gerard convince you? Didn't Father and Uncle Gaudry prove that everything about you points to prominence in the schools? I thought that they had persuaded you that if you were determined to be a cleric, the place for you was Cluny. It is not like you to go over ground that has been so thoroughly covered. What has happened?"

"Look, Humbeline, look down over those hills and beyond the fringe of that forest and think with me. Fifteen miles south of us, deep in the heart of those woods where only winds whisper and trees sigh, is a colony of men with only one business in life. To me, they are the real knights of Burgundy even though many of them are only serfs. They are the men who are tilting in the only tournament worth while; battling for the only victory worth the wounds; warring for the only King who merits man's undying loyalty.

"Our world has changed as we have grown, Humbeline. When we were children, I had only one hero besides Dad; he was Godfrey de Boullion. You remember how our knights rode away to the First Crusade. You remember how anxious those weeks and months became. You know now that the hearts and minds of everyone in France were in the East. Then came the news that set our castle ringing with more shouts than at any onslaught. Serfs were running around as though mad. Old men grew young again and gave voice to battle-cries and wild laughter even as they wept. I remember Mother kneeling like a statue of stone at a prayer that lasted hours and ended in tears. Jerusalem had been captured and Godfrey de Boullion made king. Our world became God-conscious in those years, Humbeline. Fighting men had something to fight for. They wanted the Sepulcher of Christ; and a Christ-like chivalry was born. War was civilizing our nation, ennobling our knights and stirring consciences that seemed atrophied. Do you remember?"

"Do I remember? How could I forget? I was only a youngster, but I stood in this very tower room with Mother and watched Odo, our Duke of Burgundy, ride away never to return."

"Oh, he came back, Humbeline; and he is here now."

"His body is, Bernard. Down there with those monks you talk of and whom he really loved." Bernard saw his opportunity and was quick to seize it.

"Why did he love them, Humbeline?"

"You know. You have often heard Father tell the story; how one day Odo called him aside and said, 'Tawny-beard, we have saints in our duchy at last. Deep in the marshy woods of Citeaux is a group of spiritual giants. We must help them all they will allow us. God is near. They have found Him.'"

"That is why I go to Citeaux. I go to find God. I go to become a saint."

"A what? You? Bernard, don't be impious!"

"Don't talk that way, Humbeline; you're not thinking deeply. I know that there are many who would call that attitude of yours humility. It is not. It is more nearly stupidity. You and I and all of us were given life for only one purpose. And I think that it is high time for me to stop playing at life and get down to real living. I'm going to find God. I'm going to become a saint. That is why I was created."

"Don't get excited, Bernard," said his sister as she saw the color mount to his face and a flash of fire spark from his eyes.

"Who's excited? I'm not getting excited, Humbeline; I'm more nearly disgusted. Look here. I was going to give you some pointers on love and lovers when I first came up to the tower room, for you have many knightly courtiers and I don't like them all; but instead of love, let me talk of life. It is the same thing, but very few ever realize it. Let me tell you that God is Life and that God is Love; but how many of us mortals ever reflect on that fact? Oh, it's sad! Some there are who neither understand nor seek God; and these some, I say, are dead. Others there are who understand indeed, but do not seek Him; and these I say, are impious. There are still others who seek after Him, but do not understand; and these are empty fools. But, Humbeline, there are some who both understand and seek; these are the saints; and one of them, I'm going to be!"

Humbeline had picked up a broken lance that lay on the floor in front of her; she turned it idly in her hands as her eyes took on a faraway look that told of her deep thought. Finally she said, "But, Bernard, is it only at Citeaux that you can find God?"

"No," quickly answered Bernard, "I don't say that; but I do say that Citeaux is the safest and surest place for me to do my searching for Him; perhaps the only place." Then after a little pause he turned toward his sister and said, "Humbeline, we've been the closest of pals always, but I wonder if you really know me. Do you know the fires that flame in my soul? Tell me, what do people call Father?"

"Tescelin the Tawny," came the ready reply.

"Right," snapped Bernard, "and they say that the Duke of Burgundy has never lost a battle in which Tescelin the Tawny has been at his side. And what of Mother's family?"

"Alice of Montbar," said Humbeline with an unconscious lift of her head, "was descended from the warrior Dukes of Burgundy."

"Very well, then," said Bernard. "Such is our lineage. We are sprung from a conquering race. Look at my hair, or better still, look in a mirror at your own transparent skin and catch their full significance. Humbeline, we are not children of the southern sun; we are more truly sprung from the great forests of the north. We are French in culture, but Burgundian in race; and that means passion. You think that only women were made for love; let me tell you, so was man! Passion, Humbeline, is a transforming agent; it can make a man a beast or an angel. And passion is my strength and my weakness."

"What do you mean?"

"If you know yourself, Humbeline, you know me. Tell me, have I ever done anything by halves?"

"I should say not. Mother always said that your spirit was too fiery for your delicate frame; while Father still insists that you are not brave, you are foolhardy."

"Well," said Bernard, "that's what I mean. I've got to put all that I am and all that I have and all that I can muster into everything I do. In that is my strength and my weakness."

Humbeline looked a bit perplexed and somewhat hesitatingly said, "I don't follow."

"Humbeline, I learned more than Latin while I was at school at Chatillon-sur-Seine. To tell the truth I learned a lot of things the good priests never taught us; and one was that it is dangerous to be a priest."

"You talk like a heretic."

"I talk like a brother of Humbeline of Fontaines, but a brother who knows himself and knows his weakness. You've heard of Suger, haven't you, Humbeline?"

"You mean the monk of St. Denis?"

"I mean the ambassador of the king. Do you think he left home to become the king's favorite?"

Humbeline looked at her brother sharply then said, "Why, of course not. He left home to become a monk."

"Is he one now?" asked Bernard without taking his eyes from the tree on the distant slope he had been studying.

"You mean," said Humbeline rather hesitantly, "that he is too involved in state affairs...?"

"I mean that he and many another prelate is enslaved," snapped Bernard in a tone that was almost bitter. "And that is why I am going to Citeaux." Then turning full upon his sister he said, "Here is the story, Humbeline. History says that after the fall of the Roman Empire, the Church took the barbarian nations of the north, tamed them, instructed them and achieved that paradox of a barbarian civilization. Undoubtedly in those early days the Church sanctified the state. No one can think of Clovis or Pepin or Charlemagne, or study the gradual growth of the nations of the west without marveling at the gigantic part played by the Church in the formation of our world. The Church did sanctify the state; but now, Humbeline, the state is secularizing the Church."

"You're exaggerating."

"Am I? Well I was going to say that prelates were looked upon, and many of them act, only as feudal princes; I was going to say that archbishops, bishops, abbots and even priests are under the domination of barons, dukes, counts and kings; but I see that you are skeptical, so I'll ask you who is Pope?"

"Pascal II."

"Is that so?" asked Bernard. "Have the Germans always admitted that? Did Emperor Henry IV always recognize Pascal as successor to Peter? Have the archbishops and bishops across the Rhine been unanimous in acknowledging Pascal as Pope? Indeed they have not! They have had four different popes while Pascal has been in Peter's chair. And Henry V is proving himself a worthy son of his worthless sire. Just look at what he has done this very year: he seized the Vicar of Christ on earth, imprisoned him, and then for two anguishing months kept him under such moral torture that he forced from him the grant of investitures. Humbeline, that is gross sacrilege; and that is the tempo of our times. German Emperors look upon the Pope as their chaplain, and the papacy as some sort of a fief; the feudal system is ruining the Church."

"But," put in Humbeline, "Gregory VII and Urban II and even our own Pascal have taken measures to remedy all that."

"Yes," laughed Bernard, "and so did the monks of Cluny two hundred years ago, but look at them now."

"What's wrong with Cluny?" demanded Humbeline with some show of indignation.

"Oh, nothing," said Bernard, "except that it is not for me. No, nor any other monastery but Citeaux; and if anyone should ask you why, just tell them: 'The times and my temperament.'"

"Bernard, you're barking," said Humbeline, "and you remind me of a legend I once heard about you, and which I am beginning to believe. An old retainer of ours once told me that before you were born, Mother dreamt that she had a little white dog in her womb who was always barking. A holy hermit interpreted the dream for her and told her not to worry, for the child in her womb would one day be a watchdog for the House of God, and would bark mightily against the enemies of the Faith. You're barking now; tell me, do you also bite?"

"I'll bite you if you won't take me more seriously. What is there about the mind, anyhow, that always makes it wander?"

Humbeline pointed the lance she was holding at Bernard, then touching him lightly with it said, "I'm not wandering, little watchdog; I'm only doing what Mother always did. I'm protecting you against slandering the clergy."

"Just like a woman," growled Bernard, "tell them the facts of history and everyday life and they accuse you of slander." Then turning to his sister he changed his tone as he asked, "What does Citeaux say to you, all-holy one?"

"Nothing," answered Humbeline with a toss of her head. "I've just heard that a tiny group of fanatics were there working out some reform."

"Now, Humbeline, that's not like you," said Bernard. "Come, now, and be yourself. Don't be superficial; look much more deeply and see what I see. See in that group idealized unworldliness, an argument incarnate and a protest in flesh and blood against all that I was telling you about priest and prelate, baron and bishop,

Emperor and Pope. Listen to the message Citeaux has for the world. That little group is trumpeting a truth; it is saying that man was not made just to become either serf or sovereign, but that he was made to become a saint. Open your eyes and your ears, little girl, and then think!"

"I am thinking," came the speedy reply, "and since you are so fond of straight talk, I want to know why that little group has to be so exaggerated in their articulation; I further want to know why Bernard of Fontaines has to bury himself in a marsh to find God when God is everywhere; I want to know why the scion of one of Burgundy's noblest families has to become a grubber of the soil in order to become a saint; I want to know what is the necessity of becoming a scribe and a pharisee, a faultfinder with every other existing religious Order if you are to follow Christ; I want to know why all this violence when He has said, 'Learn of me, for I am meek and humble of heart'; I want to know why one has to renounce the world that God so loved that 'for it he gave his only-begotten Son'; I want to know...."

"You want to know too much," broke in Bernard. "Let me see if I can tell you a few of the things that you want to know; but before I try, let me tell you that you are beautiful when you are aroused; your eyes sparkle like the evening stars and your face is as mobile as the ever-moving sea."

"Never mind the compliments," snapped Humbeline, "answer the questions."

"My, but you're an Amazon."

"Humph!" snorted Humbeline. "That's you, from flattery to insult in one breath." Fire was flashing in her eyes, but it shifted and shaded into a new and tender light as she said, "Ah, Bernard, why Citeaux?"

"For the very reasons you pointed out, Humbeline. It's violent. But 'the kingdom of heaven suffers violence and only the violent bear it away.' It's humble and humiliating; but one becomes a saint by going down, not by going up. I must bury myself in a marsh to find God; because He who is everywhere, to most men is nowhere. And as for exaggeration—anything that is not mediocre is by that very fact exaggerated; and if there is one thing I will never be, it is mediocre. Understand me, sister-mine, I do not mean to boast. No, indeed. I go to Citeaux not because I am strong, but because I am weak; not because I am great, but because I am small; not because I am wise, but because I am foolish. But remember that, 'the foolish things of the world has God chosen that he may confound the wise; and the weak things of the world has God chosen that he may confound the strong.'"

"But Father and the family...," interjected Humbeline.

"I've got to be true to them," answered Bernard. "A race of warriors, a family of noble knights. I've got to go to Citeaux just to be true to them. I go to tilt in the great Tournament of Love, Humbeline. I go seeking God. I go to become a vassal to the only King who can appreciate loyalty and reward fidelity. When first we came up here today, I spoke of love, Humbeline, and you misunderstood me. I said love seeks not gain; by that I mean that true love is never mercenary, though it is never unprofitable. I make myself clear when I tell you that God is not loved without reward, although He is to be loved without regard for reward. I want to love God. I want to grasp Him, and as you say 'to have and to hold.'"

"But, Bernard, is the step you plan necessary? Just look across those hills. God made them. Look to the purple haze of those distant mountains. God made them. Look to the glory of that western sky. It is God who is painting those clouds in colors no human hand can ever reproduce, and no human being can look upon without feeling a deeper beat to his heart." She turned to him, her face filled with emotion. "Can't you find God here?"

"Why, Humbeline!" exclaimed Bernard. "There's a mist in your eyes. Come! Be your brave self. Be my tomboy sister and face facts. I'm going to give up for God things that I wouldn't give up for anyone else. It is not the 'wicked world' that I give up for God. No. Thank God we have never been part of that. But it is the good and glorious world, the hills and plain and those blue-hazed mountains, the solitude of deep woods and the great silences of starry nights—that's what I give to God. And above all I give—you! But let's go down. The sun is almost set. The shadows have climbed our outer wall, the evening breeze is astir among the trees over yonder. Day is done, and yet, do you know what I feel in my soul?"

"What?"

"The heralding breeze that sweeps over the slumbering world just before dawn! Have you ever felt it? I love to feel it full on my face. It is so fresh a promise of fair things to come. It sets me breathing deeply and standing on tiptoe. It sets me tingling with expectation. That is the breeze that I feel on my soul this moment. And, Humbeline, I feel so elated that if I didn't know you so well, I'd kiss you; but I respect my ears."

"Bernard," said Humbeline as she playfully flicked her hand toward his face, "you're part poet, part chivalrous knight and part clown. Let's go down and find Andrew. Your secret is safe with me. You will be the first to announce your self-imposed knighthood. But let me say that I still think that Cluny houses holy men, and that I still hold that one can find God without losing the world, and finally that I still admire young Abelard who has become the talk of the kingdom by his defeat of William of Champeaux in dialectics. I had hoped that you would rival him. But let's go down before it's dark."

"Let's go down before you cry, you mean," and with that Bernard of Fontaines ran from the room followed by the broken lance which Humbeline threw after him as she cried, "Run, you little white dog with the barking tongue...."

Thus under running banter brother and sister hid the pain that was in their souls.

Tescelin Brings Back a Runaway

"Humbeline, where's Nivard?" It was Tescelin the Tawny, Lord of Fontaines and most trusted vassal of Burgundy's Duke talking, and there was an impatient ring to his words.

"I have asked the grooms, Father," said Humbeline as she came into the room, "and they tell me that early this morning he ordered his favorite roan saddled, refused all attendance, and rode south."

"South?" said Tescelin, and the word was almost a bark. "I know what that means. He has gone to Citeaux· again."

"If so, Father, there is no worry," said Humbeline in a tone that was meant to comfort and calm, "for Abbot Stephen Harding will send him back again just as he did last time, and you will have first-hand information about Bernard and all the boys."

"Yes, yes, child, I know," said Tescelin, "but this is getting to be too much of a good thing. This is not the first time that he has run away. Abbot Stephen told him that he was too young to join his brothers. I told him to wait until he knew what life was all about. And I have heard you talking to him like a mother. And yet, in his headstrong way, he mounts his own horse, rides without attendants, and leaves us without a word. It will not do!

What has come over this land of ours, anyhow? I'm beginning to believe that the Duke is right."

"In what, Father?"

"In saying that an epidemic of religious fanaticism has broken out in Burgundy. And, of course, he blames Bernard as the breeder."

"Is he really angry?"

"No, I wouldn't say that. He's puzzled. So are we all. More, he's a little perturbed. In a joking manner, but with a ring of earnestness and gravity, he said that Bernard had so upset things in Burgundy that instead of Citeaux being a monastery in the Duchy, the Duchy is but the nursery of the monastery."

"Is he really dissatisfied?"

"No, Humbeline, I would not say that; but he is perplexed and just a trifle worried. And I don't really blame him. Last year when Bernard took thirty nobles from our midst, thirty fighting men, knights and knights-to-be, and that at a time when war was on, the Duke and the men of the Duchy gasped. They had reason to. Burgundy is chivalrous. Burgundy is venturesome. But Burgundy has never been religiously impetuous or fanatical.

"And yet Bernard with his thirty was only the beginning. Since then, hardly a week has passed in which the Duchy has not lost a promising noble or a goodly knight. The Duke needs fighting men, you know, Humbeline. It's all very well to be pious, but we must also be practical. Burgundy is a Duchy, not a monastery; and a Duchy that lies on the borderland of two great powers. Hence, wars must be fought, justice upheld, and society propagated. The Duke needs knights even more than Citeaux needs monks. As far as I can fathom God's unfathomable ways, religious life is only for the few; the great mass of men and women are to serve God outside the cloister. Hence, this whole movement does strike one as feverish and a bit fanatical."

"Why do you say that, Father? Bernard argued so logically. I didn't see anything feverish about him. I found him coldly logical."

"It is the steady drift that I am talking about, Humbeline. It would be difficult to understand at any time, but it is doubly difficult at the present. You see, disasters, such as war, pestilence, famine and the like, turn men to God; but prosperity has never been the nurse of religious vocations; and we are enjoying great prosperity at the moment. The turn of the century saw our knights come back from the Holy Land brilliant in victory and inspiring in their holy ardor. Only recently the men of Burgundy have carved out a new nation on the Iberian Peninsula; and the first King of Portugal is a Burgundian. Such tremendous triumphs sire martial men, not monks. Then again the crops are good; the golden slope is living up to its name. Vineyards, orchards and watered plains give up heavy harvests. Peace and prosperity rule the land."

Tescelin was now in deep thought; he had begun to pace the room and he was musing out loud rather than talking to Humbeline. "Then there is the tournament," he went on. "Was there ever such an invention to stir the blood of fighting men? And the way they have adorned it with the ladies! Why, everything is exciting. And yet, many of our most promising youngsters are turning their backs on it all to do as Bernard has done. It is puzzling. Just look at Nivard. What more could a boy ask for or desire?"

"But he *is* only a boy," broke in Humbeline. "Why take his impetuosities so seriously?"

"That is the point, my good girl. Why should a boy, who has just turned thirteen, who is heir apparent to this castle and all its lands, who has the closest possible connections with the suzerain of this Duchy; why should such a boy, I ask, be so filled with ideas of becoming a monk that he closes his eyes to everything that a man usually desires, and becomes a runaway? You say that it is boyish impetuosity. Maybe so, but that is a very unusual bent for a boy's impetuosity to take."

"Maybe Bernard was right. He said that the world was becoming God-conscious; even though he seemed to be contradicting himself in almost the same breath by decrying the enslavement of the clergy."

"What else did he tell you, Humbeline? What reason did he give you for going to Citeaux?"

"He said he was going to become a saint."

"A what?" shot back her father.

Humbeline's high musical laughter held keen enjoyment in its every note. "Oh, Father," she finally said, "that is exactly what I said and that is exactly how I said it. You sound surprised."

"Surprised?" laughed her father, "I'm bewildered. Bernard should have been a king's ambassador."

"What do you mean?"

"I mean he's clever. He tells you that he goes to become a saint. Do you know what he told us at Grancy? He said he was going there to become a man. Oh, he's wise; he's wily! If he had ever tried to induce Gaudry or Guy, or Gerard and Andrew to go with him in order to become saints, they would have laughed in his face if they didn't thrash him into practicality." Tescelin started to pace the floor again as he muttered, "So he went to Citeaux to become a saint, did he? What a boy! What a boy!"

But Humbeline interrupted his muttering by asking, "Didn't he say anything to you about becoming a saint?"

"I should say he did not," almost shouted her father. Then in a calmer tone he added, "You see, Humbeline, we men have so exalted an idea of saints and sanctity that we hesitate even to aspire to them. Had Bernard spoken of them at Grancy he would have been met with a far different reception. And that is why I marvel not at his wiliness but at his wisdom.

"Look. We were at Grancy just preparing for the siege. There is high tension in camp at such a moment, Humbeline. Nerves are on edge. Blood is at fever pitch. The men are all fidgety. They are like mettlesome steeds champing at the bit. Words are few and hurried. One business alone occupies the mind—it is the battle. Into such a ferment came Bernard; told us his decision; talked of becoming a man, of laying siege to a city greater than that of Grancy, of doing battle for a Sovereign greater than our Duke, of proving his valor in a more manly and more human way than by fire and sword and slaughter. And what was the result?—His uncle Gaudry, the oldest, most matured and most famed knight of the group that listened to him, joins Bernard, even though Grancy has not yet been assaulted! Next follows his brother Guy, despite his wife and his two young children. Gerard would not listen to him that day; but you know where Gerard is this moment; and you also know where thirty other knights and nobles of Burgundy are. Humbeline, Bernard used some sort of magic."

"To me it seems that he worked some sort of miracle. Look at what happened to Gerard: wounded just where Bernard said he would be wounded; captured and imprisoned just as Bernard had predicted; then freed by means he knows not of; his shackles loosened by no key, iron or fire, the prison doors opened in some unaccountable way, and then he walks down the street of an enemy's city and, though recognized, is unmolested. I think I'd go to Citeaux myself, if I had passed through such an experience."

"Yes," said Tescelin, "that was a strange happening. But do you know what strikes me as more miraculous?"

"What?"

"That all thirty should have remained loyal through-out those long six months at Chatillon-sur-Seine. It is easy enough to understand a group persevering in their aim under an Abbot like Stephen Harding and in a monastery that has established customs and order. There they are made to feel like beginners, and discipline does the rest. But for six months these thirty men lived under Bernard, observing the regulations that he laid down, and doing whatsoever he said. Why, I expected most of them to give up the idea any day; and yet, this boy, who knew no more about the religious life than they, held them as a unit and after six long months led them to the monastery of Citeaux. I know something of men, Humbeline, and I say that that was a miracle. Ah, the whole situation is just a bit beyond me. But come, I must ride south and bring back Nivard. Will you ride with me?"

"Gladly," answered Humbeline, "but if my hearing hasn't gone back on me we will be saved the ride. Listen. Do you not hear a horse in the courtyard?"

They both listened and quite clearly came the sharp ring of iron-shod hooves striking the stones in the outer courtyard. Both started for the door, but had not reached the hallway when a voice that was not Nivard's was heard talking to the grooms.

"Why, it's Guy of Marcy, the Duke's nephew," gasped Humbeline. "He must have some message for you from his uncle."

Tescelin smiled down at his daughter and the twinkle in his eye spoke more merriment than the ironic formality of his voice as he said, "Oh, undoubtedly, Humbeline. And I am quite positive that it is my daughter's deep concern in the message of the Duke that makes her blush and breathe so rapidly. Humbeline, you're naïve; but you have told me something just now that I have wanted to know for a long, long time. You like Guy of Marcy, don't you?"

"Yes, Father, I do." It was almost a whisper.

"Good," said her father, and in that one monosyllable put more meaning than in a speech. "So do I," he added. "Now let's see what he has to say," and linking his arm in his daughter's, Tescelin the Tawny walked down the hallway of the castle of Fontaines. Just before they reached the farthest door, it opened, and a servant entered closely followed by a knight. On seeing Tescelin and his daughter the servant bowed and backed away, but the knight advanced with outstretched hand and in a vibrant voice that spoke of good health and high spirits, said, "Lord Tescelin, I have such excellent news of your sons that I could not wait until this evening to tell you."

"That's fine, Guy," said Tescelin, "and I suppose that you did not hope that this excellent news of my sons would fall on the ears of my only daughter."

Guy of Marcy smiled; it was a smile that was honest, open, almost boyish, and for that reason all the more fetching; then said, "My uncle says that you are the deepest man in the Duchy. I begin to believe him."

Tescelin looked from Guy to Humbeline and from Humbeline back to Guy, and laughed as he said, "I'd have to have cataracts on both eyes not to see hearts that are worn on sleeves and lights that leap in voices. You two are priceless. But come, what is the news?"

"Citeaux has set up another monastery in Burgundy."

"That makes the third in our Duchy," said Tescelin.

"Right," answered Guy, "Citeaux, la Ferté and now Pontigny; and, Humbeline, you could never guess who is head of Pontigny."

"Who is it?"

"A relative of yours, Hugh of Macon."

"What does your uncle say of this, Guy?" asked Tescelin.

"Oh, he's proud of it," laughed Guy, "even though he makes a lot of noise about men-at-arms becoming monks. I saw him one day on his return from Citeaux. He was beside himself. All he could do was mumble, 'They are men all right, real men; men of God. And to think of them in my Duchy!' Yes, he's proud to have them here no matter how loudly he protests about men changing armor for the cowl. If you ask me, I'd say that my uncle hides his bursting pride under a noisy protest."

All three laughed. Then Tescelin led the way to the courtyard saying, "I know you won't object to a little canter to the south, Guy. Humbeline and I were just about to ride to Citeaux."

"To see your sons?"

"No!" said Tescelin. "But to bring back a baby runaway. Nivard wants to become a man of God, as your uncle calls them, before he has become a full-grown boy. I don't want to be forced to leave Fontaines to your uncle or my serfs, and from the looks of things I won't be able to leave it to Humbeline; for by the time it becomes necessary for me to leave it to any one, I really think that she will be the wife of a certain nephew of your uncle's. I wonder if you know the young man, Guy; his sister is Duchess of Lorraine."

"Maybe you're talking about my mother's only son," came the quick reply, "I certainly hope so."

"We'll see," said Tescelin, "we'll see." And with that they reached the courtyard.

They did not ride to Citeaux that day, for before they had covered half the distance they were met by a boy riding a beautiful roan. At the sight of them he put spurs to his horse and greeted them with the triumphant shout, "Father, Father, Abbot Stephen says he'll accept me when I get a little older."

No one would take the thrill of triumph from a boy of thirteen. One does not snuff out the lights of gleaming happiness that shine in the eyes of a stripling; one never smothers the effervescence of glowing youth; so Tescelin the Tawny's voice matched the excitement in that of his son as he said, "That's just glorious, son of mine. But now, before you grow a minute older, let's have a fast ride home. Come, Humbeline. Come, Guy. I'll wager that Nivard and I reach the castle at least an hour before you."

"That's a wager that I'll gladly lose," said Guy as he smiled at Humbeline.

But Tescelin did not hear him, for he and Nivard had spurred away. As they slowed down to cross a little stream, the father turned to his son and said, "Nivard, I think I gave myself long odds in that wager," and his whole being radiated the joy of living that was in him and the peace that lay upon his heart.

Guy of Marcy's Wife Visits Clairvaux

Guy of Marcy lost that wager with Tescelin, but he won Tescelin's daughter, so nobody was sorry. But just about three years after that ride in the woods, we find Humbeline sitting in the guest room of the abbey of Clairvaux. She is making ineffectual dabs at her eyes with a dainty bit of lace that makes up in beauty what it lacks in practicality. She had been crying, but now that the ascetic-looking young Abbot is smiling down on her, the dainty bit of lace is wiping away the last little trace of her tears. She even manages a tiny chuckle as she says, "Reverend Father Bernard, you should teach your gatekeepers not to bark."

"They can't help it, Humbeline," answers Bernard, "for you know the old adage about 'like father, like son';

didn't you always call me 'the little white dog with the barking tongue'? What can you expect then, from my children?"

"Yes, but your bark was always worse than your bite. That Andrew though has a bite that is far worse than his bark; and the Lord knows his bark is terrific. Everyone in my train must have heard him. It is positively degrading to be barked at by your own brother before your whole suite of attendants. I just know that the maids and the outriders are having the joke of the month this moment, and it is at my expense."

"Well, now that you are the wife of Guy of Marcy, you are so rich that you won't mind that little expense," laughed Bernard. "What did he say, anyhow?"

"He looked at me from head to foot. Then looked at the horsemen and the coach. Then counted the number of the maids out loud. Then looked back at me again, scrutinizing everything I have on from hat to shoes; then in a very loud and very, very vulgar voice said, 'To me you look like overdressed offal.'"

"Never, Humbeline! Never!" cried Bernard as he put both hands to his ears. Then with a quiet chuckle he added, "I'm sure you have the words twisted. I feel positive that Andrew only said what I myself might have said."

"And what might you have said?" snorted Humbeline as she tossed her head and looked at Bernard—her nose very high in the air.

"Why, I might have said," replied Bernard very coolly, "yes, I might have said that you are awfully overdressed."

"Humph!" snorted Humbeline, and her hat almost fell off, so vicious was the toss of her head, "I see that Bernard of Clairvaux has the same sharp tongue as Bernard of Fontaines. Don't you like nice clothes?"

"Yes, I do," replied Bernard, smiling wryly. "But I have often wondered how many women realize that just as clothes do not make the man, neither do they make the woman. You see, Humbeline, a woman can be beautifully dressed without being a beautiful woman. Silk and purple and brightly colored stuffs possess charm, but they do not confer it. When you put such things on your body, they display their own beauty, they do not resign it in favor of your body. And when you remove these beautiful things, they take their beauty with them. So why be a display rack for clothes?"

"What would you have me do, become a nun?"

"You could do worse things than that, my dear little girl."

"Bernard," said Humbeline with a proud lift to her head and a proud lilt to her voice, "I am not your dear little girl, I am wife of Guy of Marcy."

"Good for you, Humbeline!" laughed Bernard. "That was said like a queen. But come, tell me, have you found love?"

Humbeline softened. In a tone that was caressing she said, "Yes, Bernard, I have found love. I have an adoring husband, a beautiful home and many delightful friends."

Brother and sister were seated now much in the same posture as we saw them in the tower room almost four years ago; but what a change in their outward appearances! Humbeline had flowered into the full bloom of the beauty that had been promised. Marriage had given her more than a new name. It had given her distinctiveness and dignity that rendered her really *distingué.* There is no other word for it. Because it was much more than the mere external perfection of her outward person, perfect though that was. There was something inside her, something secret, something deep that gave star-radiance

to her eyes, a conscious superiority to her gait and carriage, and created an atmosphere that called for the acknowledgment of nobility.

Humbeline, the young wife of Guy of Marcy, justly
merited her reputation for beauty. But on the other hand,
Bernard, who had been so handsome when last we saw
him with his fair hair, transparent skin and large, luminous eyes, had become emaciated. His cheeks were hollow, their bones standing out in high relief; the line of his
mouth was thinner, straighter, firmer, even somewhat
hard; while his chin, now that he had lost so much flesh,
was really aggressive. His was a face that spoke of stern
asceticism; it was the face of a warrior after a hard campaign. It would have been repellant had not the sharp
lines been softened by the large eyes, whose sparkling
beauty was enhanced now that they shone out from deep
sockets. They looked like two deep pools that were filled
with sweet, cooling sympathy, and they so set off his features that he, who could no longer be called handsome,
now deserved to be called beautiful.

Obviously Bernard had suffered much, both mentally and physically. Though he was only twenty-seven,
and had been Abbot but for three years, there was a ma-
turity about him that comes only from soul-suffering.
Every line and lineament of his face was like a telltale
scar, a permanent record of a battle hard fought. His eyes
held a light that is seen only in the eyes of those who
look the long vistas of time and discern beyond the last
horizon the realities that are timeless. Bernard of Clairvaux was not four years older than Bernard of Fontaines;
he was an eternity older. Citeaux and Clairvaux had not
only thinned him out, they had deepened him and chis-
eled him, so that Humbeline was now in the presence of
a character.

Bernard smiled as his sister enumerated the possessions that marriage had given her. "I see," he said, "that

you still maintain that love gives. You say it has given you a husband, a home and fine friends. Come now, Humbeline, tell me truly, is love a conquest or a surrender? I have heard people say that you won Guy and others say that Guy won you. Who is right? Does a lover win or does a lover lose?"

"I think I know what you mean," said Humbeline slowly. "You are asking: did I give myself to Guy, or did I acquire him. You are asking whether love is a self-giving or a self-seeking. You are asking a deep and difficult question, Bernard; it comes to this: Does a lover want to possess or to be possessed? To tell you the truth I think that love is a conquest and a surrender; that the lover wants to possess and to be possessed. Honestly, it seems to me as though deep love is a passionate grasping as much as it is a whole-souled, prodigal giving; in other words it is selfish even while it is utterly selfless. What do you say? Have you found love?"

"Yes, Humbeline, I have found Him; and while what you have said about love is true enough, I find that at its deepest depth, love is a surrender, a wholesale surrender; and once we have made that surrender, then we have conquered. Due to my own stupidities and early indiscretions, Humbeline, I have been somewhat ill; but that illness has been a mighty blessing to me. I have had time to spend among the oaks and the birches; and there, where life abounds, I have learned much of Him who is life and love."

"But, Bernard, why don't you take better care of yourself?"

"Oh, don't worry; I'm as well as God wants me to be. I confess that I overdid things as a novice; but you see, I held then, and I still hold that it profits a man little to follow Christ, if he fails to overtake Him.

"Unlike the spouse in the Canticle, I did not languish with love, I was afire with it. I told you years ago that I was going to become a saint. Well, Humbeline, I have found that it is a much bigger task than I thought. No, indeed; it is no easy task to overtake Jesus Christ; and yet, overtake Him we must if we would become saints. You see, the secret of sanctity is love. That is why I told you in the tower room that happy afternoon of four years ago, that I was going to become a lover, a lover of God. But love is an art, and an art in which we can ever improve; so I am always seeking to know more about it. I have learned much of God from nature, and I am sure that I can learn much of love for God from that love which we call human love. That is why I questioned you. Look, Humbeline, the Canticle of Canticles is Solomon's love song to his dusky bride, but hidden deep within those lines is the story of Christ's love for your soul and mine, and the secret of how you and I are to love Christ. So far as I can see now, Humbeline, it is a matter of complete and absolute surrender, or as I wrote a friend of mine a short while ago: 'You ask me with what measure we ought to love God, and I answer—let it be without measure!' You don't set any bounds to your love for Guy, do you?"

"Of course not," came the speedy reply, "I give him my all."

"Good. I am glad that you said that, Humbeline; for it tells me that you do love Guy and that you do know what love is. Ah, it is as strong as death. It does not say: It is fitting or it is expedient to do such and such a thing. No. It says rather: I will! I desire! I long to do it with all my soul! That's love, isn't it, Humbeline? See how utterly fearless and truly sublime it is?"

"Yes, indeed, and I also see that you are telling me your life."

"Oh, no!" came the rejoinder, "just my ambitions. Those are my ideals, Humbeline; the real is far from that as yet."

"Well, tell me something of the real."

"The gathering of the thirty," began Bernard with a smile, "was engrossing and fascinating by its very challenge. The six months at Chatillon-sur-Seine were a delight by their very novelty; but the two years at Citeaux were grueling. Let me tell you, Humbeline, to conquer self is a fierce struggle, and to live for God alone can be really excruciating; for one is so often left alone in the dark. You see, we are flesh and blood, but I wanted to be all spirit. I wanted too much, and my poor body is still complaining. I was exaggerated, and that, you know, is a bit of stupidity. But do you now when I learned my mistakes at Citeaux?"

"When you fell ill?"

"No, but when I tried to demand the same from my community here at Clairvaux. Our first year here was a fright, Humbeline. It is a good thing that Abbot Stephen Harding gave me my brothers and relations as companions. A brother helped by a brother is like a strong city, you know; and yet, our strong city almost proved too weak. Oh, Guy, Gerard, Andrew, Bartholomew, Uncle Gaudry and the rest have been most loyal; but it was from them that I learned that monks are men and not angels. I asked for the very best; and let me tell you, Humbeline, the best is the greatest enemy to the good! I asked too much. I was less discreet than St. Benedict. And while I still maintain that he who sows sparingly shall also reap sparingly; though I still insist that we should blush to be weak members beneath a thorn-crowned head, I must also admit that I exaggerated and that exaggeration is error. I was wrong."

"Oh, I'm so glad to hear you say that," broke in Humbeline. "You will never know what a relief it is to find the same honest Bernard in the Abbot of Clairvaux that I loved as my brother at Fontaines. Your confession reminds me of a little deceit that you practiced to win your followers."

"A deceit? What was that?"

Shaking an accusing finger at her frowning brother, she said, "You told me that you were going to Citeaux to become a saint; but you told Uncle Gaudry and the rest that you were going there to become a man. Oh! You fox."

Bernard's eyes sparkled and the thin line of his mouth lifted into a very winsome smile as he said, "I used to be a little white dog, now I am a fox. Either I'm improving or you're degrading. But tell me, does one deceive if he employs synonyms?"

"Of course not."

"Then, of what are you accusing me? To be a man, a real man, Humbeline, a man after the model we saw on the mount, the mount of the beatitudes, the mount of Tabor and very especially, the mount of Calvary, is to be a saint. So you see, my dear, I said the same thing to you and to them, though I did use different words. And let me tell you that both they and I have found out that it takes every inch of our manhood to be the tiniest bit saintly."

Humbeline leaned forward and there was just the trace of a frown on her almost alabaster forehead as she said, "Bernard dear, tell me truthfully, isn't it all quite burdensome? I know the ideal is lofty and the pious catch phrases inspiring, but how about the everyday, humdrum routine of the life? Doesn't it weary you?"

Bernard looked long at his sister; there was admiration, appreciation and even a touch of awe in his look. Then he said, "Women *are* intuitive! Humbeline, you have seen more deeply in this hour than some monks see in years. The honest answer is: 'Yes, the life is burdensome.' But here is the paradox: the more the burden grows, the lighter it becomes. I'm not joking. Christ said, 'My burden is light.' And He does not deceive. His burden *is* light."

"I don't understand," said Humbeline.

"Have you ever reflected on birds?" asked Bernard. "Oh, nature teaches us so much! Is it not the very number of the birds' feathers that raises them? Take these light burdens away from them and what happens? Does not their body, by its very weight, fall to the ground? That is an apt illustration of what happens in this life. There are burdens, very real burdens; but in all truth they bear us more than we bear them; and once again, the secret is love. Oh, Humbeline, it is a blessed life! Tell me, is not that a holy state in which a man lives more purely, falls more rarely, rises more speedily, walks more cautiously, is bedewed with the waters of grace more frequently, rests more securely, dies more confidently, is cleansed more quickly and rewarded more abundantly?"

"You make me jealous, Bernard. And I am glad to hear you speak of reward. That makes your approach more human, more natural and much more practical."

"Of course I speak of reward, Humbeline; for as I told you before: while love is never mercenary, it is never unprofitable. God is our reward exceedingly great. We seek Him. We want to find Him and say with the spouse in the Canticle, 'I have found him whom my soul loves and I will not let him go.' Oh, it's a fascinating search. I told you years ago that it would be a thrilling tilt, the only tournament worthwhile; but I did not know then how true my words were. Yes, it is glorious even though some days must be dark and dreary. Did you know that Clairvaux almost ceased to be? That was a dark day."

"What do you mean, Bernard?"

"We were literally without food our first months here. And let me say that it is hard to work even for God on an empty stomach; further, let me tell you that it takes real fortitude to sing His praises when the hunger pangs are actually gnawing. Guy and Gerard, yes, and even the staunch old soldier, Gaudry, advised a return to Citeaux."

"Oh, why didn't you let me know?" broke in Humbeline in real sympathy. "Or why didn't you send word to Father? Were you too proud to beg?"

"No, but I wanted to be brave enough to trust. I hope it was not presumption on my part, but I put it up to God to take care of us. He did. But I must say that He allowed it to become very dark before He showed us the dawn. On the day that I called dreary, the whole community was gathered outside the little church ready to walk back to Citeaux. The months had been too demanding. Prudence and common sense called for a retreat. I was almost ready to give in, but I still had trust in God, so I went into our little church and prayed. I told God very plainly that if He wanted a monastery in this Valley of Wormwood, that if He wanted monks instead of bandits in this hide-out, that if He wanted to hear hymns of praise instead of robbers' curses, He would have to provide.

"Pretty arrogant talk, wasn't it? But I had no more than finished laying down my ultimatum, than a wagon was heard rumbling down the very rough road we had dug out. That wagon was loaded with food and clothing. I doubt if any horse and wagon in all history were ever more welcome to men! We did not return to Citeaux and since then God has shown His hand continually. Our community grows. One day I will have to do as Abbot Stephen has done; I will have to send out colonies to found other monasteries. But how I shrink from that day!"

"Shrink?" exclaimed Humbeline. "I should think you'd rejoice."

"Humbeline," said Bernard, "you are a woman and know something of a woman's love. You can surmise how the child of a mother's womb is twined round her heart. Let me tell you then, that the children God has given me to raise for Him have gripped my heart in the self-same fashion. Most are older than myself, some even older than Father, but to me they are all children, and God knows I *love* them."

"Bernard," said Humbeline in a very measured tone, "these four years have changed your outward appearance greatly, but they have not changed your soul; and I thank God for it. You are still my brother with the beautiful eyes and the more beautiful heart."

"The millennium is here!" Bernard exclaimed. "My sister Humbeline is getting complimentary: I used to be a dog; a little while ago I was a fox; and now.... Oh, don't change, Humbeline, or I'll accuse Guy of Marcy of spoiling a grand tomboy."

Humbeline smiled a sad little smile as she said, "Oh, those blessed days are gone forever, Bernard; and listening to you talk just now, I begin to wonder if I haven't been somewhat frivolous during the past few years. Sitting here talking of God and the way to God makes our life in society seem so empty, vain and absolutely purposeless."

"Mother lived in society, Humbeline; and I wouldn't call her life empty or vain."

"Yes, Bernard, but that is my point precisely. The society in which Mother moved and the society in which I live are as far apart as the silence of this Valley from the bustle of our castle just before a battle. I wonder if I haven't been silly."

"Now wait a minute," said Bernard soothingly. "Don't be too hard on yourself. Newlyweds must have some outlet for their newly found happiness. They need society. Yes, and society needs them! For the world would grow completely cynical if new loves were not being continually born. Love is life's elixir and just to see it in others changes the world for us. But perhaps you have had your fling. Perhaps from now on you could imitate Mother more closely. She was so good to the poor. But don't make the mistake many make; don't let pity sway your heart and govern your donations. No. Let love be the motive, love for Christ in the poor of Christ. Humbeline, I say to you what I so often say to myself: Life is only for love. Time is ours only that we may find God. We were made to become saints. Humbeline-mine, that is the purpose of life; see to it that you do not make a mess of it. Many do! But come, my awfully over-dressed one, come and see if Andrew will now talk to you in a more brotherly fashion. I will go and round up Guy, Gerard, Bartholomew and Nivard—that boy makes a splendid monk."

His sister arose and put out a restraining hand as she said, "Before you go, tell me, isn't there anything I can do for you?"

"Yes, indeed there is, Humbeline," said Bernard with seriousness, "you can pray that I become the man and the saint that God wants me to become; or better, you can pray that I really fall in love with the God of love. I am becoming involved in many affairs. I am called from the monastery frequently and I fear for my soul. It is the work of God that calls me forth, it is true; but if the great St. Paul could fear lest he become a castaway, you can see why your brother Bernard needs prayers."

"Well," said Humbeline, "since you won't allow me to give anything, may I beg something?"

"Anything at all, Humbeline, and you don't have to beg."

"Then, give me your blessing and a parting word of advice."

She knelt. Bernard's eyes went to heaven as his hands came up, and as he prayed the blessing of God the Father, Son and Holy Spirit to descend upon his sister and remain forever, his tones and gestures seemed to change the unfurnished and only roughly finished room into a sanctuary. He lifted her up, kissed her with warm affection and said, "Remember, my sister, that 'Favor is deceitful and beauty is vain; but a woman that fears the Lord, shall be praised.' I want you to be praised highly, so be like your mother, Alice of Montbar, and even like your Blessed Mother, Mary of Nazareth." He then kissed her again and said, "I'll gather the others; you go see Andrew. He'll be more brotherly now, I'm sure." And with a smile and a wave he was gone.

The Cardinal and Chancellor Chat

"Well, peace at last! And, Haimeric, I feel spent, completely spent. These have been the longest eight years in my life." The Cardinal's whole person was a study in complete relaxation.

"I can believe you, Cardinal Peter, for I feel played out myself, but happy—happier than I have been in the past eight years. I imagine a soldier must feel the same way after a long campaign. The victory is sweet, but the whole man is so spent, physically, mentally and emotionally, that he can hardly taste the sweetness. Chancellor of the Holy Roman See is never a sinecure, but let me tell you that the past eight years have been enough to give a man perpetual insomnia. Peter de Leone as anti-pope has made an old man of me before my time."

The two prelates were seated in the Chancellor's study. Their care-lined faces, even in repose, told their own story of unselfish whole-souled service, of worries, anxieties and brain-wearying burdens. Haimeric, the Chancellor, was the older of the two, and yet when he walked or talked the animation that lit his countenance and the energy that marked his gestures showed him to be the vigorous executive, the man of rapid action, sure in his decisions, decisive in his deeds.

Cardinal Peter had more of the quiet composure that bespeaks the statesman and the diplomat, the carefully-weighing and always far-seeing consultor of the Holy See. One look at these men told that they had been under tension, but it also told that the tension was now lifted and had been lifted by victory, not defeat; for they were reclining, they did not sag. Deep though they were in the palace and stout as were the Roman walls of the house, nevertheless, every now and then a joyous shout just thinly made its way into their chamber. "Viva il Papa!" would be heard, then "Viva Bernard!"

At one of these distant yet distinct cries Cardinal Peter stirred; leaning forward he placed the small glass of wine that he had been sipping on the stand before him, then lifting an arresting finger he said, "Haimeric, what gives Bernard of Clairvaux his power? Hear the people acclaiming him? They are right; for to him more than to anyone else on this continent we owe the peace that has been won, and to him Innocent owes his papacy. What is it? What is in the man that makes him such a power?"

The Cardinal leaned back a moment and before Haimeric could reply, went on, "I was at Etampes at the time of the Council. Louis le Gros, King of France, had summoned all prelates and princes of the realm. And why? Because Louis le Gros did not know what to do. He did not know whom to recognize as Pope: de Leone who called himself Anacletus or our own Innocent. Suger, brilliant Prime Minister though he is, was in the same fix. For that matter, I guess the whole world was. De Leone had thirty Cardinals on his side; Innocent only sixteen.

More, de Leone had the City of Rome, and was actually resident in the palace of the Popes, while Innocent had scurried to France.

"It was a trying moment for everyone. And yet, when this little monk walked into that assembly, spontaneously, and from every quarter, rose the cry: 'Let the man of God decide! Let the man of God decide!' And all France awaited the decision of Bernard of Clairvaux. You know his decision, and you know how not only France, but Germany, England, Portugal, Spain and finally Italy and the whole world followed it. How does he do it?"

"Well, Cardinal," said the Chancellor as he straightened up in his chair, set down his glass and rubbed his hands together as if in appreciative anticipation of a real discussion, "I suppose that I could say that he has that indefinable something about him that marks a man for moral leadership. I suppose that I could say that he is one of those persons who, without any specific act of will on their own part, find themselves leaders, rather than make themselves so. I suppose I could say these things, but if I did, I would be saying nothing. Quite a few people talk that way about personality, don't they? Defining it as an indefinable something. That's not a definition. That's a confession of laziness. They are too lazy to analyze. I admit that Bernard's tremendous power does give one pause; and the deeper one analyzes it and the man, the more perplexed one becomes, until finally, he strikes the soul of the Abbot of Clairvaux. Then all is clear."

"Have you struck it?" The question was quiet, but there was a tone of incredulity to it.

"Yes," said Haimeric, "without any boasting, I think that I can say that I have. You see, Bernard and I are friends now; have been for over ten full years; and yet, our first contacts were anything but friendly. Many people call him the 'honey-tongued,' but when I first came in contact with him I called him the 'venom-penned,' and I did so with good reason."

"Oh, he can be sarcastic," laughed the Cardinal.

"Sarcastic?" came the quick reply, "Sarcastic? Why the man can be positively insulting. And yet, there is such a ring of sincerity to what he says or writes, that even though he pierces you to the very heart, you cannot take umbrage."

"That's true," mused the Cardinal. "The man is sincere. I suppose you put that as the first quality of his soul."

"First?" said Haimeric with a lilt to his tone that made the word a question and an indignant protest. "I put sincerity as his first, second, third and last characteristic. But let me tell you how I found that out."

Cardinal Peter took up his glass again, leaned far back in his chair, and the faintest trace of an amused smile touched the corners of his mouth as he watched the animated play of light and shadow on the countenance of the Chancellor.

"The man does not know what fear is," began Haimeric, as he rose, reached into a chest and drew forth a bulky looking dossier. "Here are some of Bernard's letters to myself, to Popes and to some of the Cardinals. I treasure these letters; in fact, I am collecting every letter I can of Bernard's. These early ones are my favorites to date, for nowhere have I met with such fire, fearlessness and naked-souled sincerity. The man takes your breath away."

"He's taking yours away right now. However, I know what you mean; I have received a few myself. He is a master Latinist."

"Oh," snapped the Chancellor, "I'm not talking about the form. As you say, it is masterly. I really think that it was due to his mastery of Latin that he first started to write. You see, the first few letters we received were written in the name of the Abbots of Citeaux, Pontigny, and in last place, Clairvaux. But it is not the form that takes my breath away, it is the matter! Just listen to this one addressed to Pope Honorius II—you remember that at the time there was trouble between the King of France and the Bishop of Paris. It seems that Bernard had gotten the Bishops of the country to lay an interdict on the King, and I believe he had the King squirming, when along came word from the Pope lifting the interdict.

"Bernard's blood boiled. Here is what he wrote: 'In the time of Honorius the Church has been deeply wounded.' That was merely to make the Pope blink. It did. Now catch the next sentence: 'Already the humility, or rather, the constancy of the Bishops had bent down the anger of the King, when alas! The supreme authority of the Sovereign Pontiff intervenes and sets up pride as it throws down constancy!' That wasn't calculated to smooth ruffled feathers; but listen to this: 'But what astonishes us is that a judgment should have been given without hearing the two parties; and that the absent should have been condemned.'"

"Whew!" whistled the Cardinal, "What a man! What a man! Was the Pope angry?"

"How could he be when Bernard's next sentence is: 'We do not blame you with rash presumption, but with the love of sons we suggest to the heart of our Father how greatly the wicked triumph because of this act, and how the poor are cast down.'"

"That's a touching turn," put in the Cardinal.

"Yes," replied Haimeric, "and done in such a way as to carry conviction. Obviously, the man is writing truth. It was the heart of a son that prompted what in any other would have been the height of bold and arrogant presumption. But after this tug at the emotions, Bernard concludes with what sounds like an ultimatum or a declaration of war. He wrote: 'How long the poor Bishop of Paris ought to suffer from this act, it is not for us, most holy Father, to prescribe; it is for you to consult your own heart. Farewell.'"

The thought of the Pope's face as he read this brought a smile to the Cardinal's. He then said, "The man jolts you into action, doesn't he?"

"Jolt is the word," replied Haimeric and then went on. "I happen to know that he wrote to the King of France on the same subject and opened with the sentence: 'The King of heaven and earth has given you a kingdom on earth, and He will bestow one upon you in heaven, provided that you study to govern your earthly one with justice and wisdom.'"

"Ow!" exclaimed the Cardinal, "The man is merciless in attack."

"Fearless is the word I use," said Haimeric. "I also happen to know that in that letter he laid down an ultimatum to the King saying: '...if you do not desist from this wrong quickly, there is nothing which we are not prepared to do within the limits of our weakness for the Church of God and her minister, the venerable Bishop of Paris.'"

"What was the 'limit of his weakness'?" asked the Cardinal.

"Oh, Bernard was so weak that he only got the Bishops of France to lay the King under interdict; that's all. But did you catch the phrase 'for the Church of God and for her minister'? There you have the soul of Bernard. The man is utterly unselfish and completely disinterested; truly, he is seeking only the glory of God. The man is the very incarnation of zeal; and that is why his 'jolts,' as you call them, are received with so much grace. He hits hard, but he hits justly; and while he may momen-

tarily rouse your anger, he seldom, if ever, incurs your
permanent enmity. You know, actually, he was at the bottom of this whole trouble."

"You don't say?"

"Yes, you see, the Bishop of Paris was the King's favorite until Bernard persuaded him to reform his life,
give up his worldly ways and act as a real Bishop. The
Bishop changed; but the King did not like the change, so
he started to persecute his quondam favorite. The same
thing happened to the Archbishop of Sens, and again,
Bernard was at the bottom of that and in the very same
way. He had gotten the Bishop to reform. You can imagine how welcome reformed Bishops are at Court."

"Odd, isn't it, that he, a Cistercian Abbot, should get
involved with Bishops, Archbishops and kings. Citeaux is
so strict, so purely contemplative and so rigidly cloistered."

Before he had finished Haimeric's hearty laughter
was ringing through the chambers. Then he said, "Those
were the very thoughts that I had just about ten years
ago. It was immediately after the Council of Troyes.
Bernard had been there, and of course was no mere spectator. It was he who drew up the Rule for the Order of
the Knights Templars. Almost immediately followed the
Councils at Arras, Chalons, Cambrai and Laon. Bernard
was at all of them, and again not as spectator but more
nearly as dictator.

"As you recall, these were the Councils that dis-
persed a religious community, deposed a Bishop and
forced an Abbot to resign. Bernard was the power behind
every move. Well, the councils were hardly adjourned
when from all sides, from princes, clergy and people
came denunciations pouring into Rome. The young
Abbot—Bernard was not forty at the time—was called a
'meddler,' an 'ambitious upstart,' a 'whitened sepulcher'
and what not. I decided that where there was so much

smoke, there must be some fire; so I sat down and wrote a letter. I was hot at the time. The letter was hotter. I told the good Abbot at Clairvaux that the Church would be much better off and the world at far greater peace if impudent Cistercian frogs would only remain in their marshes and not disturb the universe with their croaking."

"You never wrote that, Haimeric!" said Cardinal Peter.

"I most certainly did," replied the Chancellor, "and I sent it in the name of the Sacred College of Cardinals."

Cardinal Peter gasped, then asked, "How did Bernard take it?"

"Take it?" laughed Haimeric. "Take it? Listen to what he gave." Picking up a letter the Chancellor read: "'I rejoice to know that you are displeased at my meddling in matters that belong not to monks. Therein you show your prudence and your friendship for me. See to it, therefore, that your will and mine shall be satisfied. Forbid these noisy and unmannerly frogs to leave their marshes for the future.'"

"Good for Bernard!" exclaimed the Cardinal as he slapped his thigh. "That's a retort for you, Haimeric. That's paying you back in your own coin."

"Wait a while, you haven't heard anything yet. Just listen. He goes on: 'Let their croaking be no longer heard in the council rooms of Bishops or in the palaces of kings.' Now comes the climax," interposed Haimeric. "The man is a fire-eater all right. Listen and tell me if Bernard has not eclipsed himself. 'Let no necessity,' he writes, 'nor any authority have the power to compel their interference in disputes or public business of any sort. Perhaps thus your friend will escape the charge of presumption. Yet, I know not how I can have laid myself open to such a charge, for it has been my resolve and determination never to leave my monastery except on

business of the Order, or at the command of either the
Legate of the Apostolic See or my own Bishop, neither of
whom I can in conscience disobey except by privilege of
higher authority. If Your Eminence will be so kind as to
obtain that privilege for me, I shall enjoy peace myself
and leave others in the same.'"

The Cardinal's heightened color and shining eyes
showed his pleasure. "Never did Your Eminence have
anything so neatly dumped back into his lap."

"Never indeed," replied the Chancellor, "but listen
to the last sentence. After Bernard has put his opponent
prone in the dust, he always adds the finishing touch by
placing his foot upon him. When I had read thus far, you
can be sure that my ears were burning and my face was
red, but here is the Bernardine finishing blow: 'Yet,' he
writes, 'even though I shut myself up and keep absolute
silence I do not suppose that the murmurs of the Church
will cease as long as the Roman Curia continues to do
injury to the absent, in order to be complaisant to those
who are near at hand. Farewell.'"

Cardinal Peter was shaking with laughter but he
managed to say, "I don't suppose you fared any too well
after perusing that bombardment."

"No, I didn't," admitted the Chancellor, "and you
can be sure that I studied and studied that letter, for it
showed me the keen mind with which I had to contend.
But I am very glad that I did study it, for it showed me
the soul of Bernard. You have heard the motives he as-
signs for leaving his monastery. That was not temper
writing; that was truth. Bernard *is* a religious, a deeply
contemplative religious; and he is happy only when he is
in his own monastery."

"Is that a fact?" asked the Cardinal.

"Well, if you don't believe me, Your Eminence, just
look at this fact—where is Bernard at this moment?"

"I don't know," said Peter. "Where is he?"

"On his way back to France, back to his beloved Clairvaux."

"What?" exclaimed the Cardinal. "Do you mean to tell me that the man terminates the cruelest schism of the century and then waits for none of the celebration?"

"I mean to tell you that Bernard left Rome just as quickly and as quietly as possible. For him the drama was over the moment the false pope took off the insignia of office, laid them at Innocent's feet and swore fidelity to Peter's legitimate successor. Let the others take the applause. Bernard's work was done; he must turn himself to some other work for God. Peter, I have seen the man do the same thing time and time again."

"But what have we in this man—humility incarnate?"

"He would blush if you told him so," replied Haimeric, "and most likely argue with you, saying that he was only being honest. But, of course, that is his own definition of humility. He says: 'Humility is honesty; that honesty by which we see ourselves as we really are and hence, become vile in our own eyes,' which, you must admit, is not a bad definition. However, it is not his humility that I wanted to bring out, it is his utter disinterestedness and his complete devotion to Clairvaux. No one can ever say that Bernard is not a contemplative even though he is the most active man of our age. I sum him up by saying that he has the heart and mind of Mary with the hands and energy of Martha. Read this treatise on the 'Love of God' which he was good enough to write for me and even to dedicate to me. It is sublime, yet absolutely simple."

"Would you dare call Bernard simple?" questioned Peter.

"Indeed I would," answered the Chancellor quickly. "In fact I would be wrong if I summed him up in any other word. But I use 'simple' in its purest sense. You know, my good Cardinal, simplicity is not a synonym for stupidity, though a great many people seem to think that it is. No, simplicity calls for the keenest of intellects and the staunchest of wills; and that is why we have so few really simple people. You see, it demands that a man be absorbed by one idea; and that is true of Bernard. God is his one idea; his only absorption."

"You startle me with the abruptness of that statement," said the Cardinal, moving uneasily in his chair.

"I meant to," replied Haimeric. "You asked me if I had struck the soul of Bernard and I said 'yes.' I have just given you his soul. He is a soul lost in God."

"I see nothing 'lost' about a man who dominates the whole continent of Europe; dictates to Popes, Cardinals, Kings and the rest; is the ruling spirit of Councils and the arbiter of all great ecclesiastical and civil disputes."

"You're looking at the surface, Peter. Go down. Get under the skin. Probe the heart and search the soul of the man; then you'll learn how and why he does all those things. Let me tell you that when Bernard of Clairvaux writes, he dips his quill into his heart's blood, and the penetrating reader can feel his pulse."

The Cardinal rummaged a moment among his papers. "Here is a short letter he wrote to me over a decade ago. Listen to this one sentence: 'I shall make myself importunate, I know; but importunate for charity, truth and justice.' That's the Abbot of Clairvaux. I have already shown you his fire and his fearlessness. This one sentence shows you his naked honesty. He is importunate. He has summed himself up in a word, and done it better than many of his adversaries have done in a volume. Bernard is importunate. He is positively pestiferous in his persistency. But how can anyone refuse him or become permanently angry with him, when in all truth, as he himself says, he is importunate only for 'charity, justice and truth?' He has used three words there, but he means only one reality. And lest I miss the point; lest I be too superficial and fail to argue that since God is substantial truth, justice and charity, Bernard is importunate only for God, his very next sentence does it for me. This is a sentence, Cardinal Peter, that every person consecrated to the service of God might well adopt as a life's principle. He writes: "I do not regard any of the affairs of God as things in which I have no concern." That's a sentence for you, Cardinal. It tells why a contemplative must be active and how an active individual can be contemplative."

"You've been most enlightening, Your Eminence," put in Cardinal Peter in a pondering tone, "but can you tell me why he who is so 'honey-mouthed' has to be so venomous with his pen? Is there any necessity for so much vigor and force? Isn't he really intemperate?"

The Chancellor laughed. "Ah," he said, "you speak like a real diplomat, Peter. But I'm sure you will not be offended when I say that the leading spirits of any age and of every age have not been diplomats. They have a vigor about them that is next to vehemence, a fearlessness and a fire that is akin to brutality. The reason being that they think most clearly, feel most strongly and express most boldly. Bernard is that type. He is not a diplomat. I don't think that he has ever written even a long letter, but what he has written, has aroused some enmity. Diplomats never do that! But Bernard dominates in the end. He achieves. He wins his point; and that is something again that you diplomats do not always do."

The Chancellor rose and poured another glass of wine for his guest. "For example: You remember that biting, sarcastic and cruelly caustic treatise he wrote in defense of the Cistercian way of life? There is a lash to its every line and a sting to its every sentence. Actually the defense of Citeaux turns out to be an attack on Cluny, and not only on Cluny, but on the whole religious world.

That was not the croaking of a Cistercian frog; that was the bombardment of a Cistercian warrior. And what was the result? Did the world turn against Bernard of the venomed-pen? Well, when we all caught our breath we found Suger, Abbot of St. Denis and Prime Minister of France, a very changed man. He had recognized his portrait in Bernard's satire. We saw Peter the Venerable, Archabbot of Cluny, who had to bear the brunt of the whole attack, call an assembly of his priors and dictate to them a reform along the very lines of that treatise. We saw monastery after monastery in Order after Order, as quietly as possible do away with the things that Bernard had so mercilessly lampooned. Now, Cardinal, there is only one explanation for that—Sincerity! Truth! The world found that Bernard was right!"

"Yes, but the world does not always follow the man who is right," objected the Cardinal.

"Not always," resumed Haimeric, "but when the world finds that the man who is right is utterly sincere, devoid of all self-interest, and working only for the glory of God and the good of others, then—though the world be slow—it does eventually follow. Let us admit it, Peter, there is something 'messianic' about this Abbot of Clairvaux."

"That's putting it rather boldly," said the Cardinal.

"That's putting it rather briefly," replied the Chancellor. "Whether he is conscious of it or not I cannot say, but Bernard of Clairvaux is actually making the world God-conscious. He is penetrating and permeating every human activity and institution with God-consciousness, and thus bringing us all nearer to Christ. People believe in him; princes and prelates trust him; Kings, emperors, and even the Pope acknowledge him as the man of the day. And why?—" The Chancellor paused but it was quite evident that he was not waiting a reply; the Cardinal saw that he was striving for effect, and got it when he added very slowly and distinctly, "because they recognize his own God-consciousness. That is the whole secret of Bernard's power—sincerity and simplicity, or in a word, God-consciousness."

"He is a man, all right," admitted the Cardinal.

"Yes, and a man of God," added the Chancellor. "But Your Eminence has seen only one side of Bernard as yet. I have labored, and perhaps belabored, the divine side. If I stopped there I would be most inadequate. If I summed him up in the one word, God-conscious, and let it go at that I would be doing him an injustice and telling only a half-truth. To be honest, I must add what so many fail to grasp, namely, that because Bernard is so God-conscious, he is most human!

"Paradox—always paradox..."

"No, wait—let me finish. You see, Peter, God gave us two commandments, and we cannot keep the one without keeping the other. He who loves God must love his neighbor. God gave us one model, but in that model there are two natures; and, therefore, he who would reproduce Christ must be human, most human, if he will be divine. Ah, Cardinal, that is a truth that is missed by so many. Good people, pious people, even earnest religious often miss that truth. But Bernard doesn't, nor can anyone who knows him or who lives under him. I have shown you his fist in many of these letters; you yourself have seen that fist in many of his actions; but after the battle, that fist becomes an open hand to grasp you with the warmest grasp of true friendship that you have ever felt. Bernard will have enemies as long as he lives, for he sees things too clearly and states them too plainly to suit most people. But Bernard will also have deathless friends as long as he lives because of his own genuine friendliness. Look at Suger. Bernard made him the laughingstock of the realm by his caricature in the *Defense of Citeaux*; yet today, Suger loves Bernard with a moving, manly love, and Bernard returns it. Look at Peter of Cluny. Bernard simply blasted his whole Order in that same *Defense of Citeaux;* and yet, today, Peter writes more letters to Bernard than he does to his own priors. Why, I have even heard it rumored that Peter wants to become a monk in Bernard's monastery. And so it is all down the line...."

"Yes," interposed Peter as he took a last sip of wine, "right down the line to the Chancellor of the Holy Roman See. Haimeric, whether you know it or not, you love the man."

"Oh, I know it," said Haimeric with warmth, "and I'm proud of it; but prouder still of the fact that Bernard loves me. If you doubt that, listen to this last letter from him. He talks to me of my soul and does it in a way no father confessor has yet done. Bernard is anxious about my salvation, anxious with a mother's anxiety; and to me, that is love. He writes, 'A soul is a valuable thing. What shall a man take in exchange for it? Not the whole world would be sufficient. If it should perish by sin even unto death, whence shall it be restored? Is there another Christ, or will He be crucified again for it? Upon this subject I would wish that you would never forget the counsel of the wise man: *My son, remember your last end, and you shall never sin.'*" The Chancellor paused, looked at the Cardinal, then said, "Peter, only a lover would write that way to the Chancellor of the Holy See."

The Cardinal nodded in agreement, then mused aloud, "Truly a lofty soul."

"Ah, but the beauty of it all is that he is a lowly soul," said Haimeric. Then he went over to a chest against the further wall and taking out two letters said, "Peter, I'm going to let you in on a secret. Bernard gets the blues!"

"Can you really prove it?"

"That's just what I am going to do. Here is a letter," said the Chancellor as he held aloft one of the sheets of paper. "Now don't ask how I got it or from whom; but just look at the seal to see that it is genuine."

The Cardinal looked and said, "I recognize it; it is Bernard's."

"Now look to whom it is addressed," said Haimeric.

The Cardinal held the paper up to the light and read aloud, "To Beatrice—m-m-m."

"Yes, m-m-m-m," repeated Haimeric; then taking the letter he struck a pose as he read, "'I wonder at your zealous devotion and loving affection towards me.' That's the opening sentence. That surprises you, doesn't it? The man of God writing such an opening sentence as that. Well, he goes on in the same vein saying that had she been a relative all this affection and devotion might be expected. 'But,' he writes, 'as we recognize in you not a mother, but only a noble lady, the wonder is not that we should wonder, but that we can wonder sufficiently....'"

"What an exquisite way of saying 'Thank you,'" broke in the Cardinal.

"Right, but now comes my proof that Bernard gets the blues. He's a lonely man, Peter, and that despite the fact that he has his whole family under him and hundreds of monks besides. Taking up the idea in that last sentence about her not being a relative causing him to wonder, Bernard explains himself saying, 'For who of our kinsfolk or acquaintance takes care of us? Who ever asks of our health? Who, I ask, is, I will not say anxious, but even mindful of us in the world?...'"

"My!" exclaimed Peter, "that certainly is the cry of a very lonely soul."

"Isn't it?" resumed Haimeric. "And listen to this lament: 'We are become, as it were, a broken vessel to friends, relatives and neighbors. You alone cannot forget us.'" The Chancellor paused again. He had read the passage with deep pathos. He was affected. He looked at the Cardinal to see how he was taking it, and found him shaking his head in wonder and sympathy.

"Great heavens," he finally exclaimed, "I would never have believed it! That cry borders on a cry of dereliction. And from Bernard, the fearless warrior! Can it be that God shakes the souls of His saints to such depths that He almost makes them lose their minds?"

Haimeric's reply was slow in coming; when it did come it was solemn. "Peter," he said, "you have touched on a deep truth. God does shake the souls of His saints. I am appreciative of your penetration, but more appreciative of the fact that you have placed Bernard where I think he deserves to be placed—among the saints of God. Furthermore you have proved my point, namely, that a man often shows his divineness by a display of his humanness."

Then in an altered tone, one that had all his old vivacity about it he said, "But come, this is not an evening for such solemnity; nor would I end a discussion of Bernard on such a note. He gets the blues; but that is seldom. Here is Bernard is his more normal vein." And with that he flourished the other letter that he had been holding. "This also is written to a woman. But in what a different tone! This good soul was thinking of changing her manner of life. She had been in the convent for a goodly length of time when the thought came to her that she should become a solitary. She wrote Bernard asking his advice. She got it. Just listen. He writes: 'Either you are one of the foolish virgins (if, indeed, you are a virgin)....'"

"Ow!" gasped the Cardinal.

"Yes," resumed Haimeric, "Bernard's parentheses are priceless. That one is certainly pungent, isn't it? But listen to the whole argument. He writes: 'Either you are one of the foolish virgins (if, indeed, you are a virgin) or you are one of the wise; if a foolish one, you need the convent; if a wise one, the convent needs you.' That's all. Pithy, pointed, practical. That's the real Bernard." The Cardinal was laughing in keen appreciation, so Haimeric went on, "There's your man, Cardinal, and a man's man he is. He spurns miters, won't even use the one Abbots are beginning to wear; refuses Bishoprics and Archbishoprics, but will write to a wise or foolish virgin, work as no ten Bishops, or for that matter, as no ten Cardinals will work, pray like a Seraph and love like—God. That's Bernard as I see him—a lover."

"Yes," agreed the Cardinal. "And looking at him through your eyes, I see him as I never saw him before. Perhaps in your last word you have analyzed and synthesized him; perhaps in that one word you have given the best and truest account for his amazing influence. All the world loves a lover, they say; and, as you have shown, Bernard is that—a lover of God, of man and of woman."

"You won't mind if I make one little correction, will you, Peter? Don't say I have shown him—recognize the fact that he has shown himself. It was Bernard, not I, who said, 'I am importunate for charity, truth and justice'; it was Bernard, not I, who said, 'I do not regard any of the affairs of God as things in which I have no concern'; it was Bernard, not I, who laid down ultimata to the King, the Pope and the College of Cardinals; and, Peter, it was Bernard, not I, who said: 'You ask me with what measure God is to be loved and I answer: *Without measure.*' Bernard could emblazon that on his coat of arms or stamp it on his seal, for it sums him up perfectly: Love God without measure. Bernard has analyzed himself for you, Cardinal." Saying which he placed the letters he had been holding, and with which he had been gracefully albeit forcefully gesturing, on the table, picked up the decanter of wine, again filled their small glasses and said, "Let us drink a toast to Bernard the man, the monk and the lover." There was a tiny musical tinkle as their glasses met and two Cardinals drank to the honor of the Abbot of Clairvaux.

The Prior and Secretary Disagree

Some ten years after the tinkle of the Cardinals' toasting glasses had died away, two other admirers of Bernard were found discussing another toast; but the harmony and peace that had surrounded Haimeric and Peter as they chatted were noticeably missing as this other discussion progressed. So was the wine. For this latter discussion was held at Clairvaux by two of Bernard's sons—the Prior of the Abbey and Abbot's secretary. A bit of poetry was the cause.

It was 1147. Bernard had just returned from the Council at Rheims. He was tired and his face showed all his fifty-six years with their toils, troubles and triumphs. Weariness was written deeply in every line, so the Prior had refrained from asking him questions. As soon, however, as Bernard had retired to his room, the Prior summoned Geoffrey of Auxerre, who, as Bernard's Secretary, had been with him at the Council.

Geoffrey entered the Prior's little room alive with enthusiasm; his eyes were sparkling and his whole countenance alight. Before the Prior could put a single question, the exuberant Geoffrey said, "Father Prior, just listen to this, I think it exquisite." And lifting his hand as if holding a glass, he spoke in warm accents saying:

> "Here's my hosanna
> To Bernard the bard
> Who wrote love letters
> Better than Abelard."

Then without waiting for comment, he exclaimed, "Isn't that great?"

The Prior's shaggy eyebrows lowered. Two lines, looking very like exclamation points, cut themselves deep into either side of the top of his nose. He was not frowning; he was looking puzzled. The Secretary was disappointed. He looked at the puzzled Prior; and though anyone else would have been chilled, if not frozen, by the lowered eyebrows and the deep-cut lines, Geoffrey was not even cooled; he just smiled and said, "I see that I have been too sudden. Let me make a more gradual approach by giving you the opening lines of the poem as well as its close. It goes:

> Being a poet
> I had rather
> Written as Bernard
> Of God the Father,
> Son and Holy Spirit,
> Than penned the pleas
> Of passion Abelard
> Sent Heloise.

With that as an introduction, you simply must appreciate the toast that is its termination." And once again Geoffrey lifted his hand on high as if holding a glass and said:

> "Here's my hosanna
> To Bernard the bard
> Who wrote love letters
> Better than Abelard."

This time the Prior did frown. He turned from Geoffrey and looked out across the field of grain that was brilliant in its fresh greenness, out over the tops of the apple trees that were holding a heavy snow of white and pink blossoms, on and down to the brownish flow of the Aube. He muttered the lines to himself twice, then said, "No, Geoffrey, I don't like it."

"What?" almost shouted the Secretary. "You don't like it? Oh, Father Prior, is all your taste in your mouth? Why that's exquisite! You've got the whole history of the age's two outstanding characters caught, clasped and contrasted in a few short lines of running verse."

"Oh, I appreciate the concept," said the Prior. "It is arresting. And the contrast is striking and sharp. I have no fault to find with the poet's expression. He has written well. As you say he has flashed the highlights of two brilliant personalities on us in a few swift lines. But, Geoffrey, I can't share your enthusiasm, because I find it more fanciful that factual. Your poet has shown marked literary proficiency, but he has not shown profound logical or psychological penetration. In short, Geoffrey, I would say that your brilliant bit of poetry is historically unjust to both Bernard and Abelard; and I don't like things that are historically unjust."

The Secretary's smile had vanished. The glow that had suffused his whole countenance on entrance had gone; and the light in his eyes that shone from beneath lowered eyebrows punctuated by their deep cut lines, was a light of pain as well as puzzlement. In a tone that was a full gamut lower than the lilting, jubilant one with which he had spoken the poet's lines, he said, "Father Prior, lest I call you an iconoclast, will you please tell me just where my poet errs? You say, unjust to both. How?"

The Prior straightened himself, brought the tip of his right index finger to the tip of the left hand's little finger and said, "First of all with regard to Abelard: He fell. The world knows of his intrigue with Heloise. But I hold it unmanly, unpriestly, un-Christlike to sum up his whole life in that intrigue; for it is untrue! Further, every time I hear anyone speaking of that affair I am always reminded of Christ turning His back to a crowd of Jews who had stones in their hands, and seemingly regardless of the poor disheveled woman at His feet, bending over and writing in the dust. You know what He said when He arose from that writing, and you know how many stones were thrown at the poor woman. Geoffrey, we are all made of mud; every last one of us. Why, then, should we throw any of it at our neighbor? Abelard was intellectually proud; I admit that; but remember that he was intellectual! I wonder if we can say the same about every one of his critics? Remember also that it is the intellect that makes man man; it is the one talent that must not be hid lest the Master one day call us 'wicked and worthless servants.' Man was made to *know*, Geoffrey, and that means that the intellect must be developed; for man was made to know both here and hereafter. In fact, that is Christ's description of heaven. Did He not say, 'This is eternal life, that they may *know*...'?"

"Yes," interrupted the Secretary, "but no one finds fault with the intellect; it is intellectual pride that is the sin."

"True," resumed the Prior a bit more calmly, "but Geoffrey, I have noticed that those who speak most glibly of intellectual pride are usually bogged down and almost inextricably mired in intellectual sloth; which, to my way of thinking, is the greater sin. But apart from that, suppose I grant that Abelard was guilty of intellectual pride; what follows? Is not that but a proof that he is brother to you and me? Has there been any son of Adam and Eve who has not been tainted with that pride? Why, Geoffrey, if you watch people closely you will find that the most ignorant are always the most arrogant; and paradox though it be, their very ignorance is the cause of their intellectual pride. Come now, be a true son of Father Bernard; do as he so often exhorts us to do—look to the end. How did Abelard end?"

"Cluny's Abbot Peter never wearies of telling the world how humble, how holy and how truly devout were the last years of this intellectual giant."

"And Heloise; what of her since that fall of long, long ago?"

"She has been a nun, and such a nun that they elected her Abbess. I have never heard anything against her. In fact, Father Bernard made a visitation of her monastery of the Paraclete and found fault with only a phrase of the "Pater noster.'"

"Don't you see, then, how much more charitable, how much more Christlike and how much nearer the truth it would be to talk of these things, rather than of their sin? Abelard retracted and repented. Heloise lives a respected nun. May their critics have as holy an end."

"You sound like a disciple of Abelard...," said the Secretary with the beginnings of a smile.

"I sound like a disciple of Bernard and a disciple of Christ, I hope," quickly interposed the Prior. "Now to my second point," he continued as he brought the index finger of his right hand to the ring finger of his left, "your poem is unjust to Bernard."

"That's going to be much more difficult to prove; for his sermons are like 'love-letters to God the Father, Son and Holy Spirit.'"

"Once again I say that your poetry has an exquisite concept. It is poetical. But don't you see, Geoffrey, that anyone who does not know our Father intimately and who reads that poem must conclude that Bernard's whole life is summed up in his conflict with Abelard?"

"And wasn't that one of his greatest works and greatest triumphs? I was there that day; and though it all happened seven years ago, it is as fresh in my mind as what happened yesterday at Rheims. But why wouldn't it be? That was the meeting of the century. Why, Father Prior, there was no one in France, no, there was no one in all Europe who was anxious to face Abelard in debate.

"Many felt uneasy about his teachings. You remember how William of St. Thierry wrote to our Father Bernard about them. He had discovered Abelard's errors; but he wanted Bernard to refute them. So it was with many another. They knew the errors, but they were afraid to face the author of them. And why? Because he was king of all debaters. As a mere boy he had defeated William of Champeaux, the master dialectician of all France; and from that day until June the third, eleven hundred and forty, he had ruled the roost! Abelard was unconquerable. So he thought and so thought the world. But what happened? There before one of the most brilliant audiences he had ever faced, there before King, Apostolic Legate, Bishops and Archbishops, before Abbots, Priors and clerics, before a whole horde of scholars, the great Abelard was reduced to utter silence by our thin, weak-looking and very sick-looking Abbot.

"I'll never forget that assembly as long as I live; no, nor the fear I experienced at Abelard's entrance. How small, frightened and worried our Father Bernard looked in comparison. Abelard was late; I think that was for effect. He made an entrance that can only be called 'majestic.' There was vigor, confidence, command, power and imperiousness about his whole person and in his every move. He strode down the aisle with that fiery and fierce-looking Arnold of Brescia at his side and a whole swarm of disciples in his wake. These were already buzzing as if the victory were theirs. When he reached the sanctuary, Abelard stopped, looked at the King, the Legate, and the Archbishops, swept the rows of miters with a glance that was half disdainful, half patronizing; but Bernard put an end to this display of dramatics and brought a hush to the holy house by rising and reading in that high, clear voice of his a series of propositions gathered from Abelard's writings. They were obviously heretical. I saw many a mitered head jerk as Bernard read on.

Oh, he was succinct and pointed that day! Then he stopped; looked at Abelard, and said: 'Defend them; amend them; or deny that they are yours.'

"The whole assemblage seemed to catch its breath as that triple imperative fell from Bernard's lips. It was a moment that tingled with awe, fear and amazement. The suspense was broken as Abelard stirred. The audience stirred with him. His partisans were aglow with anticipation. They seemed to be looking at Bernard pityingly; but their faces fell at Abelard's first sentence. He said: 'I will not answer the Cistercian. I appeal from this Council to the See of Rome.'—And before the assembly had recovered from the shock, Abelard was gone! What a triumph! Only a short while before Bernard had called Abelard a veritable Goliath; I wonder if he had any inkling that he was going to play the part of David.''

"Did our Father feel elated?" asked the Prior.

To which Geoffrey replied, "Father Prior, that is one thing I cannot understand about our Abbot. Before the battle and in the battle he is all fire and passion. In the victory, he is utterly unconcerned. Why, some of the things I had to write to the Pope, the Cardinals and others about Abelard, made me wince. Our Father Bernard is merciless in attack. He said, 'Abelard knows everything but his own ignorance!' called his writings, 'ravings' and his theology 'Foology.' He even intimated that he was a greater danger that Peter de Leone had been, saying, 'We have escaped the roaring of Peter the Lion (de Leone) only to encounter the hissing of Peter the Dragon.' He called him 'a monk without a rule, a prelate without subjects, and an Abbot without a community.' Honestly, the charges in the letters before the Council were like dynamite. Then in the Council that triple imperative—'Defend! Amend! or Deny!' was a thunderclap. But once the condemnation came from the assembled prelates, our Father Bernard was a different man. He did not show the interest of the most disinterested spectator; he cared not to discuss the errors or the erring one; he had only one thought: Let us get home to Clairvaux. In our triumph our fiery Father Bernard is as cold as ice. He is positively disappointing and disconcerting."

The Prior looked kindly at the secretary and good-humoredly remarked, "I suppose that you would have preferred to stay behind with the prelates and do a little crowing. Geoffrey, there is much of the rooster about you. But tell me, hasn't it ever struck you that our Father Bernard is interested only in truth? Didn't you ever suspect that his battle was not so much against Abelard as against Abelard's errors? Have you ever heard him gloat?"

"Never. But don't you see what a violent contrast he strikes when a warrior and when victor? It's not human. He has two distinct and different personalities. One is violent. Honestly, Father Prior, the things he says in letters, yes and in battle.... Why, only yesterday, when de la Porée was giving a masterly address, piling up reference after reference from the Fathers of the Church and setting syllogism after syllogism in formidable array, our Father Abbot breaks in on a discourse that had the assembly spellbound, with the terribly direct, blunt and almost brutal words, 'A truce to this rhetoric. Come to the point. You are charged with holding that the Divine Essence is not God, but the form by which God is God. Tell us plainly: is that your opinion or is it not?...'"

"What did the Bishop say to that?"

"Oh, he was angry at such an interruption and shouted loudly: 'The *Divinity* is not God but the form by which God is God.'"

"What happened then?"

"I broke in."

"You?"

"Yes. I was so astounded that involuntarily I exclaimed: 'But this is contradictory to what you said at the Synod of Paris.'

"He did not blink an eye; just coldly answered: 'Whatever I said at Paris, this is what I say now.'

"'That's all we want to know. Let the Bishop's confession of Faith be written down,' said our Father Abbot.

"That stung de la Porée and he showed it by blazing the retort: 'Yes, and let your own doctrine be written down.' Then Bernard the battler made answer: 'Aye, let it be written down with a pen of iron on a slate of adamant.'"

"That sounds like him at his best," put in the Prior. "How did it all end?"

"As you say, our Father Bernard was at his best. It was quite evident that the Cardinals present were all in favor of Bishop de la Porée; after the debate they very dignifiedly retired for conference, consultation and discussion. So our fighting Abbot very quickly gathered the Bishops and got them to submit, through Abbot Suger, a confession of Faith that our Father Bernard had drawn up, saying to the Cardinals: 'Here are two confessions, ours and de la Porée's. Take your choice.'"

"That is Bernard the battler, all right."

"The Cardinals resented it very much, at first, saying that this was dictating to them. In his own way Bernard smoothed out that wrinkle and the Cardinals approved the confession submitted by Suger."

"So de la Porée stands condemned?"

"Practically so. The Pope will have him retract and the case will be ended. But as far as our Father Abbot is concerned it is all over now. At the moment, he is Bernard the victor, hence he acts as if there never had been a Council at Rheims or a Gilbert de la Porée. He acts as if there were only Clairvaux and his community of contemplatives. I tell you he is most disconcerting."

The Prior was amused at Geoffrey's distress and said, "Perhaps you are nearer the truth in that last remark of yours than you realize. Perhaps there is only Clairvaux and his community for him."

"Huh," snorted Geoffrey. "It is easy to see that you are only Prior. If you were Secretary for a day you would learn that our Abbot's interests are as wide as Christendom, as long as the world and as deep as death. Without any violation of confidence I can tell you that a great many people are saying that Bernard is Pope and not Eugene; and they have good reason for so saying."

"I don't know whether to call that calumny, slander or just plain lie," said the Prior.

"Call it appreciation, and you'll be nearer the truth. But to prove my point and to defend my poet I'm coming back to Abelard."

"Which one?" asked the Prior, "the one who 'penned passionate pleas to Heloise,' the erring theologian, or the repentant sinner?"

"I'm serious, Father Prior," said Geoffrey. "My claim is that Abelard was the greatest danger of our day; and when I say 'Abelard' I mean him and his disciples. For Gilbert de la Porée would never have had to be refuted if he had not at one time sat at Abelard's feet. And the same can be said for that even greater menace, that one whom our Father Bernard is hounding from kingdom to kingdom and state to state, Arnold of Brescia. Take these three men as representative of a movement; look upon them as the spearhead of an attack on orthodoxy; recognize them as the battering ram that smashes against the wall of the Church; then you will see how aptly our Father Abbot's life can be summed up by contrasting him to Abelard."

"You've got a strong point there, Geoffrey," said the Prior. "And yet, you must not forget the schism of Peter de Leone. As anti-pope he split the ranks of the faithful and kept them split for almost eight years. To have re-united those ranks was a tremendous work."

"True," said Geoffrey.

"Nor must you forget the work he did against the heresy of the Henricians, or if you prefer, the Albigenses. You were with him on that tour. That was only two years ago. (You yourself told me of the many miracles he per-formed on the sick, the crippled, the blind, the deaf and the dumb.) That was actual heresy; and, as you said, sur-prisingly deep-rooted. And the schism of Peter de Leone was actual schism. Now don't you think that it is a greater thing to accomplish wonders against actualities than it is to accomplish them against possibilities? You tell me that you can never forget this triumph over Abelard at the Council of Sens; didn't you say the same thing about his converting the whole city of Albi?"

"I did, and I do," said Geoffrey rather thoughtfully. "In fact, Father Prior, that was one of his greatest miracles."

"Good," said the Prior as he warmed to his theme. "Now, Geoffrey, you made the recruiting tour with our Abbot. You saw him whip an unsympathetic Europe to a heated enthusiasm for this Second Crusade. You wit-nessed and wrote down the accounts of so many and such astounding miracles that if you did not have the support and substantiation of Hermann, Bishop of Con-stance, of the Abbots Baldwin and Frovinus and of the other clerics in the party, we would have found it difficult to believe you."

"I can understand that, for I had difficulty believing my own eyes and ears."

"All right," continued the Prior, "so you saw our Fa-ther Bernard send the flower of France's chivalry to the Holy Land; and that over the protest of Abbot Suger, the King's Prime Minister; you saw him convert the stubborn Emperor Conrad and send every real knight of Germany to the East. Now tell me, which is the greater triumph, to have silenced one man and his theological errors or to have set the whole of Europe shaking to the thunder of marching feet? And before you answer, let me remind you again of the stamp of approval put on that work by heaven; you say that hardly a day passed without some astounding miracle. That diary kept by you and that group of attendants takes one's breath away."

Geoffrey became more thoughtful. Rubbing his chin with his left hand, he looked up at the Prior and smiled somewhat sheepishly as he said, "I think I called the conversion of Conrad Bernard's miracle of miracles, didn't I? And really," he went on, "it was!

"On Christmas Day our Abbot spoke, but Conrad was unmoved. No. Germany was not going to the Crusade. The Emperor was adamant. But just two days later, when Bernard turned from the altar and gave a sermon on the last judgment and arraigned Conrad before the world, enumerating the gifts God had given him, then asking him to give an account of his stewardship, the Emperor was seen to weep and a few seconds later I heard him say, 'I begin to be grateful. Give me the Crusader's cross.' Yes, that was a miracle."

"Uh-huh," interjected the Prior, "so we have the countless miracles performed during the campaign of the schism caused by Peter de Leone, countless miracles performed during the campaign against the heresy of the Albigenses, and countless miracles during the campaign for the Second Crusade. Unquestionably, Father Bernard was God's instrument in these three great campaigns, and yet you burst in on me this morning with:

> 'Here's my hosanna
> To Bernard the bard
> Who wrote love-letters
> Better than Abelard.'

And expect me to wax enthusiastic."

Geoffrey laughed as he said, "Don't rub it in. I still think it an exquisite piece of poetry, an exceptionally clever contrast and a very just tribute to our Abbot. I admit now that it is not adequate. But let me remind you that poets are not historians; they are not expected to give the whole biography of a man in their ten or twelve lines of running verse. Haven't you ever heard of the poet's license?"

"Don't joke, Geoffrey," said the Prior. "You happened to hit upon a subject to which I have given much thought of late. And now let me tell you that your poet is right in fundamental concept of our Father Bernard; more right than most historians are or will be. Listen, Geoffrey, this very moment most people in Europe look upon our Abbot as what?—as the great voice that sent our knighthood to the Orient, the miracle worker who even raises the dead to life; some will remember his work at Albi and his healing of the schism and call him the savior of Christendom and the champion of the Pope; while a few others like yourself view him as the scholar and think only of his triumph over the genius Abelard and his erring followers.

"But, Geoffrey, all are wrong! Great, every one of these works was, but no one of them merits the name of his 'greatest.' No. Your poet has caught the truth and he has named our Abbot rightly when he calls him, 'the lover.' He is the lover of God the Father, Son and Holy Spirit! And let me tell you that his greatest miracle was not worked at Spires, at Albi, at Rheims or at Sens. No. His miracle of miracles was worked and is still being worked right here at Clairvaux. First, last and always our Abbot is a monk, and a contemplative monk at that; and his greatest work, which I call a miraculous one, is to make of other men, monks—and contemplative monks.

"For over thirty years now he has been taking men from all walks of life, with every variety of background—

intellectual, economic and social—and moulding them to the likeness of Christ. He takes serf or sovereign, bandit or baron, knave or knight, seemingly it makes no difference to him, and he teaches them what he taught Emperor Conrad, he teaches them to begin to be grateful to God. Geoffrey, for over twenty years we have been sending out, on an average, two colonies of monks a year to found other monasteries; we have daughter-houses all over the continent. They are generously sprinkled here, there and everywhere in France; they are in Germany, Spain, Portugal and Italy, in Ireland, England and Scotland, in Switzerland and now they want us in Jerusalem. Every one of these houses is due to Bernard, and every monk in these houses is his spiritual child.

"Think what that means, man! You were thrilled at Sens when he silenced Abelard; and at Albi when he set the church ringing with the orthodox profession of Faith; you say that you were just about overcome when he brought Conrad to his knees, and with all Christendom you thank Bernard for the termination of that awful schism; but to me, and I am quite sure to our Abbot, these things, mighty as they are, are only accidentals and incidentals; his life and his life's work is here at Clairvaux teaching men how to love God. Geoffrey, the external works dazzle; but honestly, I am convinced that the most dazzling of Bernard's works is the one that does not even shine!

So—Hosanna to Bernard the Moulder of men
Who twists us to God, from pleasure and sin.

"Oh, I'm not a poet I know, but I think that I would be close to truth were I to say something like your real poet said, but put it—

Here's to Bernard the masterful potter
Who can fashion a saint out of rounder or rotter.

"No," said Geoffrey, "you are not a poet, but you certainly can be eloquent when you want to be. But tell me, why so much insistence on the rawness of the material that our Abbot handles?"

"Simply because it is so awfully raw," answered the Prior hurriedly. "Don't you ever marvel at Brother Constantine?"

"A fine religious," said Geoffrey.

"Yes," said the Prior, "but he used to a very fine highwayman. Our Father saved that man from the gallows. Actually, I'm telling you no secret when I tell you that. Constantine would tell you the story himself if he could. He was being led to execution before the Count of Champagne when our Abbot happened along. Bernard asked the Count what was going on; when told an execution was to take place, he asked to be given the felon. The Count saw that our Abbot was not joking so he started to tell him on how many scores this man deserved to be put to death. 'Give him to me,' said our Father, 'I'll see to it that he dies daily.' He got the bandit; and as you see, we got a splendid lay brother."

"Great heavens!" exclaimed Geoffrey, "that does sound like romance."

"Just a proof that 'truth is stranger than fiction,'" said the Prior, then went on with, "Just look at that batch of knights we received a few years back as postulants for the choir. That was what I call raw material and a miracle: They will furnish your poets with some exquisite material. They were on their way to tournament. They were out for honor, glory and the smiles of the ladies fair. They stopped here for a little refreshment. Our Abbot chatted with them, chided them for their vanity, spoke to them of a higher chivalry and of the glory of God, and told them that at Clairvaux there was held the constant tournament of love.

"They listened respectfully, but nevertheless they prepared to ride on. Then Bernard invited them to have a stirrup cup. To that there was no demur. Our Abbot blessed the wine; they drank; they rode off; but before the hour was up our gate-keeper was brought to wide-awake attention by the thunder of horses' hooves. On they came at a gallop, and flinging themselves from the saddle, begged to be admitted as novices in the tournament of love. Look at them now—knights of Jesus Christ! Ah, Geoffrey, to turn men to God, to make lovers of the Crucified out of worldly souls, to make near-sighted individuals focus their gaze on eternity—that is a miraculous work; and that is Bernard's greatest."

"I really believe that it is a case of 'not seeing the trees for the forest,'" smiled Geoffrey. "I must confess that I am so taken up with letters to outsiders about outside affairs, and have been such a constant and close companion to our Abbot on his many journeys and been witness to so many of his great works, that I have been blind to his greatest. I begin to agree with you. Clairvaux is the scene of his mightiest miracle; and moulding monks out of the extremely raw material of worldly men, making us forget our tiny but very assertive selves as we focus our whole attention on God, is a greater triumph than the vanquishing of Abelard."

"What makes me marvel most," said the Prior, "is the way he goes about his task. I have been studying his sermons on the Canticle of Canticles, and I am amazed at their essential simplicity."

"Oh, sometimes he soars," objected Geoffrey, "and soars too high for me."

"Granted," resumed the Prior. "He does wing his way to the far reaches at times. But, Geoffrey, to take them together and read them one after another, the thing that stands out is his simplicity and his searching penetration of the hearts of men. I am convinced that he knows us perfectly only because he has studied himself so exhaustively. Ah, but honestly, isn't his greatest sermon his everyday life? He has never asked us to do anything he hasn't done himself; in fact, he has never asked us to do the half that he has already done. Example is the greatest teacher, after all. But isn't it marvelous to realize that a sickly man, well past his fiftieth year, can take us as we are with all our faults and failings, our smallness and our selfishness and get us to 'prefer absolutely nothing to Jesus Christ'?"

"That is his aim, isn't it?" said Geoffrey. "And he seldom misses it."

"I sometimes marvel at myself," went on the Prior. "Geoffrey, I hate pain. I shrink from all suffering, be it mental or physical. I love peace and moderate comfort, the company of men and of books. Ah, books! I could live with them. And yet, here I am living a life that in itself is painful, a life that is hard both mentally and physically, a life that deprives me of the company of my twin loves, men and books; and I am living that life with greater peace and joy than I ever had before. Yes, I marvel at myself until I look at Bernard; for then I look at the man who changed me. He has changed me, mind and heart, will and soul. He has given me fortitude in place of my cowardice, and strength in place of my weakness; he has given me eyes that look beyond time and a pair of hands that want to be wide open so that God can take from them whatever He wants to take and place in them whatever He wants to give. Now let me tell you, that *is* a change!" The Prior's emphasis only lightly concealed his momentary self-consciousness.

Geoffrey was touched by his superior's confusion. "I can make the same confession, but I never have, because I have never reflected as much or penetrated as deeply as you have just done. It strikes me ever more forcibly that the secret of Clairvaux is Bernard."

"Oh, that's unquestionable," said the Prior. "He is the magnet, and he has drawn iron and steel of every temper and cast to this Valley of Light. Then, like a real magnet, he performs that miracle of magnetism: he converts us into other magnets, he converts us into lovers of Jesus Christ. That is Bernard's whole secret; he is in love with the crucified Jesus."

The Prior paused, looked away, seemed to be weighing something very carefully, but then gave a quick lift to his head and a piercing look at the Secretary as he said, "Geoffrey, I am going to tell you a real secret; one that I want you to keep. Tell nobody. Understand?" The Secretary gave an almost imperceptible nod, so the Prior went on, "I have just said that Bernard loves Christ crucified. That is no secret; we all know that. But what all do not know is that Christ crucified loves Bernard in a surprisingly intimate way."

The Prior paused again, but this time Geoffrey could not wait; with a gesture that betrayed his tenseness he asked, 'What do you mean? Tell me, quick."

Unconsciously the Prior lowered his tone as he said, "A short while ago, our Father Abbot was praying before the life-sized crucifix in the church. One of the community happened in and found him there alone. Seeing him totally absorbed in prayer, this religious stopped where he was lest his lightest footfall disturb the Abbot. He was not there a minute when he saw the arm of the crucified Christ loosen itself from the wood of the cross and encircle the shoulders of our Father Bernard."

Geoffrey's jaw dropped. His two hands rose and opened wide in a sudden, involuntary gesture of amazement. "O-o-o," was all that he could say for a moment. Then a little later he added, "I feel frightened. I wish you hadn't told me that secret. I'll never feel free in the presence of our Abbot again. But you've more than proved your point, my poet...."

"Your poet," interrupted the Prior, "had a real inspiration when he called Bernard the lover who writes of God the Father, Son and Holy Spirit. He has found the one word that best sums up our Abbot. He is a lover. You know, that little book of his on *The Love of God* reads to me like his autobiography. He has given the aim of his life in the opening sentence—to love God without measure; and in almost every chapter I find him renewing his resolution, spurring himself on to that measureless love. And what I love most about the man is his honesty and humility. In one place he says, 'My God, I will love You with all my strength. That is not as much as You deserve, I know; but it is as much as I can give.' Doesn't that just about sum up his doctrine to us? Isn't he always saying in one way or another, 'Love God with every last ounce of your energy'?

"Yes, your poet has struck him off. All that I objected to was summing up his whole life as a conflict with Abelard. It is not! It is a conflict with the world, the flesh and the devil, a conflict with all who will not love God with all their might, a conflict with the stubborn clay in the make-up of man which he would convert into the heart of a lover. And yet, were you to ask him to sum up his life, he would most likely say what he said in that sermon of his on the religious life, 'My life is a giving of the widow's mite.' Do you remember?"

"Indeed I do!" answered Geoffrey. "He said something like, 'I possess only two mites; two very worthless mites—my body and my soul. Or to speak more strictly, I have only a single mite—my free will; and shall I hesitate to give that up?'"

"He hasn't hesitated," put in the Prior, "nor will he allow us to hesitate. He takes all hesitation from you; and to do that in my case, and in the case of many another, is a miracle. So, Geoffrey, whenever you write poetry or prose and speak of our Father Bernard, give him his proper title. Call him 'The Lover.' And when you mention his greatest work speak of it as the moulding of monks. Then above all else, make him what he is—human! He has many divine traits, it is true, but it is his humanness that characterizes him best. Never forget that. Now run along; you've taken up too much of my time already."

The Secretary laughed as he said, "That's gratitude for you! I give you all the news I have and then am told that I am taking up your time." But he left.

Darkness in the Valley of Light

It was August 24, 1153. The Prior of Clairvaux sat in his little room motionless; his head was resting heavily in his two hands, his elbows were on the desk and his eyes were fixed in an unseeing stare on the mass of paper before him. A knock on the door came. Mechanically he gave the signal to enter, then somewhat wearily turned to see who had entered. Relief showed on his countenance and relief was heard in his voice as he said, "Oh, it's you, Geoffrey. Come in. Come in. You are just the man I need at this awful moment. I feel lost. My heart is leaden and all my spirit chilled. I am wondering if I shall ever feel warm again and if there will ever be light again in this Valley of Light."

Geoffrey's voice in answer carried the same somber qualities, "I understand, Father Prior. We called him the magnet, the power, the moving spirit of the Abbey; but we never fully realized that he was the life and the light that made this valley, the Valley of Light. Only four days dead, and yet, it seems an eternity. But come! You are Prior; you must take his place at the moment."

"No one can take his place, Geoffrey; no one!"

"Someone has to! And you are that someone," said Geoffrey with a little show of spirit. "Come, Father, brace up! Don't you remember how our saintly Bernard always used to say that the dead could and would help us more from heaven than they did while on earth? Well, he'll help you now; for if ever any one of ours went straight to heaven, Bernard is the one. So, come! There is a tremendous amount of work to be done. We must send letters to his many, many friends. You must do the dictating; I am only the scribe. Come, make a start. It will ease your pent-up sorrow to talk about one we loved more deeply than we knew."

"Has that realization beaten in on you, too, Geoffrey?"

"Yes, indeed," replied the Secretary. "I thought that I had shed my last tears years ago. Weeping has always seemed such a womanish thing to me. But I have been weeping. No, not weeping; I have been crying like a lonely and lost child for four full days. Indeed, I loved him more than I knew. But come. I think that our first letter should go to his baby brother Nivard, down there in Spain. What we say to him we can practically duplicate for his other brother, Abbot Bartholomew; he is nearer to hand. What shall we tell Nivard?"

"The truth," said the Prior, "the whole truth. Tell him that his brother Bernard's last years on earth were very like our Savior's last week in Palestine. Tell him that the Tabor on which his brother had shone so brilliantly for a quarter of a century, turned to a Calvary. Tell him that his brother Bernard had to look out upon the world from Clairvaux just as our Lord had to look down upon Jerusalem from a neighboring hill. Tell him that Bernard wept for that world just as Christ wept for that city. Tell him that the 'Hosannas' that sounded so long in his ears, were changed, even as they had been for Christ, into cries of condemnation even to crucifixion." Tears were flowing fast from the Prior's eyes, but a new verve had come into his voice and Geoffrey, after one gasp of amazement, jotted down note after note; for he knew that a strong man's heart had opened, and love was gushing forth in a flood of real eloquence.

"Yes, go back to the time of the Second Crusade and tell young Nivard that although his brother never left the kingdom, every disaster, from the foul treachery of the Greeks to the disgraceful intrigues of Queen Eleanor, was blamed on him. Tell him that the Catholic world was wounded to the heart's depths by the unexpected debacle of what had begun with so many manifest signs from heaven; tell how that wounded world, reeling in its agony, sought balm for its tortured soul by a frenzied attack on the man whom only two years before it had called 'God's angel.' Tell him that because the flower of Europe's knighthood lay withered and dead, flung upon the wayside of Attalia or in the passes of the Phrygian mountains, Europe turned in fury upon a sick and aging man in the Valley of Clairvaux. Tell him that when our chivalrous King Louis, who had departed at the head of a proud army of over a hundred thousand, returned with a handful of sorry knights and a wife who had disgraced him, the kingdom turned on Bernard as if his had been the hand that struck down our warriors and his had been the heart that had played truant to the king. But oh! Tell him above all else, that when the voice of all Europe was at this wildest and weirdest pitch, when it cried out with as much unreasoned fiendishness as did that rabble before Pilate twelve centuries before; oh, tell him that then his brother stood as silent, as majestic, and as unresentful as He stood of whom Pilate said, 'Behold the man.'"

The Prior wiped his eyes as he mused, "Ah, man can be so unkind to man!" Then turning again to Geoffrey he went on.

"Nivard knows how sensitive was the heart of his brother; hence, he will know how like the agony in the garden and the night in the dungeon this groundless and merciless attack was. He will see in it Bernard's crowning with thorns. But then go on and tell him of the Judas kiss given him by his own secretary, Nicholas. Tell him how this ingrate stole the Abbot's seal, forged letter after letter in which he recommended worthless men for positions of honor and importance, denounced worthy abbots, bishops and whole communities, advised things that were rash and wildly imprudent, and thus threw the whole Roman Curia into consternation. Tell him that to this day we know not how widespread these forgeries are, for the ingrate fled with our seal and the seal of his brother. And don't forget to tell how patient, lenient and long-suffering Bernard was with this Judas. Tell him that just like Christ, to the very end Bernard called him 'friend.'"

The Prior paused and looking at Geoffrey intently said, "God almost takes sanity from His saints before He has fully fashioned them. He makes them almost lose their minds. I wonder if that is the lesson of the cry of dereliction that escaped Him on Calvary?"

Geoffrey made no answer. The Prior looked like, and talked like, a man who expected no answer. He was stating facts in question form. At length Geoffrey, looking down at his notes, said, "This is a rather sad letter of consolation."

With a trace of fierceness the Prior turned on him and said, "You are writing to Bernard's brother. The same blood runs in his veins as pulsed from the heart of our great warrior saint. He was born of the same father and mother, and schooled in the same hard school of Citeaux. Bernard was more than brother to Nivard; he was also his spiritual father. So tell Nivard the truth. He'll find consolation in the very fierceness of the facts. He'll find consolation in the reading even as I do in the dictation,

consolation in the truth that Bernard walked the Via Do-
lorosa, thorn-crowned and cross-laden, consolation from
the fact that our Abbot followed in the very footsteps of
Him whom he so loved." The Prior stopped—then a look
of grim determination came over his face. His next words
were slow and deliberate.

"And lest Nivard wonder if his brother's side was
opened and his heart pierced, tell him how Rome, how
Pope Eugenius, his beloved child of former years, turned
against him because of Cardinal Hugh. Tell the whole
stupid story, how Hugh was raised to the Cardinalate
from the abbacy of Three Fountains, how, when his favorite was not elected to fill his place, he turned on
Bernard with all the fury of one demented, and vomited
forth, in public and in private, all sorts of vile calumny
about the man who loved him deeply and who had nour-
ished him in the early years of his religious life. Tell him
that the whole Roman world, even Eugenius himself, accepted the calumny. Then tell him what his brother wrote
to this unjust and angry Cardinal; tell him how he ended
his letter of apology and explanation with the words, 'As
for the rest, I thank God that He has mercifully deprived
me before my death of a consolation to which I have been
perhaps unduly attached—I mean the friendship of Pope
Eugenius and yourself.' Ah, Geoffrey, that is the sentence
of a saint. That is resignation that drains the heart.
Bernard loved his friends to love's last prodigality. How
he suffered from that misunderstanding!"

"Shall I tell him of the reconciliation?"

"If you wish," answered the Prior. "But Nivard is old
enough to know that healed friendships always show the
scar. However, you must tell him of the loneliness of his
last years. Tell him how the death of Abbot Suger wrung
from his soul the cry, 'You precede, but you do not de-
part from me; for our souls are bound with bonds that
cannot be loosed or broken. One so loved can never be

lost to me.' Tell him that the deaths of Emperor Conrad and of Abbot Raynaud gave his brother a homesickness for heaven, and that when he heard that Pope Eugenius had gone to his reward he exclaimed, 'Come, Lord Jesus, come.'"

Geoffrey looked up from his hastily written notes and asked, "Should we not also tell him of that last ride his brother made with the charity of Christ as his spurs and death riding *en croup?*"

"Would you omit anything from the passion of Christ? By all means tell him! Tell him that the prelates and princes of the kingdom and the world stormed Clairvaux during Bernard's last months seeking a final blessing and a parting word of advice; but they found a man who had his thoughts fixed in another realm. Tell him that though his brother had told the Bishop of Langres that, 'he had done with the things of this world,' when the Archbishop of Trèves came with the news that Metz was divided into two hating and hostile camps, that two thousand men had been killed in the first battle, that only the Moselle now separated the two armies as they prepared for another battle, and that only one voice in all Christendom could prevent it, that a dying man rose, flung himself into a saddle and road the many torturing miles to Metz. Tell him that he labored a whole hot summer's day without results, but that during the night the leaders of both parties came to Bernard's tent and the following sun-up saw the soldiers of both armies exchanging the kiss of peace. Then say that his brother rode back to the Valley of Light to keep his rendezvous with death."

"What shall I tell of his death?" asked Geoffrey.

"Just the end. You can say that he suffered torments for months, being unable to take any food, and that a tiny bit of water was his only refreshment. Yes, but tell him that his brother said Mass as long as he could stand.

Then write that on the morning of August the twentieth we administered the Last Sacraments, and when his brother saw the community in tears, he mustered up enough strength to give us a final instruction. Tell him that it was of one piece with all the others, that it summed up the only message his brother ever felt he had to give the world, the only message he had ever used to guide his own life. Tell him that Bernard's parting words were, 'In the name of Jesus Christ I beg you to go on loving God as I have taught you.'"

The Prior choked with emotion. Geoffrey himself swallowed hard and said, "The last message of the lover was a message of love."

"Right," continued the Prior, "and his last act was an act of love. Tell Nivard that we all begged his brother to stay with us a little longer and that his brother lifted his big, beautiful eyes towards heaven and said, 'I know not to which I ought to yield: the love of my children which urges me to stay, or the love of my God which draws me to Him. I will let God decide.' Then say that God decided against us and took to Himself the heart of His lover, the great heart of Bernard of Clairvaux. Sign my name," said the Prior, "but add that it is the name of a man who is living in darkness in this Valley of Light. That is all, Geoffrey. Write it quickly. Nivard will want the details."

Geoffrey gathered his notes, rose, bowed and left the Prior to his loneliness and love.

A little over twenty years later, on January 18, 1174, Pope Alexander III solemnly enrolled Bernard in the catalogue of the saints and published a Mass and office which he had composed himself in the new saint's honor. Since then, title after title has been given this Abbot of Clairvaux; to some he is "the mellifluous Doctor," to others, "Mary's troubadour," and some have gone so far as to call him the "Last of the Fathers," because they find his writings so like those who centuries before really earned the name of "Father." But to us, Bernard will ever be the boy and man who fell in love with God, determined to love Him without measure, and lived his resolve to the hilt.

Part 4

THE YOUNGER
MEMBERS

His Partner
in the Service of Love

"No humor ever came from hell."

"Guy, I envy you. I have just been talking with Tawny-beard and he tells me that everything is settled for you and Humbeline. Boy, you've got a prize, a pearl, a rare, rare woman! Yes, I envy you."

"Well, Your Excellency, that makes it just about unanimous. I think that every noble in the Duchy can make the same confession. I'm a much envied man. Humbeline has made me what I have never been able to make myself."

"What is that?" asked the Duke of Burgundy with a twinkle in his eye.

"Conspicuous," confessed his nephew, Guy of Marcy.

"Yes, she has made you that, all right; but let me tell you that she has made you more; much more. For she has made you more of a man! You've had more energy, life and alertness about you this past year than you've shown in all your previous life. In fact, I'm beginning to have hopes that she will make you a worthy nephew of mine yet."

Guy was used to his gruff, old uncle. He understood Hugh's backhanded compliments; so the harshness in his voice as he grated out, "worthy nephew" told Guy that his uncle was very pleased with his nephew, with Humbeline, and most of all with himself. Taking advantage of the moment, Guy made bold enough to ask, "What were you raving about yesterday when Jacques and his brother were here?"

"Raving?" said Hugh as he flashed a dark look at his smiling nephew. "I wasn't raving. I was telling those numbskulls about your bride-to-be. Ah, they make me mad, these superficial men who never see deeper that the skin. Can you imagine anyone praising Humbeline for her beauty?"

"Can I?" exclaimed Guy with warmth. "Well, I should say I can! In fact, I can't imagine anyone with two eyes who wouldn't praise her for her beauty. Why, Uncle, she's the talk of the Duchy. Her eyes are like stars. There is a light in them that is seen only in the scintillant orbs of the heavens. Her skin is velvet and the rose of her lips unfurls only to show an even row of gleaming pearls. And I have seen lights dancing in her raven black hair. Why she has a face that will do more than did the face of Helen of Troy...."

"Oh, stop your nonsense!" growled the Duke in disgust. "I know she's beautiful. I don't have to have you tell me that. I have two eyes. And I know all about Helen of Troy, Cleopatra and the Queen of Sheba, for that matter. But if that's all you see in your bride-to-be, you're as stupid as Jacques and his brother, as dull-witted as that ox Benoit who thought he had coined a phrase when he said, 'Her neck is like a swan's.' Great heavens, boy, look deeper than the skin! Humbeline is a beauty. No one can question that. But I've seen countless beautiful women. It is not the eyes, the teeth, the skin, the lips or the hair that make Humbeline the prize that she is, even though these are exceptional. No! Nor is it her beautiful voice.

And if all you see and all you can say is what you have already said, you shouldn't be allowed to marry her."

This outburst startled Guy. Duke Hugh II almost always growled when he talked and flashed fire from below bushy, overhanging eyebrows; but his nephew knew him well enough to realize that a new depth had been sounded in this question of Humbeline. It was, therefore, with a feeling of awe that he asked, "What do you mean, Uncle?"

"I mean that you've got a woman. Do you hear?—a woman! Not a pretty-faced female. Humbeline of Fontaines has fire, spirit, soul. That's what makes her the beauty that she is. Not her eyes and teeth and cheeks. Why, I've seen that girl ride in a hunt with all the recklessness of a knight. I've seen her crash through briars and brambles that had some of the nobles circling them. I've seen her take high hurdles and get up from a fall with all the speed and unconcern of a warrior. She was in at the kill! And that couldn't be said for all the men. Do you begin to understand me? Humbeline of Fontaines has backbone; and to me, that's a whole lot more than a face."

Guy thrilled to the Duke's furiously voiced character sketch and could not refrain from laughing at his last sentence. "Well, Your Excellency, let's call her Diana, the goddess of the hunt."

"Call her nothing but Humbeline," growled the Duke. "These goddesses and heroines of literature never lived; your Humbeline is flesh and blood. Yes, and let me tell you she has a mind! I heard her arguing with her brother Bernard one day and I was astounded."

"At her fire?" asked Guy.

"No," thundered the Duke, "at the force of her logic. She has the mind of two men and a half. Which gives me another reason to rejoice for your sake."

"Meaning that she'll make up for my deficiency?" smiled Guy.

"Exactly!" snapped his uncle. "If after all your years of courting you can only enthuse over her complexion and the carriage of her head, you'll need a wife with brains. Why, Guy, it's character you want in a woman, not complexion. Look at her eyes, yes! and see starlight if you will; but then look deeper and see if you can see the glow of her baptismal candle in her soul's depths. Look at her lips, yes! and see the ruby of the rose, if you must; but then look closer and find out if those lips can be firm; find out how often they are rubied by the Blood of Christ. See lights dancing in the raven blackness of her hair if you will, but find out if a halo of holiness, a halo of genuine holiness, can as fittingly be placed there. In other words, Guy, find out if she is a "woman." Find out if the girl of your dreams has real beauty, the beauty that comes from a strong personality, a lily-pure soul and a character of sterling worth. Beauty lies not in the skin, my boy; for that wrinkles and withers and cracks; but a woman who has character possesses a beauty that never dims but always develops. Humbeline of Fontaines is such."

"Thank you, Uncle," said Guy as he arose. "You have told me things I never knew before. Things about yourself that very few know."

"Huh?" grunted Hugh. "I've been talking about one of the grandest persons in the Duchy, your wife-to-be."

"I heard you," answered Guy, "but I also heard you telling me much about yourself. And now let me tell you something about Humbeline that perhaps you don't know. She says that she is more male than female, and has lived a topsy-turvy, delightful life. Being the only girl in the family forced her to be boyish. She says that she spent her childhood wishing half the time that she were a boy and half the time that she weren't so boyish. Just at present she confesses to a great loneliness, for she claims that only a woman can understand a woman and that if her mother had not been more of a companion than a parent her life would have been terribly empty. Bernard, she says, was always understanding; but then she shakes her head and adds, 'But even the greatest 'tom-boys' will ultimately seek a woman to find full and sympathetic understanding.'"

"Her mother was a remarkable woman," broke in the Duke.

"Yes, and I think that Humbeline has most of her remarkable qualities," continued the nephew. "You speak of backbone, and you're right. She's got daring, drive and determination. But, Uncle, she's got more! She's got a God-consciousness that scares me and shames me."

"A what?" snapped the Duke with a sudden turn of his head and a black frown.

"A God-consciousness she calls it, and I accept the term. She talks as easily and as naturally about God as you and I do about the tournament. She says that her mother brought them all up in an atmosphere that was charged with the Divinity. She was surprised to find me surprised. She thought that every good Catholic mother did the same. So you see why I say it scares me and shames me. You talk about the superficiality of men regarding the beauty of woman; I've learned from Humbeline the superficiality of most of us regarding something much more important—the beauty of the Godhead."

"Don't you start," growled the Duke. "Tescelin talks that way often; and when he does I feel lost. I feel that he is talking about matters entirely beyond me, but matters which I ought to know. It's a shame-filled feeling."

"I'm glad to hear you say that, Uncle. I thought I was the only one who felt that way. So her father can talk of God, too?"

"So easily and intimately that I feel like a pagan," came the gruff reply.

"And I thought it was just empty piety."

"There you go again! Superficiality! First of all, there is nothing, absolutely nothing about Humbeline that can be labeled with that derogatory adjective 'empty.' Get that clearly! She has the character, the mind, the will, the heart, the everything of a heroic woman. As for her physical beauty, that is so striking that to label it 'empty' is to desecrate one of God's choicest creations. Secondly, genuine piety, that is, a filial turning to God, a God-consciousness, as you called it, could be and should be the foundation and the crown of our manhood."

"But it isn't," said Guy with warmth.

"I know it isn't," fired back the Duke, "but that doesn't prove that genuine piety is feminine; it only proves that you and I and rest of us are not real men. But I'm beginning to sound like Tawny-beard. Let's have done with this. Here, my boy, a toast to your girl who has been and is so boyish, to your woman who is so much a man, and to your bride-to-be who will make you my worthy nephew." Saying which he poured a liberal goblet and drank it with relish. As Guy finished his and put the goblet back on the table the Duke said, "Just remember, my boy, that beauty is more than skin-deep. Then you'll understand me when I say Humbeline is a beauty!"

Bittersweet

The Duke and his nephew thought that they had made a profound analysis of Humbeline's character, but actually, they had only touched on truths. It was true that Humbeline could ride a horse better than many a knight, and would ride recklessly in a hunt. It was also true that she had been a 'tom-boy.' But how could she help it? She was the only girl in a family of seven; Guy, Gerard and

Bernard were above her, while Andrew, Bartholomew and Nivard came after. Thus she had all the advantages and all the drawbacks of being in the middle; she was looked up to and down upon. Many a time great, salty tears had welled up into her pain-filled eyes as some one of the brothers had said, "No! You can't play. This is a game for men. You're only a girl." But she knew supreme delight when asked to play "The Queen of the Tourney" or heard her father insist that "gentlemen always yield to ladies."

Small wonder then that she called her early days 'topsy-turvy.' It is true that she played more with a soldier's spear than with a little girl's doll and would rather ride a horse than play house. It is even true that this preoccupation with the games and interests of growing boys influenced her adolescence. But what Guy and the Duke had so lightly touched was what had the deepest and most lasting effect upon the character that they so much admired. It was Alice who gave Humbeline her greatest beauty; for, wise mother that she was, she taught her daughter those crowning virtues of womanhood—simplicity and modesty.

What gruff old Hugh really admired in Humbeline, though he did not know it, was the surprising combination of strength and gentleness, of recklessness and resourcefulness, of comeliness and competency. It was the woman, the valiant woman, that shone through the cloak of the girl that had this growling old warrior eloquent in his admiration. And that woman had been formed by a wise mother. Could Hugh and Guy have listened to the conversation that was going on at Fontaines at about the same time that they were drinking their toast to Humbeline, they would have learned much.

Tescelin had said, "Well, little queens grow up, don't they, Humbeline?" Only to be met with the answer, "Not to those to whom they were little queens."

"Meaning?" questioned her father.

"Meaning that as long as I live I will be your "Little Queen." I have grown up as far as all others are concerned. I can no longer be called 'little girl'; but to you, Father, and with you, I always want to be just 'Little Queen.'"

"Ah, that's a sweet fancy, my Little Queen, a bittersweet fancy. The hard fact of life is that you *have* grown and must take your place in the world of grown-ups."

"Oh, time flows on," answered Humbeline. "I know I am a woman; and I know all that means. But just as I will always be your daughter, so I always want to be your 'Little Queen.' They say that all things change, Father. But they are wrong. There are certain relations that never change. I will always be a child of God, and I will always be a child of Tescelin the Tawny."

"You say that with a touch of sadness, Little Queen; what's wrong?"

"Oh, nothing, Father; but the word you just used is a perfect summation of my life."

"What word?"

"Bittersweet," said Humbeline with a wistful smile. "I find so few, so very, very few things that are completely bitter or completely sweet. Mother's death was very bitter, but oh! the sweetness it brought when it gave me so much of you. I would never have known my Daddy the way I do, for I could never have been to you what I have been, had God not taken Mother. That's why I call even death bittersweet.

"And the same with Bernard's going. It was bitter, very bitter. Do you remember how I carried on? I never knew how much I loved old 'Big eyes' until he had locked himself away at Citeaux. But now that he is Abbot of Clairvaux and has all my brothers there with him working away for God alone, the thought thrills me. But even that thrill is only bittersweet; I miss him still. And now, Daddy, as you say, I've got to take my place in the world of grown-ups. I'm going to get married. I know I've got a very faithful and truly adoring man. I think I really love him. And yet, the thought of marriage is only bittersweet."

"Why so?" asked her father anxiously, and received the sweetest tribute of his life as his beautiful daughter walked over to him, put her two arms around his neck and laying her head on his breast like a little child, said, "Because of you."

Tescelin was touched. Humbeline was his "Little Queen" again. For a moment he rested his cheek on her raven black hair where the green and gold lights danced. It seemed so good to feel her head against his heart. But then he straightened up and taking a long breath said, "Little Queen, you must not think that way about me. I'll not be lonely. I have my work; plenty of it. And what's more, you must never divide your heart! Be Guy de Marcy's wife whole and entire. Don't be old Tawny-beard's little girl."

Humbeline never stirred as she asked, "Can leopards change their spots?"

"No," answered Tescelin firmly as he lifted her head and looked deep into her eyes, "and that is why I want you to be true to yourself. You've always been a thoroughbred. Life has many high hurdles and some very dense thickets. Take them as you've always taken them, bravely, boldly, fearlessly, with your eye ever on the quarry. A new life begins for you, Humbeline. The old must go."

"Oh, it's not fear, Father," came the sweet-voiced reply as two crystal tears trembled on the edge of long, black, silken lashes, "it's longing for you. What have you got from life? Mother has gone to God. The boys, all of them, have gone to religion. And now I must go and get married. It doesn't seem right. It doesn't seem fair."

"Come, let's sit down," said Tescelin gently as he led his misty-eyed daughter to a chair. When he had drawn his own up close to hers he took her two hands in his own and said, "Little Queen, let me make a confession. You are twenty-two years old. I married your mother before she was sixteen."

"That was very young, Daddy; very, very young."

"I know it. But she never regretted it; neither did I. But now I wonder if I have been selfish in your regard."

"You? Selfish? I should say not!"

"Hold on now, Little Queen. Did you know your hand was asked for the year your mother died?"

"No."

"Well, it was; and I hesitated."

"Oh, I'm so glad you did! Just think what the past five years would have been for you if you had consented."

"That's exactly what I've been thinking of," said Tescelin slowly. "And that's why I'm afraid that I've been selfish."

"No, Father," said Humbeline firmly. "Not one bit selfish. You were considerate of me, that's all. I would have been miserable if I could not have been at your side the past five years; just miserable. So you see, it was kindness and consideration for me, not selfishness."

Tescelin smiled. "Humbeline," he said, "you can turn things beautifully. And my old heart wishes that what you say were true; but I'm afraid that it is just your delicately sensitive and loving mind. However, now I can say that I am thinking only of you. You are twenty-two. You must be married this year. It is my will, and I feel sure that it is the will of God."

"Yes, Daddy, and I feel that the past five years have been His will, too. Mother always insisted that there are no accidents with God. What we so foolishly call accident is all part of His wise, providential plan. And see how kind He is! Suppose you had married me off, as they say, in 1110—what heartache there would have been all around. I don't think the boys would have had the courage to follow their vocation if they did not feel that I would make up for them to you."

Tescelin squeezed her hands feelingly as he said, "Right, Little Queen; and let me say you have made up! Ah, what a wonderfully big heart you have, my girl; you have filled the void made by death and the one made by religious vocations; you have been Alice as well as Humbeline, Guy and all the boys rolled in one. Little Queen, I'm grateful!"

Humbeline was awe-struck by the tone of her father's voice. Never a demonstrative man, this deeply emotional expression of affection and appreciation surprised her. She heard a trembling in his throat and with a woman's quick intuition she knew she must still the tempest before it conquered a strong-souled man. So returning the pressure of his hands she said, "Thank God, Father, not me. He made the heart. I only use it.

"Which reminds me of Mother," she continued with a smile. "One day I heard her talking to the Duchess. It seems that Her Highness was of the opinion that I and all little girls should be kept humble by being told that they were ugly and awkward and whatnot. Mother gave that musical trill of a laugh that was hers and answered, 'But, Duchess, there are mirrors! And I would rather have my daughter, while looking in hers, find the beautiful features God has given her and to make an act of thanksgiving to Him for them, than to look very closely and find there the face of a liar—her own mother's!'

"The Duchess did not immediately agree. She said I should be told that I had ugly, straight hair and the slightest little cast in my right eye to keep me from being vain. Mother did not laugh this time but quietly asked, 'And what will my daughter think of me when she finds out that her eyes are perfect and her raven black hair a glory? Won't it seem strange to her that a teacher of virtue should be unvirtuous? Now, Duchess, isn't it a sounder tactic and a surer way to true humility to exclaim: Humbeline, dear, what beautiful hair the good God has given you! And He must have robbed the radiance from the stars for your eyes! You must thank Him and thank Him and thank Him for these gifts. You are His little girl, you know.'

"From my place behind the door I could see the Duchess's face. You should have seen her eyes and mouth pop open when Mother began to exclaim about my hair and eyes. I thought she was going to faint. But when Mother ended, the good Duchess just sagged and sighed, 'Oh-h-h!' Then after a little while she rose and said, 'Alice, you have taught me a deep Christian truth. I thank you. I shall never forget it.'"

Tescelin chuckled at the perfect pantomime of the Duchess that Humbeline put on as she rose and drew herself up into a majestic pose. "Ah," he said, "she is an honest woman. Not all would have admitted their lesson."

"Yes," smiled Humbeline, "she is an honest woman and honesty is true humility. You know, Daddy, Mother taught me thoroughly. I could have been a very spoiled child, a bold, brazen little upstart. The way you and the boys always made so much of me and the nice things all the visitors used to say to me! I think I've passed the age of silly vanity, and I can see now how wise Mother was to tell me the truth all the time and make me refer it all to God. Oh, how she drove home that lesson that I am God's girl first, last and always!"

"I have to smile as I look at you and hear you say 'girl,' Humbeline."

"That's because you do not see my heart, Daddy. I know I have the physical appearance of a woman, but way down deep in here I am only 'little Humbeline.' Don't you think we always remain children at heart, Father?"

"In a certain sense, yes," answered her father.

"Do you know what I think it is? I think it is the eternal in us, the everlasting child, the one that shall never grow old, God's child. That's why I love the 'Our Father.'"

"And that's why I love you, Humbeline. There is something everlastingly young about you. Maybe, as you say, it is the child peeping through the eyes of the matured woman. Whatever it is, may it ever stay such!"

"Amen," said his daughter with a smile. "And now, old Tawny-beard, let us be off to bed. Tomorrow will be a busy day. But remember Guy de Marcy's wife will always be just your 'Little Queen.'"

"I won't forget," said Tescelin and his smile was a benediction.

A Surrender That Cost

Six years later a very similar scene was enacted, but in Tescelin's place sat Guy de Marcy. He and Humbeline had been discussing their "in-laws." Elizabeth, the wife of Humbeline's oldest brother, who was at present Superior of the convent of Jully furnished the liveliest topic.

"She's been happy," said Humbeline, "very happy."

"I wonder," said Guy in disbelief.

"I *know!*" insisted Humbeline. "I've visited her and a woman can always tell when another woman is only pretending. I know that there are many who doubt about her happiness. They think that she was more or less forced into the convent by my brother's departure for Citeaux."

"Can you blame them, Humbeline? She was wife. She was mother. Hardly a novitiate preparation to become a nun."

"Guy dear, only men and shallow women talk like that. Men because they don't know a woman's heart; shallow women because they don't know themselves. Let me tell you that her years as wife and mother prepared her to be what she is now—a real, fully understanding and genuinely sympathetic superior. There is a certain warmth of sympathy that can come from one who has felt the paralyzing chill that comes from making a total surrender. Elizabeth has plumbed those depths, scaled those heights and made that surrender. I am convinced that it was God's way of fitting her for her present position. She is the mother of many virgins now. Had she not married my brother Guy and borne him two children, perhaps she would only be superior of a community and not the mother that she is."

"That may be true for those under her, Humbeline. But how about herself? In the depths of her soul, is she satisfied?"

"Before I answer, Guy, I must ask you a question. Why were we made?"

"To be happy, Humbeline," came the prompt reply. "Happy here as well as hereafter. I have no sympathy with those who reserve all the happiness for the next life. They make of God a torturer; equivalently saying that He has surrounded us with beauty, given us almost infinite capacities for pleasure and insatiable appetites for joy, only that we may renounce them, deny them or starve them entirely. It doesn't make sense! No, I hold that God made me to have happiness here and a greater happiness hereafter."

"I see that I have asked a question that you have answered before," smiled his wife.

"Yes, I've answered it before. It is a subject on which I can grow eloquent. There is some queer poison in the air of the court these days, Humbeline. Men are talking as if we were nothing but sinks of iniquity; as if our bodies were vile, and all that we could do was sin. Why, I even heard one say that marriage was an invention of the devil. As far as I can trace it, the poison comes from the south. I think that Languedoc is the plague spot and Albi the center and source of it all. In one discussion I heard your brother Bernard and all Cistercians with him labeled as followers of this accursed doctrine. One of the lords said that the austerity of Citeaux and Clairvaux was but a mitigated form of that practiced by 'the perfect' of this sect. He then proceeded to point out the parallel by citing Bernard's disregard for his body and his denial of all natural cravings. It was a startlingly strong argument; and one that convinced very many, I'm sure.

"There are many in our own circle talking now as if we were never to have a single bodily pleasure, never to take a crumb of creature comfort or taste a scrap of genuine human satisfaction on earth. They insist that this is a land of exile and that all happiness is reserved for heaven. Why, according to some of them, suicide is a saintly act. And that lord I made mention of a short while ago said that your brothers and all the Cistercians were doing nothing other than committing a slow suicide. It's awful! What a monster they make out of our good God! Of course they try to dodge that difficulty by blaming it all on the devil. But that only makes matters worse, for that is to make Lucifer equal to God and thus deny God's supremacy and actually to make two gods! Why,—oh excuse me, Humbeline dear, I'm getting heated."

His wife was visibly pleased at this sudden confession. "I never knew my husband was such a fiery orator. But of course, you're right, Guy. God made us to be happy here, as well as hereafter. He has been kind enough to connect pleasure with the proper use of every faculty. Look! Color delights the eyes, melody thrills the ear, velvet tickles the touch, the perfume of roses pleases the smell—but why go on? Life would be agony, and suicide the only sensible step, had God not only made us for happiness here, but made it very easy to be happy. Why, see how delightful it is for you and me to sit here exchanging ideas. Indeed, there is a great pleasure in the proper use of our faculties of both body and soul. I'm very glad that we agree that God made us for happiness, for now I can ask a deeper question. What produces the greatest happiness, acquiring for self or giving to others?"

"You're getting subtle now," Guy said, humorously suspicious, "and I think you're laying a trap for me. We started to discuss Elizabeth's position...."

"That's exactly what I'm leading to," broke in Humbeline, "but I want to be sure that your hounds are on the right scent before I allow you to plunge headlong after them."

"All right," said Guy, "I'll throw you off the scent by answering your question this way: I say that I can't give to others without acquiring for myself! Why, Humbeline dear, some of the greatest happiness of my life has come from making your eyes shine with delight. Oh, there is nothing like it. I wanted to make you happy, very happy, it is true; but I derived my greatest happiness from that very accomplishment. So you see, our greatest generosity is nothing but a subtle and very refined selfishness. Now what do you think?"

"I think that you're confusing terms a wee bit. But I'm going to accept your terms just for the sake of argument and say that sacrifice, genuine sacrifice, is nothing but selfishness in its most exquisite form."

"I'll accept that," said Guy. But he was wary. He knew that his wife, who was obsessed by the idea of unselfish living and unselfish giving, would never have taken his terms unless she had seen further than he had. So it was with keen anticipation that he awaited Humbeline's next remark.

"Then we are in at the kill!" she said triumphantly. "And you, on your own logic, must admit that Elizabeth de Forez has the greatest happiness on earth, has been the wiliest and wisest of all self-seekers and has acquired more than most other women simply by sacrificing more!"

"Brilliant," Guy cried as he clapped his hands. "You allowed me to dig my own trap and then fall into it. Logically, I have to admit. But now, pyschologically...."

"Ah! You're going off again. No, Guy dear, let us not play with words. We have touched a truth that I want to discuss with deep seriousness. To be happy, one must give; to have great happiness one must give generously; to have supreme happiness one must sacrifice oneself totally. That is why Elizabeth de Forez is so surprisingly happy. She has given most. She has given all! She gave home, husband, children, life. She reserved nothing whatsoever. Hers was a complete surrender. And by what you think a subtle contradiction, she has received most; for at this moment, she possesses all! It is not a contradiction; it is but one of Christ's paradoxes and promises fulfilled. The grain of wheat must die; and if we would save our life we must lose it. Why, Guy dear, I have experienced it in my own life...."

"How?"

"In our first year of married life we had a great deal of pleasure, didn't we? We entertained and we visited; we traveled here and there. We were like two excited children. We spent a lot of money that year. It seemed that we were determined to outdo the rest of society in every way...."

"And we did!" put in Guy. "At least you did, Humbeline; for you were universally recognized as the best-dressed lady in the Duchy. I was proud of you."

"Uh-huh," said Humbeline. "Well, Guy dear, I'm ashamed of it now. But as I was saying, we had a great deal of pleasure. To deny that would be to stultify oneself. I love nice clothes and you lavished them on me. I felt the admiration of the men and the envy of the women, and was glad for your sake. I really think that you got as much, if not more, pleasure out of my costly wardrobe than I did. Then the social life that we led was engrossing. I found it truly intoxicating. I loved the excitement of it all. It kept us so very much alive. Undoubtedly it was a year of exceptional pleasure; but since then, Guy dear, I've had happiness! And I find that the difference between pleasure and happiness is almost infinite."

"What do you mean?"

"Our pleasure was selfish. We were living only for ourselves. Others mattered only in as much as they interested us, or entertained us, or could furnish us further contacts. We were gadabouts, Guy; just a pair of young, excited, thrill-seeking gadabouts. Bernard says that it was inevitable in our first year; and that it was good for us and for our acquaintances. Maybe he's right; but I know now that all we had then was pleasure; what we have now is happiness. One lies on the surface of the senses, the other goes down to the very marrow of the soul. People used to talk about the clothes I wore and the unbounded liberality with which you allowed me to buy them. What do they talk about now?"

"To tell the truth, Humbeline, they don't talk about us so much at all. When you stopped gadding about, as you call it, and began to give your attention to the poor, they talked a great deal. Many of the society leaders imitated you, for they thought that you were merely introducing a new fad into society, and they did not want to be the least bit behind. But when you persisted in your work and the novelty wore off for them, they criticized you—and me! Today they don't talk. They neither praise nor blame. But if I am any judge, they admire and envy, even as they cannot fully understand. The older lords and ladies drop a remark now and then, and they are very sweet to hear. Only the other day one dowager said, 'Your wife will be held in as high benediction as is her mother.' To me that sounded like a tremendous tribute."

"Wouldn't you prefer that to, 'the best dressed lady in the Duchy'?" asked Humbeline with a smile.

"A hundred times," came the enthusiastic response.

"Well, there you are then, Guy. My point is proved. We have sacrificed the past five years; sacrificed much. And if society has stopped talking, serfdom has begun. Only yesterday, as I was leaving his little hovel, an old man looked up at me and said, 'May God bless the generous heart of that husband of yours!' To me that was greater praise than I ever heard about you from anyone, even from your gruff, grouchy but adoring old uncle, Duke Hugh."

Guy smiled his pleasure and exclaimed, "By heavens, Humbeline, you're waking me up to something. I'm beginning to believe you're right. We have been happy the past five years and it has come from giving pleasure to others. I can see the truth of your proposition by looking into my own heart. I never counted the costs when you were buying clothes, for I loved to see you wear them. When you kept on asking for as much money and even more to clothe the poor, I must confess that I knew a secret misgiving. But the light of happiness in your eyes as I handed over the sum was reward enough for me and did much to dispel the misgiving. Yes, I admit it, I've been most happy when I gave the most pleasure."

"And now will you go one step farther with me?" asked Humbeline as she drew her chair nearer the table.

Guy leaned forward, resting both elbows on the tabletop as he said, "If it teaches me as much as the last few, I'll be glad to."

"Will you admit that there is a proportion between giving and receiving? A strict proportion according to which the more it costs us to give to others, the more happiness and greater satisfaction we receive once we have given it? Will you agree that the greater the sacrifice the greater the reward?"

"Hmmm," mused Guy, "that calls for thought."

"Oh, not so much," said Humbeline quickly. "Let's take it out of the general and abstract by looking at actual cases. Let's take Elizabeth de Forez again. She'll prove the point. Guy, are you afraid of death?"

Her husband started. The question was so sudden that he was nonplussed for a moment. "Afraid of death?" he repeated quietly. "Why—yes, Humbeline, I am a little afraid of death. I think everyone is."

"Why?"

"It's hard to say exactly, but I think it's part of our very nature. We were not made to die, you know. Death is a result of sin. I suppose our instinct for life then, is nothing but the deepest depth of our original nature struggling against this thing that sin brought on. And then again, I don't suppose it is death we fear so much as it is the judgment."

"Ah! That's it. Wouldn't it be lovely then to live without a dread of death or judgment? Wouldn't it be happiness supreme to face those fearful facts and be unafraid? Wouldn't that be conquering life's greatest fears?"

"Yes, it would. But I'm afraid that you're back in the realm of theory again."

"Oh, no I'm not!" exclaimed Humbeline happily. "I'm in the realm of realest fact. Elizabeth de Forez and all her nuns live that way! Bernard and all my brothers live that way! My father died that way! Every soul that gives itself entirely to God laughs at death and longs for judgment. And why not? For to them death is a friendly liberator and judgment the time for reward."

Guy folded his hands on the edge of the table and studied his thumbnails. It was evident that Humbeline's enthusiastic response had struck deep. "Death a liberator," he muttered, "and judgment the time for reward. Mmmm." His wife was watching him closely. She seemed most anxious that he would believe this truth. His muttering excited her. She grew afraid that he would not accept her statements. "Guy dear," she pressed, "it seems incredible, I know; but that is because we think so superficially. Now tell me: Were you not more ready and without fear to face your uncle after you had done some heroic deed in battle, after you had risked your life and sacrificed safety than you were after some escapade or boyish prank? Bring the principle to the touchstone of everyday life and you'll see its force. When did you face your uncle most gladly?"

"After I had sacrificed, as you say," came the thoughtful reply. "That is certainly true in the case of any knight."

"Then don't you see the parallel?"

"I do, Humbeline; more clearly than ever before. And I see that I have sacrificed very little for God. I can believe that religious souls such as Elizabeth de Forez and your brothers, if not completely without fear, are certainly more ready to face God than any of us in the world. It is most reasonable."

"And you have touched the real reason, Guy. It is *giving to God!* I am growing more convinced that life has only one purpose: that God gave us everything simply that we might freely give everything back to Him again. Daddy's death at Clairvaux last year taught me that most forcefully. I saw then that happiness here and hereafter is to be found in God alone."

"Do you mean that the world should be one large monastery?"

"Never!—But I do mean that everyone in the world should live as do the inmates of the monastery; that is, fully God-conscious, God-centered, God-absorbed! My sister-in-law has more happiness here than any hundred society women, and she is more sure of happiness hereafter than any thousand of them. And why? Because she has made the total sacrifice and the unconditional surrender. She has given her all!"

Guy buried his head in his hands and remained in that bowed posture for some minutes. Humbeline thought she·saw his shoulders shake once, but was not sure. After watching him for some little while she reached across the table and, lightly touching his head asked, "Guy dear, what is it?"

His head came up then and Humbeline saw a furrowed brow and pain-filled eyes. "I was thinking of my sister, the Duchess of Lorraine," he said. "She has everything that a woman naturally craves; but I see now that Elizabeth de Forez is much better off. And I was thinking of myself. How little I have sacrificed to God! Yes, I fear death because I fear judgment, and I fear judgment because I have not been what you say we all should be— God-conscious, God-centered, God-absorbed. But you have opened my eyes, Humbeline. I see a way out. I see a way of doing something that will have me as ready to face God as I am to face my uncle after doing something great. You say that religious laugh at death and long for the judgment simply because they have sacrificed themselves. Well, I can sacrifice something greater! I can give God something I love more than myself, and I will! I can give God—you!"

Humbeline caught her breath in an audible gasp. Five years ago, timidly and with tears, she had proposed this very sacrifice to Guy. He had kissed away the tears and smiled away the proposal. He told her that she was under an emotional strain after her visit to Clairvaux. He allowed her full liberty to indulge her zeal in charity to the poor, even agreed to curtail their social life, but he would never hear of her going to a convent. During the ensuing five years she had never once repeated the proposal, though she had often given expression to a holy envy of those who could live their lives for God alone. If she had meant these as bait, Guy had never bitten; so now this sudden declaration sent her heart to her throat. Both hands went there in a gesture of fright as she murmured, "Oh-h!"

"Yes," said Guy fiercely, "if you are generous enough to give yourself to God, I'll be more generous. You are my heart, my life, my all. I love you this moment as I never loved you in all my life before. I see you tonight more clearly than I ever saw you. Humbeline, my Queen, you are at the height of your physical beauty, the full bloom of radiant womanhood is just upon you. Your hair, your eyes, your mouth, your every feature, your very carriage—all, all are adorable. Yes, and what the eye does not see is more beautiful still—your soul! You say that sacrifice pleases God; then I'll please Him as I never pleased Him before. You say that life is all paradox. Then I'll live one. I'll tear out my heart and give it to God so that God may give it back to me at the judgment. Yes, life of my life, you may go. Make your sacrifice as I've made mine. Let us both live for eternity; and since that is won only by death in time—let us both die! I die as I yield you to the stronger Lover—God! Come, my sweet, seal our sacrifice," and he held out open arms to a woman who walked into them as if hypnotized.

Holding her to him Guy went on passionately, "Don't think this sudden, Humbeline dear. I've watched you through the years and I've known that you wanted to go, but were too loving and too loyal to mention it.

Tonight, by what seems merest accident, you have cut the last cord that held my selfish heart captive. You've been talking to me about eternity and the Eternal One even though we spoke about people we know. I see now why religious are so happy. For at this moment as I make the sacrifice of my life, God gives me a happiness I've never known before. My very soul is trembling, Humbeline. You may go, my sweet, and I know that you'll think of me always just as I will never for a moment forget my wife, my Queen, my little savior, Humbeline."

They kissed then and Humbeline could only sob, "Oh, Guy, you *are* a nobleman!"

Partners in the Service of Love

It is hard to say who made the greater sacrifice that night, Guy or Humbeline. He gave up life's most desirable possession, she renounced the world's best gifts. And yet, I am tempted to think that Guy's was the greater sacrifice, and I feel sure that God rewarded him for it with a high place in heaven, even as He blessed Humbeline's surrender with sanctity.

As soon as matters were arranged she went straight to Jully and was welcomed by her sister-in-law, Elizabeth, and her niece Adeline. There were no Cistercian nuns at the time and Jully, a Benedictine convent, offered Humbeline the closest possible approach to the life her best loved Bernard was leading. When she was at Office she would close her eyes and see him standing beside her, blending his voice with hers as they hymned the praises of God. When she was at work she would often look at the sun-dial to see if Bernard was working at exactly the same hour. When she was making her spiritual readings she would picture 'Big eyes' at her elbow doing what she was doing and doing it for the same end. To Humbeline it was childhood all over again, but with no "make-believe" and no sad disillusionments. They were really one now as they had never been before, and she coined a title for herself and Bernard, calling him and herself, "partners in the service of love."

Elizabeth de Forez nodded her head many a time and said, "Your title is most apt, Humbeline; for you *are* a female Bernard." But it was in a scolding tone that she said it, for Humbeline had plunged into the life with the same vehemence and violence that had marked Bernard's early days at Citeaux and Clairvaux, and Elizabeth knew that the young Abbot had ruined his health by these early exaggerations. She wanted Humbeline to be holy, but also wanted her to be healthy; so she often had to insist, "Jully is Benedictine, Humbeline, not Cistercian! Stop being like your brother and be more like yourself." Humbeline would smile and say, "I'm sorry, Elizabeth. I'll remember in the future. I know that obedience is better than sacrifice."

It was this winning docility that saved Humbeline from excess. Elizabeth de Forez was right. Humbeline was a female Bernard, and her heart was aflame with eagerness to do great things for God and to be merciless toward herself. If she had lacked that saving docility she would have been a thorn in the side of the community and a whole crown of thorns to her superior; for runaway zeal causes more havoc than a thunderbolt. As it was, she realized that she had come to give up her own will, and she gave it up. That is why she became Elizabeth's pride and the community's delight.

When Bernard first visited her he exclaimed, "What is this? What is this? Why, Humbeline, you are more beautiful as a nun than you ever were as the Duchy's toast. The wimple brings out your features more arrestingly than any headdress you ever wore. I think I shall have to call this a saintly coquetry." They had a splendid chat that day. Humbeline was all questions, but Bernard was not all answers. He had learned his lesson at Clairvaux. He was developing prudence, so he shook his head to many a proposed practice, simply smiled at some questions and turned others aside with, "Let your Superior decide." They had many a laugh over the days that were gone and as he was preparing to leave Bernard said, "You'll become a saint, Humbeline. I can see that."

"What are the signs?" she asked smilingly.

"You've kept your sense of humor. You can still laugh, even at yourself. That's almost an infallible sign. No humor ever came from hell!"

He was right. Judged by externals Humbeline was still the same beautiful woman of old, possessing all her charming personality and captivating qualities. She had lost none of the luster of her glowing beauty of body, mind and spirit. It was only the interior that was deepening as she strove to live to God alone. This is evidenced by the fact that in 1130, when Elizabeth left to make a foundation near Dijon, the community, without a single dissenting vote, elected Humbeline as her successor.

The only surprised person in the convent was the newly elected Superior. She could not believe the announcement. She felt as if she had just arrived and had not really started on the road to perfection. She felt young and unworthy; and it was this very feeling that made her an outstanding success as a Superior, for it drove her to a blind trust in God and gave her a delicacy in her dealings with her subjects that completely captivated them. She had the strength and gentleness of her Spouse, the Christ.

Elizabeth de Forez had done much for Jully; Humbeline now did more. The report of Humbeline's holiness went the length and breadth of the Duchy. The report of her superiorship affected the female nobility in much the same manner as Bernard's roundup of twenty years previously had affected the male. Jully was soon overcrowded with the very best of Burgundy's daughters. One after another Humbeline sent out groups to make new foundations; and though she mothered twelve new daughter-houses in the few short years of her superiorship, her own convent was always crowded.

One morning, her Assistant, coming into her room early, found her tacking up a little square of parchment just over her desk. She looked at it and saw in bold, black print the two words, *"LOVE SERVES."* She looked at it again; read it aloud; then said, "What in the world is this?"

"That," said Humbeline abruptly, "is the whole science of sanctity compressed into two words. I put it there to keep me from losing my mind, my tongue and my time." Then she smiled. "You see, Sister, I'm only human, and there are times when I could explode. This little card is a whole deluge of water that will put out my raging fires. There are other times when I get terribly weary. This community is large and every single member of it is an individual concern to me. When my spirits flag, that little card will reinvigorate me. Countless are the occasions that I look at you and the others going to prayer when duty shackles me to this desk, and I envy you. That little card will change that capital sin into a source of merit."

Sister Assistant looked from Humbeline to the card, and touching the latter said, "What a magical little piece of parchment. Where did you get it?"

"Can't you guess?" replied Humbeline. "That's Bernard's whole life in two words. He sent it to me, for I guess I must have been complaining to him in my last letter. You see, Sister, I long for solitude, silence and great interior union with God. That was my ambition when I came here. But you see what has happened. I never have a moment that I can call my own, and the dear Lord has to take my incessant activity as my loving converse with Him.

"I must have mentioned my distress to Bernard, for that is his whole answer. Just two words, but what a long, long treatise they contain! 'Love serves!' Yes, they tell me why I live; why I must give and give and give; why I must grow weary but never give in; know irritation but never show it; long for solitude but never be allowed a moment to myself. For you must remember, Sister, it is not the motto we hang on the wall that counts; it is the motto we live! Bernard can be brief. Bernard can even be bitter. There is a fierce condemnation of my murmuring in those two words. But Bernard is always inspiring. This little card has given me more food for thought than many a book I've read. Only this morning at mental prayer the thought came to me of how true a title those two words make for the crucifix. More true even than the one about which Pilate growled, 'What I have written, I have written.' I'll have to thank Bernard for his furious call-down and inspiring uplift of two words."

The Assistant had watched Humbeline closely during this talk. She saw the earnestness and sincerity of her soul leap into her eyes as she spoke out her determination to live the motto: LOVE SERVES. But she saw other fires there too, and these so intrigued her womanly intuition that she said, "You love Bernard, don't you?"

Humbeline, who had been studying the card, turned on her quickly, "Do I love Bernard?" she asked in a surprised tone, then added, "If you doubt it, just say something against him. Why, Sister dear, Bernard is half my heart. He is my dearest brother; has been my pal all my life; is my love, my inspiration, yes, I dare to say it, he is my adoration. My love for him scares me at times, and were I not sure that we *are*, 'partners in the service of love,' that we both are striving with all that we have and are to give to God all that He expects from us, I'd be in despair because of my absorbing love for that brother of mine. But you see the proof—this little card. Bernard loves me the same way I love him, but just look at the rebuke he sends me. Do you know what that little card says? It says, 'Humbeline, your Beloved is a jealous God who will have no rapine in the holocaust. Work yourself to death for Him, and do it with a smile!' Bernard knew that I would catch every shade of meaning hidden in those two little words. He knew that they would bite right into the heart. Yet he sent them. And that, to me, is proof positive of a sincere and saintly love. I am not ashamed to confess my love for Bernard. It is God-given, and I try to keep it ever God-directed."

"If you didn't confess it, Sister Superior," said the Assistant with a smile, "we'd all guess it anyhow. Your eyes tell us so. They are the wide-open windows of your soul. You'd be surprised to see how those windows light up at the mere mention of your brother's name. But I'm glad I asked the question."

"Why?" asked Humbeline with just the shade of a blush.

"Because I love human saints! I have heard others say that we should hate father, mother, brothers and sisters...."

"Oh! Oh! Oh!" cut in Humbeline quickly. "I have no time for such people. They do not know how to read their Bible. That line is in there; right from the lips of our Lord, but He only means a love of preference! He only means that I must be ready to hate even Bernard rather than give up my vocation. Oh, no! Our God is a God of love. He wants us to love all men. Only those who know not Christ ever interpret those lines literally. It's so silly! So utterly stupid! But come, Sister, 'Love serves'; we must go to work. Sit down and suggest twelve names for a new foundation."

The Assistant was used to Humbeline's fiery way, so she sat down and picking up a list of the community ran her finger down the line until she came to Jeannette. "I think she could be one. Jeannette?"

"I don't," said Humbeline. "She doesn't sit her saddle loosely enough."

"Hmmm," said the Assistant; but she could not repress a smile at the aptness of the metaphor. Jeannette *was* too tense. "How about Matilda?"

"She'll do. There's common sense there."

"And Marianne?"

"Her name should be Martha; she's always troubled about so many, many things. But she'll do."

"How about Leone?"

"No, too meek. This foundation will mean work and perhaps real suffering. Give me some with joy in their hearts, a joy that bubbles to the surface no matter how black things get."

"Then Bertha, Vincentine, Margarite and Lois will do."

"Indeed they will! But you mustn't rob me of all my 'sons.'"

"Your what?"

"My 'sons'—women whom God loves so much that He trusts them with bitter trials. The quartette you just named are among the liveliest in the house, aren't they?" The Assistant nodded her head. "Well, I can tell you privately that they have each suffered more than anyone guesses. They have backbone. They can and have taken and carried real crosses. Believe me when I say that I call them my 'sons' with good reason: with very good reason! But I'll sacrifice them. You have six now; select six more of like material and give me the list at noontime. But don't rob me of all my 'sons.' I must leave you now. I have an engagement."

Humbeline left then and as the Assistant watched her stride down the corridor with energy, ease and grace, she exclaimed, "Well if you have 'sons' in this convent, I know who their 'father' is! Just look at that woman! Who would ever suspect that next to her tender skin is a rough hairshirt? Who would ever dream that she curtails her sleep and only toys with her food? She won't allow anyone else such penances, but claims that she owes them to God on account of the vanities of her early married life. What a woman! What a woman!" Then she added, "What a saint!" and turning to the little square of parchment over the desk, read it musingly, "Love serves—I'll say it does! And I'll further say that if you sum up Bernard's life, you also sum up that of his 'partner in the service of love'!"

"How Happy!"

Sister Assistant was right. Humbeline did perform heroic penances and said that they were for the vanities of her early married days. In fact, her life was simply prayer and penance; for although she longed for and lacked the quiet so conducive to contemplation, she was a contemplative and a deeply contemplative soul, for even in the midst of her works she was conscious of the God of her heart who was in her heart. Like Bernard her God-consciousness had so developed with the years that it was now God-absorption. Humbeline had fallen in love with God; she could not be but a contemplative! Bernard had taught her much about the religious life, but nothing better than that it was no more than a means of falling in love and a manner of showing our love to Him who is Love. That she had grasped the lesson fully was never more in evidence than in August of 1141, when she was seized with what was to be her last illness.

The community could not believe their eyes when they saw their indefatigable Superior crumble. To the last minute she was at her post, smiling, alert, efficient. The little placard, "Love Serves" was before her and it held her up long after normal reserves had been exhausted, but finally she smiled to it and turned to her Assistant and said, "The spirit is willing, Sister, but the body is worn out. I think one phase of love's service is just about ended. I must go to bed and prepare for the second phase."

She went to bed and the wise Assistant sent word to Bernard that his 'partner in the service of love' was ready to receive her reward. The Abbot was shaken by the suddenness of the call, but quickly summoning Andrew and young Nivard, who happened to be on a visit to Clairvaux, set out for Jully.

They found Humbeline smiling, perfectly conscious, but very, very weak. Bernard recognized the signs and bending over her said, "You know you are dying, Humbeline?" She nodded her head slightly then said, "I know it, Big Eyes; and I want you to know I am happy, oh! so happy! and all because I followed your advice."

As Humbeline lay back almost exhausted by the effort, a series of scenes flashed before Bernard. He saw her as she was at her first visit to Clairvaux; then the five years that followed of being charity incarnate to the poor; he saw her at his first visit to Jully, afire with anxiety to give all to God; he saw her as Superior, and he well knew all that it had meant to her. He sighed, and as he did so memory played one of her tricks on him and showed him Humbeline as a little girl at Fontaines. This was the flash that showed Bernard how short life is at its longest. It seemed but yesterday that he had been playing with that little girl in the courtyard and castle of Fontaines and now here she was dying. His heart flooded with tenderness and bending over his sister again he said, "I'm happy, too, Humbeline; so happy and proud to have had you as my 'partner in the service of love.' It has been a hard service for you; very hard. Prayer and penance make no easy life for a nobleman, much less for a noblewoman; but now, dear girl...."

Then Humbeline startled them all by breaking in on Bernard with, *"Laetata sum in his quae dicta sunt mihi...."* The words came forth in a gush of gratitude. There was a ringing joy in the voice and her face was suffused with an unearthly radiance. The three brothers had recognized the opening words of the one hundred and twenty-first psalm—*"Laetata sum in his quae dicta sunt mihi"*—"I rejoiced at the things that were said to me...." They looked at one another in startled surprise, then turned to their radiant sister into whose eyes had come a look of ecstasy. With bated breath they waited for her next word. It came as she stretched out her two arms and softly, rapturously, wonderingly said, *"In domum Domini ibimus"*—"We shall go into the house of the Lord." Then as Bernard put his arm under her shoulders she dropped back—dead.

Appreciation

Bernard preached no eulogy of Humbeline as he had of Gerard. No, there are times when the heart is too full, and times when the heart is too empty for words. This was one of those times. But his tears told their tale, and many of those who watched the weeping Abbot as he celebrated the funeral Mass, and listened to his tear-choked voice as he read the prayers at his sister's grave, echoed the words spoken of Jesus as He had stood weeping beside another grave; they said, "Behold how he loved her!"

As the three brothers made their way back to Clairvaux Bernard suddenly turned to Andrew and said, *"Laetata sum in his quae dicta sunt mihi: in domum Domini ibimus!* Weren't those Humbeline's last words?" Andrew grunted, with a nod. So Bernard asked, "Do you think she was talking of the past or the future? She had just said how happy she was to have followed my advice, so they could have referred to the past. And yet, I wonder. What do you think?"

"I don't know what she meant," came the abrupt reply, "but I do know that it's a beautiful way to die."

Whereupon Nivard said, "I feel sure she was talking about the future, Bernard. That look in her eyes told me that she saw much more than we saw. I feel positive that she was talking about heaven when she said, 'Into the house of the Lord we shall go.'"

"That's what I like to think," said Bernard.

"Most likely she was talking about both," said Andrew. "Remember that she was a saintly girl long before she put on the Benedictine habit. She had reason to rejoice over that past once she had given up her foolish finery. You two can think what you like; I'm going to think that she summed up her past and told us of her future in that one verse of the psalm. God has been very good to us to have given us such a sister. I hope you two appreciate it." With that the three brothers lapsed into a meditative silence.

Humbeline lived and died a Benedictine. But an appreciative Cistercian Order has always honored her in a most exceptional manner. She is one of the very, very few not of the Order whose feast is kept with a special Office. Pius IX on February 7, 1871, issued a decree giving papal approbation to this Office in honor of Blessed Humbeline, and the grateful Order of Citeaux sings it in praise of Bernard's "partner in the service of love" on February 12. Its lessons end with Humbeline's own words, *"Laetata sum...I rejoiced."*

The Man Who Kept the Gate

"To give up arms is stupid."

"Well, what sort of a day have you had, my love?" asked Tescelin the Tawny as he drew his chair closer to the open hearth and smiled to his little wife who was busy with her needles on a bit of fancy work. It was evening and the early March winds whistling in the courtyard of the castle made the leaping flames seem all the more friendly. The children had all gone off to bed, leaving to the Lord and Lady that blessed hour which fathers and mothers know when little voices are stilled and the quick patter of little feet unheard, for tired tots are fast asleep.

"Oh," said Alice cheerily, "about as usual. Humbeline fell and cut her knee while playing 'knight.' That girl's the greatest soldier of them all. Little Bartholomew surprised everybody and scared me by climbing on the back of that new colt you bought. Nivard was found up in the tower, if you please: and when asked what he was doing he answered, 'Lookin' for Dod. Mummie says He lives up high.' That's about all of interest, I think."

Tescelin who had been all alert, drinking in the anecdotes avidly, now settled back in his chair and stretched his legs toward the fire. But just before he was completely composed and comfortable Alice laid her work on her lap and said, "Oh, yes, there was one other thing. Will you please walk across the room at your usual pace? I want to see something."

Tescelin arose, smiled good-naturedly and walked the length of the room twice saying, "It's hard to be natural when people ask you to be that way; but I think that this is about my normal gait and carriage."

Alice watched him closely, then clapped her two hands as she said, "Well, that boy is the limit! He has seen something I have never noticed."

"Who saw what?" asked Tescelin as he came over to the hearth again and stood resting his hands on the high back of his chair.

"Andrew," laughed his little wife. "Look! I found him doing this today." And she got up, laid her lacework on the table, then assuming a stiff pose, lifted her left shoulder and threw it noticeably forward, then in that peculiar posture walked back and forth twice. Keeping the same strained position she said, "I watched him for a while and noticed how determined he was to have this shoulder up and out. You should have seen his set little face. My, what determination! After he had paced the room two or three times I quietly asked, 'What in the world do you think you're doing?' Keeping the same strained stance he bravely said, 'Walking like my Dad.' And by heavens, Tescelin, he's right. You do carry your left shoulder just the least little bit high and forward."

"Well, well, well," said Tescelin with a laugh. "What a compliment from my son. Imitation, you know, is the subtlest and sincerest form of flattery. And from Andrew!"

"He's an odd one," said Alice resuming her chair. "only eight and at times he looks as serious as forty-eight. He's the strangest one of my boys."

"No, no, Alice. Not strange; just a serious streak in his character. That's all. I've watched him at play. He's so intent and determined that one wonders if he is at play. He seems to make of it the most serious business of his life. It's a good trait in a child, but it seems quite early for a boy to manifest it so clearly."

"I didn't mean strange, Tescelin. I should have said he's the soberest of my children; and yet when he *screams!*"

Tescelin laughed, for more than once he had been drawn to the courtyard by those very screams, only to find that all were intent in some game of soldiering, with Andrew more intent than the rest. "Yes," he said, "the boy can and does scream; but never forget, Alice, eagles scream."

"Well, let me tell you I often wish Andrew were an eagle; for they scream only when they are high up and far away."

"Oh, don't you worry about that lad, Mother; if I am any judge of children, he'll be like the eagle in more than his scream. That boy is going to soar!"

It was thus that the late evening hour was always spent in Fontaines castle. Alice recounted the incidents and accidents of the day, and Tescelin commented on his growing boys and his "Little Queen." His comments on Andrew seldom varied. He admitted his seriousness, soberness and determination, but claimed them as portents of a brilliant future. Truth is, Andrew intrigued Tescelin. He found something in the boy that struck a sympathetic chord in his own heart and kept it vibrating for hours at a time. He thrilled to see the determined little frown come on the lad's forehead, and to note the firm set of his lips. It was Andrew's earnestness that fascinated his father, for it seemed so out of place in a child of eight.

What gave the mother many a laugh and many an embarrassing moment was the youngster's outspokenness. The strange part of it was that Andrew was an exceptionally quiet child. He was actually so sparing with words that one who did not know him well might judge him to be shy. But when he did speak it was right to the point and startlingly so. Tescelin enjoyed this directness, insisting that it was another eagle trait, and he passed off many an embarrassing direct hit made by the lad by saying, "Eagles scream and eagles strike straight and true."

Keen Observers

Just eight years later Tescelin knew his eaglet was soaring, but found himself embarrassed by the fact. He was standing before Duke Hugh, while over to one side sat Ranier the Seneschal and Seguin of Volnay. Hugh was scowling blackly; while Ranier's compressed lips told of determination.

"Tawny, I don't know whether my Seneschal is accusing me of favoritism or foolishness. He says your boy Andrew is too young to be knighted. I say that birthdays have nothing to do with bravery. I don't dub men knights because of their age but because of their acts. They tell me that Andrew is only sixteen. Is that a fact?"

"That's a fact, Your Excellency," came the cool reply.

"Is it also a fact that he can ride anything that trots, that he can keep his saddle despite a spear-splintering jolt, that he is afraid of no man living and respects, reverences, and worships womankind?"

Tescelin watched the fire that flashed from the Duke's eyes punctuating his every phrase with fierceness; he was inwardly thrilled by the tribute his sovereign was paying his son, for Burgundy's Duke was extremely sparing with compliments. The surprising eulogy just delivered by Hugh made Tescelin wonder whether his liege lord was intent on honoring his son or on worsting the opposition of the Seneschal. He looked at Ranier to ascertain his reaction, but found his face unreadable. His eyes were cold, his lips, one straight even line, his chin, firm but normal.

Tescelin knew Ranier for a sincere, conscientious counsellor and immediately concluded that his objection to the Duke's proposal was not mere personal antagonism, but must have some foundation in fact. As these thoughts were flashing through his mind Tescelin shifted his weight from foot to foot and said, "Your Excellency, you are asking a prejudiced witness. Andrew happens to be my son. My testimony in his regard is next to worthless."

"Not so!" barked the Duke. "Any other man, yes! But Tescelin the Tawny, no! If anything you'll bend backwards and not give credit enough to the boy. I know you and your exaggerated honesty. What do you say, Ranier?"

"Your Excellency, interested parties should never be heard in a dispute. But I agree with you in this case. I'll take Tawny-beard's word for anything."

"Gentlemen, you embarrass me. I am sensitive to the high honor my sovereign proposes for my boy. I would not be a father did I not desire it for the lad. But I am also a counsellor of the Duchy and I must say that I have never known our Seneschal to object to anything without solid reason. Before I answer in my boy's behalf, may I hear our Seneschal's grounds for objection?"

"I've just given them to you," barked the Duke. "He says he's too young. And I insist...."

"Your Excellency, I cannot believe that that is the Seneschal's real objection. Andrew is only sixteen but he is as strong as anyone twenty-two, is much more mentally mature than many who are twenty-eight. I feel sure that it is not his birthday that bothers Ranier. What do you say, my Lord, am I right?"

"It is my turn to be embarrassed," smiled Ranier, "but, Tescelin, you are right. And now without casting any aspersions on your boy's character, I will say that my real ground for objection is what happened at the last tourney when Andrew was tilting against His Excellency's nephew, Guy de Marcy. Seguin here noticed what I noticed. Andrew deliberately lowered his lance and refused to touch the Duke's nephew."

"I saw that myself," broke in Tescelin. "What do you deduce from it?"

"Ranier was silent. The Duke flashed around on him and growled, "Speak man, and speak straight. No more of your diplomatic dodges."

At this juncture Seguin arose and approaching the Duke and Tescelin said, "That's where the embarrassment comes in. Ranier and I have talked it over and concluded that only one of two motives could have prompted the lad; and no matter which it was, it shows him young, very young; too young to be knighted. So you see, Your Excellency, the Seneschal's insistence on Andrew's age was not exactly a diplomatic dodge."

"What are the two motives?" came the gruff question as thunder gathered on the forehead of the Duke.

"Well," smiled Seguin, "what could have prompted the lad but the fact that Guy de Marcy is a knight and the Duke's nephew?"

"Speak more plainly yet!" barked Hugh in angry command.

"Your Excellency, we judged that the boy was either afraid of the knight or was seeking the favor of the nephew."

Tescelin blanched and his lips closed tight over clinched teeth. The Duke stared for one terrible moment then fell back in his chair and let a roar of derisive laughter smite the ceiling. "So that's what my two worthy counsellors observed and concluded, is it? So that's how keen the eyes and minds of Burgundy's leaders are, eh? Well, you two idiots! Come over here! You, Seguin, sit there," and he pointed to a chair on his right. "You, Rainer, there," and he indicated a chair on his left. "Now, Tescelin, stand where you are and answer every one of my questions briefly, honestly and promptly. Do you understand?"

"I do, Sire," came the immediate and sharp reply.

"Do your boys tilt in their own courtyard?"

"They do, often."

"Do others sometimes joust with them?"

"Occasionally, yes."

"Has my nephew ever ridden against any of your boys?"

"Frequently."

"Has he ever unhorsed any of them?"

"Not to my knowledge."

"Has he ever been unhorsed?"

"He has."

"Who unhorsed him?"

"Andrew."

"How often?"

"Almost as often as they tilted."

On that answer the Duke turned from Tescelin and glaring first to his right then to his left bellowed, "Do my keen and observing counsellors hear? Andrew has unhorsed my worthy nephew almost as often as they have tilted!" Ranier and Seguin shifted uncomfortably in their chairs. The Duke let them writhe a moment or two, then went on, "That's point number one. Now, Tawny, tell us why Guy and Gerard, your oldest sons—and knights of

this Duchy—I want my observant counsellors to note—
why have they stopped tilting against Andrew? Was he
too rough?"

"No, he was too good. He has beaten both of them;
and older brothers do not like to be beaten by younger
brothers."

"I admire their prudence," growled Hugh, and turning to Ranier and Seguin in turn said, "and knights don't
like to be unhorsed by youngsters who have not yet been
dubbed! Do you grasp that, my far seeing ones? That's
point number two. Now, Tawny, tell us: Have you ever
ridden against your boy?"

"Oh, often."

"Has he ever thrown you?"

Tescelin laughed. "No, Your Excellency. He is not
quite up to that yet."

"What do you think of his skill?"

"It's uncanny. He's the quickest, coolest and most
agile of my boys."

"Now tell these two keenly observant counsellors
what you saw in the last tourney. Why did Andrew lower
his lance?"

Tescelin hesitated.

"Out with it, man!" growled the Duke. "It is my will
that they learn a lesson."

"Your Excellency," said Tescelin kindly, "it is not my
purpose to teach Seguin or the Seneschal a lesson. They
fell into error because of an oversight; that's all. We are
all human. They bear no malice toward my boy, and certainly none toward you."

"Are *you* going to teach me, too?" roared the Duke.
"I told these two that I was going to knight your son, and
they implicitly accused me of favoritism. I bring you as a
witness against them, and you begin to speak in their
favor, implying that I am unjust. Who is Duke of Burgundy, anyhow?"

"You are, my Lord."

"Then answer me!" cried the Duke pounding the table before him. "Why did your boy lower his lance as he charged against my nephew?"

"The girth on your nephew's mount had broken. He could have been unhorsed by a puff of wind. My boy saw the situation and refused to take advantage of it. Besides," said Tescelin softly, "my daughter Humbeline was in the grandstand."

Both Ranier and Seguin started noticeably at Tescelin's first sentence. They looked at one another in openeyed amazement. Then the Seneschal sprang from his chair and grasped Tescelin's hand saying, "Tawny-beard, Tawny-beard, I'm grateful for the humiliation." Still holding his hand he turned to the Duke and said, "Knight him, knight him, by all means knight him and make him Seneschal in my place."

"Humph!" grunted Hugh.

"Wait a minute," put in Seguin. "You say Humbeline, your daughter, was in the grandstand, Tawny. What does that add to the case?"

Before Tescelin could answer, Hugh crashed the table again with his fist crying, "Another example of your keen observation! Numbskull, don't you know that Humbeline and Guy are practically engaged?"

Seguin, who was unmoved by the Duke's fury, quietly arose and walking over to Tescelin's side, took his left hand and said, "Left hand is nearest the heart, Tawny. Let me congratulate you on a chivalrous son, a boy who deserves to be dubbed knight if ever any man in the Duchy did. He's a chip off the old block, all right. Like father, like son! And forgive me my foolish judgment."

"Well now," said Hugh as he looked up at Tescelin flanked by the two counsellors, "that's the way I like to see my aides. Are you all agreed that Andrew of Fontaines shall be dubbed knight, even though he is only sixteen?" They nodded and smiled. "And do you two on the outside see that deeds count, not dates, when there is a question of dubbing?"

"We do," confessed Seguin and Ranier.

"And do all three of you begin to respect my judgment of men?"

"We never questioned it, Your Excellency," said Tescelin with a chuckle. "How could we? Just look at the three you have chosen for counsellors."

"Tawny-beard, you always manage to say the soothing word. Come, let's drink to the health and the heroism of our knight-to-be." And with that he grasped a decanter and poured four liberal goblets of his best Burgundy.

A Mother's Smile

To say that Andrew was proud of his knighthood is to understate truth; yet he never swaggered or boasted, he simply carried himself with greater dignity. Congratulations, of course, were heaped upon him, but the greatest thrill he knew was an interior one; it was the secret joy of having been just a wee bit better than his older brothers! Guy and Gerard had been knighted, it is true, and had really earned their honors; but neither of them had knelt in the presence of all the knights of Burgundy to have Burgundy's Duke lay the flat of the sword on their backs at the early age of sixteen! Yet Andrew was not satisfied. He felt that his victory was only a relative one. What he longed for was something absolute; and in the fall of 1111 he felt he had his chance.

The three brothers were at Grancy laying siege to the town, and Andrew was straining at the leash; for he was most anxious to prove himself just a wee bit better than his brothers in actual combat, but the Granceyans would not come out to let him do it. They preferred to remain behind the stout walls of their castles, and this sent young Andrew into an impatient ferment.

While in this seething condition and while he was trying to devise ways of outdoing Guy and Gerard, he met Bernard, who broke in on his planning with the invitation that he come along to Citeaux and become a monk. Andrew looked at his brother coolly and the tiniest scornful curl appeared on his lips as he smiled and said, "Are you serious, Bernard?"

"Of course," replied Bernard in evident surprise.

Then Andrew laughed. It was a hard laugh and there was harshness in it. Bernard could read the thoughts that were flashing through his brother's mind as he kept on laughing his high, disdainful laugh. "Oh, I know I'm not a knight...," began Bernard.

"No, you're not even in the army!" snapped Andrew. "Why, Bernard. You're ridiculous! Do you realize that my knighthood is but fresh upon me? Do you realize that that town yonder gives me my first chance to prove my mettle? Do you realize that those walls are going to be shattered or scaled and that I'm going to be among the first to set my foot in that town? Do you realize that my life.... But no! Of course you don't. You couldn't. Excuse my outburst. But do understand me when I say that your proposition is not only laughable, it's positively ridiculous and completely absurd! To give up arms at any time is stupid; but to give them up at this moment would be nothing short of monstrous. I understand your mind, Bernard. Try to understand mine. You and I live in entirely different worlds, have altogether different ideals, think different thoughts. Yes, I understand you, and now I hope you understand me. Good day!" And with that Andrew, who had delivered the last part of his speech with all the candor, coolness and condescending pity of an utterly superior being, turned on his heel and walked away.

Bernard was torn between the temptation to laugh at the airs his younger brother assumed and the temptation to go after him, wheel him around and drive some sense into him. He yielded to neither, however: first, because Andrew strode away too quickly; secondly, because Uncle Gaudry appeared on the scene just then to take all of Bernard's attention.

Andrew gave no more thought to Bernard or his proposal. It was so extravagant an invitation as to appear farcical to the young knight. He would not condescend to become indignant or angry about it; he would not even lower himself to be disgusted. He simply haughtily ignored it and went about the manly business of planning ways and means to outdo the knights of the family. "Let Bernard ride home!" was Andrew's final thought on the matter.

That was the first encounter. But Bernard came back! He met Andrew just as the latter was leaving a group of veteran knights who had been reminiscing. The lad had heard tales of bravery that had made his heart pound. As he walked along now his brain was racing and his imagination piling up fancy on fancy about what he could do if...and what he would do when.... He was brought back to reality by the sharp command, "Andrew, come here!" It was Bernard commanding.

The young knight obeyed, for he was not fully out of his reverie. Bernard grasped his two arms, shook him slightly and said, "You look upon Uncle Gaudry as a worthy knight, don't you? A brave man? A wise man?"

"I do," came the quick reply from the now aroused knight.

"Well, he's brave enough and wise enough and knight enough to join me. We are going to give ourselves to God."

"What? Uncle Gaudry?"

"Yes, Uncle Gaudry. He's going to come to Citeaux with me; and so are you if you have any sense."

"Now, Bernard, listen! We've been over that already. I'm a knight. I'm going to be...."

"You're going to be a monk; do you hear? If you have any love for God..."

"I'm going to be.... Oh! Look!—It's Mother!—She smiles!" Andrew kept staring over Bernard's shoulder in awe.

Bernard was lost for a moment. The evident rapture of Andrew struck him speechless. He saw the reverence, awe and wonder in his brother's gaze and the light of love in his eyes; he turned to see what had so transfixed him, but he saw only space. Andrew murmured softly, "Mother! She smiles. Mother! She smiles." Bernard turned and looked again, but saw nothing. Then when Andrew said, "It's Mother. She smiles," for the third time, Bernard snapped at him saying, "Yes, and her presence here means only one thing: Come along to Citeaux."

"Yes," said Andrew. "She smiles more sweetly. Mother, I'll go. Oh! She's gone! Bernard, she's gone! Mother's gone!"

"I know it," said Bernard calmly, "and it's time for you and me to go. Come let's ride home." And he started to lead the young knight away. Andrew offered no slightest resistance, but walked with his brother to the wood where the horses were tied. He was shaking with nervous excitement and only asked, "Did you see her, Bernard? Did you see Mother? She smiled so sweetly. I'll have to go. I'll have to go just to please her."

When All Glamor Is Gone

Andrew kept the promise he made that day, but it almost broke his heart. When he took off his suit of armor and hung up his shield he wept. He felt as if the sun of his life had burned out and nothing but blackness lay ahead. He took furious rides through the woods and on the highways, driving his charger until he was flecked with foam, and though he came home physically spent, the burning was still felt in his brain and the awful ache in his heart. For days he was inconsolable. Then Bernard took him aside and read to him the list of all those who had promised to go to Citeaux. As knight after knight was named Andrew gasped and gasped. When Bernard had finished he jumped up and shouted, "Great heavens, Bernard, that reads like the list for a tournament!"

"And what do you think we're riding to—a burial?" replied Bernard with a laugh. "Let me tell you, Andrew, you never tilted in a tournament like the one to which we ride. Call it 'The tournament of love,' and remember it was your lady's smile that sent you into it to triumph."

"I won't forget, Bernard. I can't forget. I saw Mother as clearly that day as I see you now. She wants me to go, so I'll go; and I'll stay! Give me a look at the list again, will you?"

"You can have it," said Bernard handing it over to him. "Study it and see if you can be a better knight than anyone on it. You're traveling in select company, Andrew. Be prepared!" And he walked away leaving the younger brother engrossed in the list of names.

That Andrew was prepared is evidenced by the fact that he flung himself into the new knighthood with the identical abandon that had marked his days in Burgundy's army. He learned quickly, for he was young and very enthusiastic. Nothing seemed to bother him. The long hours of Office, the equally long, but more wearying ones at work, the silence, the diet, the seeming sterility of it all fazed our young knight not a whit. He went through the year of novitiate with so much relish that even the wise Abbot, Stephen Harding, was a bit uneasy. He knew that the glamor of the new life held the growing boy in its spell, but he wondered and worried about his reactions to it all when the glamor had gone. So just before vow day Stephen summoned the youngster and said, "How do you feel about taking your vows, my son?"

Andrew looked at him and a radiant light leaped into his eyes as he said, "Reverend Father, I thought I was anxious for the day of my knighting to dawn. I thought that the sands had stopped falling in the hour glass the morning I was to kneel before Burgundy's Duke and have the flat of the sword laid on my back. But I see now that I did not know what anxiety was. Now it is that I am learning how slow time can be. How do I feel about taking my vows? Why, Reverend Father, I cannot wait for the day; I have told those vows to God a hundred times in the past week."

Stephen smiled. "You do not find this life hard, do you, my boy?"

"Hard? Why, no, Reverend Father. I have found it most interesting. I enjoy the work. I love to sing. The day goes so quickly I hardly have time to think. The time we have for reading and study is too short. There are so many things I want to learn about God and how to be a real religious."

"Don't you miss the excitement of the camp life; the rivalry of the tourneys; the lure of greater honors?"

"Oh, I did in the beginning a little bit. There were moments when I thought I had made a mistake; moments when this life seemed empty and foolish. But I remembered my mother's smile. That steadied me. Then I'd look at the rest of our band of knights. They helped me considerably."

"What was it—a case of misery loving company?"

Andrew smiled. "No, Reverend Father, not exactly. I really think it was a case of an actor loving an audience. Since I've been here I've looked into myself and I find that I play to the grandstand a great deal."

"Play to the grandstand? What in the world do you mean?"

"I mean that if there wasn't a goodly gathering in the grandstand at a tourney, I wouldn't make half the effort I was capable of. I mean that I am conscious of eyes and greedy for applause."

"But you don't get that here...."

"Don't you though! Oh, Reverend Father, applause can come from more than hands. There is a glance of tribute, there is a look of envy, there is an effort at emulation; all these constitute applause for the glutton for applause; and I'm a glutton."

"I see," smiled the Abbot. "You mean that you indulged in a sort of rivalry even here."

"Indeed, I did. Bernard said that we were riding to 'the tournament of love,' and I resolved to tilt better than the best of them. If I did it for the ladies, why not for the Lord? If I was anxious to win the eye of the Duke, why not the eye of God? You see, Reverend Father, my mother taught us how to supernaturalize the natural. It was a wonderful lesson. But here everything is so supernaturalized that I had to reverse her teaching and naturalize the supernatural. It simplifies matters considerably."

"Yes," said Stephen thoughtfully, "you've told me that before. I know how you've learned from watching the older monks then imitating them. You say that is how you learned to walk correctly, ride a horse, handle a sword and a spear. Andrew, you are a keen observer, and from observation you've gone to imitation. That's a sound practice as long as your models are good. Never forget what I have always insisted upon...Christ is your Model. Observe Him with the same keenness and you are a real contemplative; then after observation imitate Him with the same fidelity and you'll be what He wants you to be and what I pray that you become—a replica of the God-Man. Man is imitative by nature. I like to think that when Christ said, 'Learn of me,' He was really saying, 'Use your natural instinct.' But I sent for you today to teach you a more homely lesson."

"I'm anxious to learn any truth, Reverend Father, be it homely, ugly or beautiful."

Stephen smiled. He was used to Andrew's generous ways and his clever turns on words. He even encouraged it from time to time by retorting. Now he said, "Truths are sometimes homely, Andrew, but never ugly. But now to talk more plainly, you're in the throes of an enthusiasm at present. What surprises me is that the enthusiasm has lasted so long. You came to a new life and made of it a new adventure. You were aglow with eagerness and energy from the first. I understand how the choir, the work and even the routine of the day is filled with attraction for one of your temperament. The older monks inspire you with awe. Those who entered with you stimulate you to rivalry. Andrew, my son, you've lived for a year on the glamor of it all. I know it is a grace from God and I know you have cooperated with it generously. But I've got to tell you now that the glamor will go!"

"Do you really think so, Reverend Father?"

"I know so, my son. I know that a day will come when the choir will weary you and seem a tedious routine...."

"Don't say that, Reverend Father."

"I've got to, son. It happens to everyone at some time or other; and forewarned is forearmed. One day you'll look at your toil-worn and calloused palms and say, 'What in the world is the son of a nobleman doing with such hands?' You'll look at the menial labor that is your life and ask yourself if God ever meant noblemen to demean themselves thus."

"I'm more than the son of a nobleman, Reverend Father, I'm a son of God."

"Good!" exclaimed the Abbot. "Very good! That is the *one* answer; the only answer! But when all glamor is gone, it is an answer that is very difficult to find. But you've given it yourself now, and I'm glad. Burn that realization into your being, then take all the consequences that flow from it, and I won't worry about you."

"Just what do you mean, Reverend Father?"

"Andrew, my son, you've lived with men of breeding all your life. Refinement, culture, courtesy have been in the very air you breathed. Gentlemanliness, kindness, consideration for others was met with on all sides. Now, all that is changed; and in the future will be even more greatly changed. Some of your companions, your brothers in Christ, will lack breeding and will not only appear, but will actually be boorish; they will have no sense of refinement, delicacy or gentlemanliness, no knowledge of the niceties of conduct or of sensitivity to consideration. That's going to bite into a nature like yours. You like to have finesse in everything. There is a certain native neatness to you, and you've cultivated it and developed it to a high degree; why, even your speech is neat. Not all men are like that. Many of your future brothers will be anything but that. You're going to suffer from them."

"I think I'm ready for it, Reverend Father," said Andrew as the Abbot momentarily paused.

"I know you're willing, my son; but I'm not sure that you're prepared. And that is my whole purpose at the moment: to prepare you for the day when all glamor is gone. Now is the time to prepare, and there is only one preparation: Be mindful of Christ! Be mindful of Christ!"

"How do you mean, Reverend Father?"

"There is the crucifix and there is the tabernacle. Study both. They are the only tangible justification for our life. They will speak to you much more forcefully than ever I could. Listen to what they say and you'll learn how to act when all glamor is gone. There is nothing attractive about the cross in itself; there is nothing attractive about being buried in bread either; but Christ allowed soldiers to nail Him to one, and He still allows men to call Him down into the other. And you know why. Love must give. Love must be near. Oh, my son, saturate yourself with Jesus Christ. He is your only salvation!

"The dull monotonous routine of our life can be maddening unless we recall the eighteen years of dull monotonous routine He lived in Nazareth. The lack of refinement in our companions can so play on our sensitivities that we are ready to shriek; and we shall shriek unless we remember how rough, uncouth and unpolished were the fishermen and the tax-gatherers. Your nobility of birth and breeding will prove a hindrance to you unless you remember that by His Blood we have all been born again and made divinely noble. My son, you've got to be steeped in Jesus Christ if you will live and die a true Cistercian. There is no other way. He explains all things, all persons, all happenings. He is the answer to every question, doubt and difficulty. He is the reason for living and the reason for dying. He furnishes the only solution to the puzzling thing you are prepared to do tomorrow. He is the one key to the whole perplexing situation. Why should you make such a wholesale dedication of your life? Why should you swear to God to live and die in this swampland? Why should you bind yourself to a living death by vow? Only because He did it before you, and still does it! Only because there was a crucifixion and there is transubstantiation. Do you understand?"

"Perfectly, Reverend Father. It's what I've been doing more or less."

"I know it, my son, but there can be no more or less about it. I want your Christ-consciousness to be greater if possible than your self-consciousness. I want you to be absorbed by and in Jesus. Andrew, my boy, listen! You've lived a life of rivalry. Emulation is in your blood and bone. You always wanted to go higher. You did. In the world you succeeded. You were knighted at an exceptionally early age. That shows spirit. Keep that spirit. It is a gift from God.

"But now you've got to face this fact: you may spend the rest of your life in the ranks. You may never know what it is to be a superior. But that does not mean that your natural spirit of rivalry, your tendency, yes, your passion to emulate is to be stifled, or to die the death. No! Make your life a life of rivalry; but let it be rivalry with Jesus Christ! See if you can equal Him, strive to outdo Him in going down. He came down to earth; He went down to Nazareth; He went down to death; He went down to Limbo; and He still comes down and can be found under the lowly guise of bread and wine. When the natural glamor has all gone—and it will go—then create a supernatural glamor by making this Cistercian life a romance, a rivalry with Christ, a tournament, as Bernard calls it, a tournament of love. Do you think you can do that?"

"I most certainly can try, Reverend Father; and with the help of God's grace I'll succeed."

"Good. But just remember this: what sounds so fanciful is factual. This life is a rivalry with Christ or it is insanity! But that rivalry must be carried on in the ordinary, everyday events of our life. You said something about an actor loving an audience. It sounded original, and yet I think St. Paul has something about a 'cloud of witnesses,' hasn't he?"

"Yes," smiled Andrew, "he has."

"Then be an actor, my son, and be ever mindful of that audience. Be an actor and remember the character you are to portray—you are to reproduce Jesus Christ. But once again let me insist: you do that in the ordinary events of everyday life. There is nothing really dramatic about our life; actually it appears drab; yet it is the greatest drama ever enacted. And if you will be conscious of the part you play, you'll come to love routine, to love rough, uncultured, uncouth companions; you'll come to love the weariness of the work, the silence, the sufferings, the solitude and all that is entailed in that consecration and dedication that you make tomorrow."

"Oh, Reverend Father, I'm so glad you talked as plainly as you did. Don't you see what you've done? You've repeated the lesson my mother taught me. You say take my nature as it is and use it for God. You know my keenness for rivalry. You don't say: Stifle it. No! You say: Develop it; but make it a rivalry with Christ. Oh! That's just like Mother; and isn't it something like what I have been doing, though I called it naturalizing the supernatural?"

"It is, my son. But my point is that Christ must glow when glamor goes."

"I will pray. I will work. I will study to make my life a tilting with Jesus; a contest, a rivalry with Christ. Oh, I'm so grateful for the wider horizons you have given me and the new vistas you've thrown open."

Stephen blessed him then and when the eager youth had left his room, the Abbot turned to the crucifix on the wall and said, "Do you think he caught the full force of what I was trying to teach him, Jesus? I was trying to say that this life can be agony and often is a crucifixion, but that it is always glorious as long as we remember You."

Thirty Years on the King's Highway

In 1113 Abbot Stephen Harding had some doubt about Andrew's grasp on the lesson he tried to teach him about looking to Christ when glamor had gone, but in 1143 St. Stephen Harding could not have the slightest semblance of doubt; for in that year he could look down from heaven upon a son who for thirty years had walked the royal road traced by Christ and never once faltered. He must have chuckled as the echoes of Andrew's answers to an aged knight reached him.

Stephen had sent Andrew with Bernard and the rest of his brothers to found Clairvaux. Bernard had made him porter of the monastery, and porter of the monastery he remained from 1114 to 1144. That was worse than staying 'in the ranks,' as Stephen had hinted; and it was far from being a superior; but Andrew had made of it what Stephen had suggested—a rivalry with Jesus Christ. Of this Andrew made no secret, and by his outspokenness startled many a visitor.

In 1143 an aged nobleman, whose step was slow, but whose erect carriage and direct, bold and commanding manner of address bespoke the knight, came to the gate of Clairvaux. He looked at Andrew for a moment, then asked, "Do you know me?"

"Do I know you?" came the answer. "Yes, and your every peculiarity. Do you still feint at the heart, then strike to the visor?"

The knight laughed and holding out his hand said, "Andrew of Fontaines, I'm glad to see you."

"And Andrew of Clairvaux is not a bit sorry to look upon Charles the Deceiver. Won't you come in? Our Abbot is away at the moment...."

"Oh, I don't want to trouble you, Andrew; I'm on my way to Troyes; I've ridden far today and I'm not as young as I used to be. I'd appreciate the hospitality of the monastery for the night."

"The night? You can stay a fortnight if you will. Come in. You're welcome."

"Thank you. But I won't trouble you for that length of time; however, since I am here, I am going to find out a few things. The first is: Aren't you sorry you left the knighthood?"

Charles had walked in and seated himself while Andrew was making a sign to a brother to stable the aged knight's horse. Andrew came in smiling thinking to himself that thirty years had not changed the arrogant, incisive and derisive Charles one bit. He knew he was in for an interminable series of slurring questions unless he put his guest on the defensive, so he cheerily asked, "If a Burgundian knight goes to Jerusalem and lives there, does he cease to be a knight? Or better still: When Charles the Deceiver rides to Troyes, out of his own Duchy, does he cease to be Charles the Deceiver?"

"No," answered Charles quietly, "but what are you driving at?"

"You." Andrew's tone implied that he was ready for whatever was to come. "You asked a question that shows that you forget the axiom: Once a knight, always a knight. I never left knighthood, Charles, for the simple reason that knighthood cannot be left; it is not a mere ceremony or a suit of mail that you put on from without; no! it is a growth from within, which, once cultivated and matured, never dies. Didn't it ever strike you, Charles, that dubbing is quite similar to Baptism? It stamps a character on your very soul. Of course, just as some men will stain their baptismal character or allow it to tarnish, so there are some knights who will insist on performing unknightly deeds. But that does not change matters; the stamp is still there; always there, Charles, to their honor or dishonor. Once a knight, always a knight."

The guest shifted sideways in his chair, crossed his knees, cupped his chin in his left hand and said, "Yes, and once a fiery talker, always a fiery talker. You were quick-tongued as a youngster, and now you are—how old are you anyhow, Andrew?"

"If you reckon by the years, I'm just two below half a hundred; but if you reckon by all the foolish questions I've been asked, I must be a few centuries older than Methuselah."

"I see, Sir Knight, since you insist you are still a knight; well since you don't like foolish questions, let me put you a wise one. Aren't you sorry that you have lived a delusion?"

Andrew had learned many things in the thirty years that he had opened and shut Clairvaux's gate, but one of the most important was to measure his man quickly, and just as quickly to suit his own attitude to the man. He had known Charles before, and from the two questions now asked he saw that he had not changed his mental modes in the slightest. He was still a scoffer. So Andrew very quietly asked, "What's the delusion, Charles?"

"Why, this! This whole thing! The life you've led. You spent a few years in a swamp, then buried yourself in this Valley of Wormwood and called it a life. Why, man, you've never lived! This is not life. This is death! Yes, you're dead and have been for years. Why, every time I pass the castle of Fontaines I cross myself. I'm afraid of being bewitched as were you and your brothers and even your noble father. Oh, that house is haunted all right. God never meant you to live as you have lived. Never! You, a knight before you were seventeen; and now what have you been for all these years? I call it a delusion to be polite; to be exact, I think it is a derangement."

"That's right, Charles," said Andrew quite calmly. "Derangement it is, and delusion it has been. But what I think you are trying to say is that myself and my family are nothing but a pack of fools. Isn't that it?"

"Well, to speak plainly, yes! What else can any sensible man call you?"

"And those more than five hundred monks back there in the monastery," asked Andrew with a gesture to the buildings farther down the Valley, "are they all fools, too?"

"More than five hundred?" gasped Charles, but recovering his disdainful attitude quickly, he said, "Yes, if they were all nobles, as were you and your brothers."

"And what are we now, Charles, serfs?"

"Well, you're not nobles! Nobles do not live like this. They realize that God has stratified society; and they stay on the upper crust where God has placed them. This life is degrading; and God never meant that. He meant us to ennoble ourselves, not to ignoble ourselves."

"Is that so?" inquired Andrew. "Well, didn't He teach His lesson in a peculiar manner?"

"What do you mean?" said Charles as he swung around in his chair.

"Well," said Andrew very calmly, "He said, 'Come, follow me,' and when you accept His invitation, the first place he leads you is to a cave for cattle and shows you Himself there between an ox and an ass. Remember, Charles, the Babe of Bethlehem is the God of the living and the dead."

Andrew was showing more warmth now. "The next place He will lead you will be Egypt, a foreign land, which means that you'll know the loneliness of exile. Then back He'll bring you to Nazareth, and He'll keep you there practically all His life. Have you ever realized what it means to be a Nazarene, Charles? It does not bespeak nobility as you conceive it. No, not in the slightest! It means to be looked down upon and despised. And from this despised town, where will Christ lead you? To a criminal's cross on the rocky hill called Calvary. Jesus Christ, Charles, was born like a beggar and died like a thief. Do you know why? Do you know why? To show knights the way to chivalry, nobles the way to true nobility and men the way to God! Listen, Charles, I have seldom been out of this monastery in the last thirty years and yet I call myself a highwayman. Do you hear? A highwayman. Yes, I have been for the best part of my life a highwayman on the King's Highway. Call it delusion if you will, or even derangement; but admit that it is a happy delusion and a blessed derangement, for it has sent me stumbling in the footsteps of the Red Cross Knight of Calvary, the Noble of all nobles, the very Son of God."

"Aw, you're talking romance! What have you got to show for your thirty years as highwayman?"

"What He had after thirty-three years as wayfarer—a clear conscience, a happy heart, a hope of reward, the satisfaction of having done the will of my heavenly Father."

"You talk like a fanatic."

"I talk like a follower of Jesus Christ; a Christian, Charles; do you understand? A Christian, an adopted son of God, a brother of Him who walked Judean hills and wrote His own love story in flaming letters of blood on the hill we call Golgotha."

"Love story. Bah! Talk facts!"

"I'm talking the realest fact of all history. Jesus Christ the Son of God loved you, lived for you, was a baby for you, an exile for you, the carpenter's son for you, Judea's wonder-worker for you, and then—and then, Charles, he became a mangled, bloodless corpse for you! That's the love story that makes Clairvaux the home of the chivalrous, makes this delusion and derangement wisdom, and your slurs pitiable. I pity you, Charles. You're a man well on in years now, and yet you talk as if you did not know yourself or your Christ."

"Never mind me," came the haughty reply. "I'm talking about you. Your brother Bernard has achieved something. He at least has made himself known. This sort of thing is all right for him. He would never have made a knight. He had not the build. But you and all the others? What sort of madness seized you, anyhow, to induce you to bury yourselves alive in this place? No one ever hears of you."

"Charles, you're using the wrong measuring stick. Manhood is not to be measured by a knight's spear. No! Jesus Christ changed all that. There is only one measuring rod now; only one. It is the cross of Christ. Bernard without his fame would still be a follower of Christ, whereas I with my knighthood, and that alone, might not have been."

"But what does it get you? You've been gate keeper for thirty years, you say. What a position for a son of a noble and a knight of proud Burgundy! And what have you done for your fellow man?"

Andrew looked out the window to see how far the sun had thrown the shadow of the church's steeple. He found it much farther to the east than he had expected, so he turned to Charles quickly and said, "It is much later than I thought. So, I'll have to be very brief, Charles, but I hope not one bit obscure."

"You're seldom obscure, and you're almost always brief," said the aged knight.

"Well," resumed Andrew, "you've asked questions that are very familiar to me. I've heard every one of them ringing in my head, pounding at my heart, beating a loud tattoo, demanding answer. They got their answer; for a wise old man told me once that I would hear these very questions and he told me where to look for their reply. Perhaps you've heard of him? His name was Stephen Harding.''

"I remember. He was Abbot of Citeaux.''

"That's he. Well, he told me that when such questions rose I was to look to the cross and the tabernacle. I did; and I found my answers. Charles, Bethlehem was obscure, Nazareth was obscure, why, even Jerusalem was comparatively obscure, for Rome was mistress of the world. Yet, Jesus Christ saved mankind by such obscurity. I don't mind being buried alive when I think of that. 'What have I got to show for my years?' you ask. The answer is: Nothing; absolutely nothing! Nothing that you can see, weigh, measure or count. Yes, I've kept this gate for thirty years and I have as much to show for it in the material line as Jesus Christ had to show for His thirty-three years on earth. But I hope to have something like what He had to show in the spiritual line. Do you know what that was, Charles? Well, I'll tell you—it was the salvation of the world!''

"What!'' gasped Charles.

"Yes, I said it. The salvation of the world is my aim; for if I read the Gospel aright, the world is saved by those who do nothing! Look at the nothingness of Bethlehem's cave! Look at the nothingness of the thirty years of the hidden life! Look at the nothingness of the cross! When Jesus could have been preaching and teaching and showing men the way to God, where was He and what did He do? Bethlehem, Egypt and Nazareth are your answer. And when He was on the cross, what did He do? Did He preach and teach? No! He prayed and suffered. That's all. Did He come down when they taunted Him to? No. He stayed there until He died.

"And, Charles, look at the obscurity, silence and nothingness of the tabernacle! Isn't it frightening? Yet, He saved mankind by His crib and His cross, and He sanctifies man by His sacrament. I am walking in His footsteps, Charles. I have silence, suffering, obscurity and prayer. With Him, in Him and through Him I am striving to save the world. I am a highwayman on the Highway of the King of kings, and by being such I'm aiming to be a savior. If I am living a delusion, as you say; then Christ must have been a dreamer! But I don't think even Charles the Deceiver will dare say that."

"No! No!" exclaimed Charles hastily. "I don't say that. Never. And while I don't fully understand all that you've just said, I must admit that you sound like a man who was fully convinced of the righteousness of his stand."

"You don't fully understand, Charles, because you have never studied the crucifix and you take the tabernacle for granted. You're unappreciative because you've never been penetrating. But come, I'll take you over to church. You can assist at Vespers and pray to the Light of the World to shed light on His world."

"What are you trying to do, make one who came to scoff remain to pray?"

"That's it, Charles, and I would ask you to pray for me. Pray that I stay on the King's Highway and overtake Christ."

"Why, do you find it hard?"

"Well, I'm always saying, 'Nunc coepi'—Now I begin; and I have to accent both the adverb and the verb! But, Charles, you just ask God to give me the strength and courage to keep on saying, 'Nunc coepi' until it is time to say, 'Nunc dimittis'; for if I do that I'm sure that the King will be pleased with His highwayman. Come, let's go over." And Charles went.

Nunc Dimittis

Tescelin's eagle made his last and highest flight, and Charles the Deceiver's fool ended his delusion in 1144. In that year he not only caught up to Christ but was actually caught up by Christ, and his, *"Nunc dimittis"* on earth was his, *"Nunc coepi"* of heaven.

Bernard was away negotiating peace between Louis VII of France and Theobald, Count of Champagne. Bartholomew was Abbot of La Ferté and Nivard, Prior of de Buzay. So Andrew died practically alone. He did not mind, however, for this made him the perfect highwayman. His King had died practically alone; could His follower expect anything different? The King's Highway leads all to the lonely hill of Calvary, but once over that hill, they find dawn breaking on the Eternal Vale!

The Menology of the Cistercian Order calls our gate keeper "Blessed Andrew" and makes mention of him on April 5. The Bollandists give him no other title than, "Brother of St. Bernard." But don't you like to think of him as "The King's Highwayman" with his ever ready, *"Nunc coepi"* and his replies that sometimes scorched?

THE GUILELESS ONE

"A difficult thing
for men with minds to do. .."

Humbeline's heart was like the sky—heavy, low, and very dismal. In the late afternoon of New Year's Day in 1112 she had come to her room in an effort to throw off the loneliness that seemed to be closing in on her. She had meant to busy herself with some correspondence, but had been drawn to the window by the sheer beauty of the falling snow; and there she had been held spellbound by the soundless, ceaseless and seemingly endless fall of hush-filled whiteness. The storm had been noisy in the night, but as the day wore on the winds died and all the world was held in the solemn stillness of the fast-falling flakes.

"How dead that courtyard seems!" muttered Humbeline to herself as she noted how the branches drooped under their weight of wet whiteness. Looking out over the crested walls of the castle she saw the smooth, still and unbroken surface stretching to the dim hills and the far forests. "Oh, what a lonely waste!" she exclaimed. Then peering up through the thickening greyish flakes to see if there was a break in the skies, she was met with nothing but murkiness. "Beautiful! Beautiful! Beautiful!"

she breathed. "I can't deny that. It is beautiful; but it is a stark, cold and lonely beauty. I never felt so alone in all my life. Nor did I ever hear such a hush. It seems as if the whole world were dead and I were left alone in a wilderness of white."

Just then from out of the north there swept over the snow-crested walls and into the silent courtyard a flock of restless snowbirds. They alighted suddenly, nervously flitted here and there, hopped about, chirped sharply, then took off to the farthest tree by the postern gate. Humbeline felt an impulse to fling wide her windows to welcome in these vagabonds of the storm, the only live things in a dead, white world. She would have yielded to her impulse, but just then there came a knocking on her door and her father's voice was heard calling, "Humbeline." In a few, quick, graceful steps she was across the room, and opening the door she said, "Won't you come in, Father dear, and share with me the loneliness and loveliness of this storm? I was just about to invite a whole flock of snowbirds in when you knocked. They are down by the postern gate. Come, see."

"I hope I make a good substitute for the finch family," said her father as he followed her to the window.

"Oh! There they go! Across the wall and out into that wilderness of white. They seem such homeless, harried things, I'd love to take them in," cried Humbeline as her father watched the numerous flock sweep across the wall and become lost amid the thickly falling flakes.

"Well, Little Queen, you might learn from the snowbirds that storm time is time to flock together. Why hide yourself away up here while downstairs a blazing hearth, Nivard and myself will make you forget the snows?"

"Ah, Father dear, I'm lonely today. More lonely than I can tell. And nature is in sympathy with my mood. Won't you sit here a while, watch the lovely snowfall and answer me a few questions?"

"Gladly, child," said Tescelin as he took the chair Humbeline had drawn over for him. "Nivard was reading by the hearth. If he gets lonely, he'll come up. Now tell me: What is it that distresses you? Is it the fact that Guy de Marcy left so early? He had a long ride ahead of him, you must remember; and the storm was getting worse."

"Oh, no, Father. It is not he. I think it was darling of him to ride through the snowfall just to say, 'Happy New Year' to us all. I'm lonely for Bernard and the boys...."

"Ah!" exclaimed her father, "I thought so. I guess you and 'Big Eyes' were more brother and sister than you suspected."

"Oh! How I miss him, Father. But tell me: Is the world as bad as he pictured it?"

Her father looked out at the storm for some minutes before he answered. "I don't know how badly he pictured it for you, Humbeline; but I can tell you it is pretty bad. The Church is not the unit she should be. Henry V of Germany did a sacrilegious thing a year ago when he forced our Holy Father Pascal to grant him the right of investitures. The princes and people of Italy and of our own France will not stand for it. They know what the great Gregory VII battled for, and they feel sure that this concession was extorted from Pascal. A schism looms, I'm afraid."

"Oh, Bernard did not draw as frightful a picture as that," cried Humbeline. "And yet," she added, "it was more frightful! What he lamented was the condition of religion among religious, and especially among the hierarchy. He said something I find almost unbelievable. He says that there are many in the Church now who, after being raised from a mean condition to an honorable rank, from penury to affluence, have become so proud that they forget their former state and even disdain to acknowledge their humble parents. Is that possible, Father?"

"H-m-m-m," murmured her father, "what else did he say?"

"He said there are some wealthy persons who aspire to all kinds of ecclesiastical honors, and as soon as they have changed their dress but not their morals, congratulate themselves on their sanctity and attribute to their own merit what they have purchased with their own money—the honors of the rank."

"Did Bernard say that?"

"He did. I was arguing with him about his proposal to go to Citeaux. I said that such exaggeration was unnecessary. His only reply was a number of facts that shocked. Why he even said that the vain woman is now outdone in her own special art by religious who look more to costliness in matters of dress than to use or necessity."

"Where did he learn such things?"

"I don't know. He was always an observant and reflective lad. He cited Suger, the King's favorite, as a horrible example of what religious are becoming. He says poverty is gone because humility has been abandoned."

"He's down to bedrock there," mused Tescelin. "The boy is deeper than I thought. Poverty has gone, Humbeline, from many a religious house; and of course, that means ruin. Humility is a rare virtue. Bernard is right. But I never thought along those lines exactly; my eyes have been on the powers that rule states."

"Oh, Bernard gave me enough about them, too. But again he arose, or descended—whichever you prefer—to the principle behind it all. Henry V of Germany is ambition and avarice incarnate; but he, according to Bernard, is nothing but the logical conclusion or natural growth from feudalism. Bernard says the Church is enslaved, enfieffed, nothing but a vassal."

"That's what she was becoming. But a great man saw that long before Bernard was born. In fact, it was just at the time I married your mother. In 1076, Gregory VII excommunicated Henry IV, father of the present emperor; and for the very reason Bernard asserts. He was treating the Church as his vassal and the Papacy as his pawn. By that act Gregory started a reform that shook our whole system of government. The grant extorted from Pascal last year, if universally accepted, will throw us back to where we were when Henry's father looked upon the Pope as his chaplain and the hierarchy as his lieges. But it won't be accepted. It isn't accepted now. And I heard that the Pope has summoned a Council at the Lateran for next March."

"Then Bernard is right in going to Citeaux."

"Why do you say that?"

"Because he claims that the only battering ram that will ever break down the towering walls of wealth, arrogance, ambition and avarice is the battering ram of poverty wielded by men who are humble. He says a frontal attack must be made, and the only ones he can see who are ready to make it are the religious of Citeaux. There, he says, poverty and humility are supreme."

"It's sound strategy, Little Queen, very sound."

"But, Father dear, don't you mind the fact that he has taken all your boys? Nivard is downstairs now; but you won't hold him here with a span of horses when he grows a little older. Mark my words."

Tescelin turned from the snow and looked long at the troubled face of his beautiful daughter. At last he gently asked, "Isn't that the thought that has brought on your awful loneliness today, Humbeline? Hasn't my Little Queen been grieving more for me than for herself?"

"Well...yes, Father, I suppose I have. It seems so cruel to you. I can look around and see other lords whose lives are blessed in their sons. The upper stretches of their years are made golden by the prowess and presence of their stalwart boys. Yours were going to be that way until Bernard... "

"No, Humbeline, stop there, and listen to me," broke in Tescelin. "This is New Year's Day. I've made a resolution to be God-minded this year. You give me a chance to put my resolution into effect right away. Now tell me: Who is sending this snow? Who could have fashioned those crystals of white fluffiness? Only God. You know that. He and He alone is behind everything and everyone. You call Bernard and your brothers 'my boys.' You must never forget, Humbeline, that they are mine only as a loan. In absolute truth they are God's boys! Yes, God's boys who have been entrusted to me for a time. It is my God-given duty to see to it that they get to eternity. And you know how that is done—only by obeying His word and His will. I'm lonely today, Little Queen; very lonely. But there is joy in my loneliness, for I feel sure that Bernard and all with him at Chatillon-sur-Seine preparing to go to Citeaux, are there in answer to God's call."

"Oh but, Father, it seems so useless!" broke in Humbeline. "What a waste of talent. Bernard promised so much. Why bury such riches? Why hide such light? Why waste such lives? Oh, Citeaux looks like a sepulcher to me. Could God mean that?"

"Little Queen, there are several ways of answering that objection. It looms large to most minds, I know; but that is because we are creatures of sense. We want to see and feel and handle and count results. We want tangible return for our every effort. But you believe in the efficacy of prayer, don't you?"

"Of course I do, Father! What a question!"

"Then why object to a life of prayer? Why call it inefficacious?"

Humbeline gasped. Her lips parted and she stared in amazement. "Why, Father," she finally exclaimed, "how simple, yet how substantial an answer! It's complete. Nothing more need be said. If prayer is efficacious, why not a life of prayer? I never thought of it at all. Perhaps it's because I've never thought of a life completely dedicated to prayer."

"Nor would I have, Humbeline, if Bernard had not decided to go. You see, I thought the life at Citeaux an utter waste, too. But as I was staring at the snow-capped Juras one day last Fall, shortly after the boys had decided to go, I learned a lesson that changed my whole outlook. Could anything seem more useless than those snow-capped mountains, I asked myself. And I answered, No! Yet this Golden Slope of ours would be anything but Golden Slope if seemingly useless snow did not rest on those mountains. Our grapes, our grain, our orchards with their blossoms and fruit are due to the seemingly useless flakes that fall and rest on the Jura caps. Life, Humbeline, life comes to you and me and thousands in this valley because there is seemingly useless snow on mountain peaks. You see the application. The Cistercians, though buried in a swamp, are the seemingly useless snow on spiritual mountain peaks. Grace will gush forth from them and sweep through valley and plain, to render fertile our sterile and dust-dry souls. Isn't it obvious? Why, look at the seeming uselessness of this storm! What good can you see from it?"

"None," said Humbeline. "It only makes me feel more lonely than ever."

"And yet," rejoined Tescelin, "those flakes mean joyous flowers in the spring, blossoms on our vines and trees, and luscious fruit in the fall. Humbeline dear, it has struck me lately that the most powerful forces in nature are either hidden or silent; and I'm sure it is equally true of the super-nature. Just think of the power hidden in the soil and in the silent sun. Growth, Little Queen, growth and all it means to men is soundless and unseen. Water, the life-blood of the earth, and an essential for ourselves, bubbles up from springs we seldom see or hear. While the tremendous energy of the sun and the ever active solar system produces its effects in a perfect hush.

"So I have ceased to worry about the uselessness of silent, hidden Citeaux. God is the one author of nature and the super-nature; and I do not question but what His greatest forces in both realms are hidden and solemnly silent. Our world needs spiritual energies, Humbeline; maybe God will use Bernard and the boys as His hidden instruments."

"Oh but, Father, think of young Bartholomew. He's not sixteen. Could God be calling one so young and to such an inhuman life? My heart aches for him. He is such a guileless, simple, lovable boy."

"I've thought of him, too, Little Queen. In fact, I almost forbade him to go to Chatillon-sur-Seine. But just as I was about to do it, a frightening contrast came to me from out of the Gospel. You remember the story of 'the rich young man,' don't you?"

"The one who 'went away sad because he had great possessions'?"

"That's the one. Think of it, Humbeline, he went away from Jesus! That's a terrifying thought. And after Jesus had said, 'Come, follow me.' Then I thought of that other young man who was working with his father, mending nets, when Jesus came by and called to him. Immediately he left father and nets and became—now listen, Humbeline—and became 'the beloved disciple.' Think over that title—'the *beloved* disciple'—beloved by Jesus Christ, true God and true man. You can see why I gave Bartholomew my blessing even though he is but fifteen. He is leaving father and fishing nets every bit as promptly as did St. John. I hope he becomes the beloved disciple!"

"That's a beautiful thought, Father; but John, the beloved, was more than fifteen when Jesus called to him. Do you really think that Bartholomew knows what he is about? He left here with more enthusiasm than Bernard. You'd think he was setting off for some exciting adventure rather than his own entombment."

Her father raised his eyebrow at her last word and said, "You certainly have no love for Citeaux; that's evident. But, Little Queen, don't let appearances deceive you. I have seen the same nervous excitement and enthusiastic energy exhibited by men who knew they were riding to death. You'd marvel at the spirit of high adventure that seizes the knights just before battle. It's a form of recklessness and abandon that used to puzzle me greatly. I wondered about them as you wonder about Bartholomew. I wondered if they realized what they were riding into. It seizes the younger knights with a greater frenzy. They laugh and sing and shout while death is hardly a lance-length away. I think there is a twofold explanation. Some are blind to the danger. That is unquestionable. God makes them that way, I think; but most are 'whistling in the dark.'"

"What do you mean 'whistling in the dark'?"

"They realize what's ahead. In their soul's depths they are frightened. I've felt that fright before every combat, Little Queen; and it will conquer the strongest if we do not sing and shout to keep up our courage and keep out that paralyzing fear. Men whistle in the dark, Humbeline, not because they are fearless, but because they are afraid. So, maybe Bartholomew knows that he is burying himself alive at the age of fifteen. That would be a crime were it not a magnificent consecration to God."

Tescelin had addressed most of his words to the window and the falling snow. He seemed to be meditating aloud rather than talking to his daughter; and his last sentence was spoken in a hush. Humbeline felt a strange fascination whenever her father spoke thus. She watched him now as he looked at the steady fall of flakes and she saw that he had been carried out of himself by memories of the past and visions of the future. She took almost the same hushed tone as she said, "You say that with deep feeling, Father. You have thought of it long."

"Tescelin rose and walked to the window saying, "Long—long—long! Indeed long have I thought on it. A father's responsibility can be crushing unless he trusts in God." Then after a pause he turned to Humbeline and said, "And that's what I would have my Little Queen do more fully. Trust in God. Think of God. You're thinking of me and the return that is mine after raising my boys. Worry about God and the little return He gets from His children and you'll see why my loneliness brings happiness; the ache in my heart, joy; and my sadness, jubilation; for it means that I'm giving something to God.

"Humbeline dear, Bartholomew is in a better position right now than Gerard, isn't he? Poor Gerard is spending his New Year's in a Grancy prison, and I don't know when the Duke will ransom him. God could have taken him by death as well as by capture that night of the sortie; and I would have had nothing to say about it. Why then should I say no to a boy of mine who wants to give his life to God? Put your hand in God's hand, Little Queen, and you'll feel less lonely when it snows or grows dark. As for me, I'm happy, and would be much happier if I could take that tiny frown from your forehead and that light of pain from your eyes."

At those words Humbeline managed a smile and said, "You make me feel ashamed of myself, Father. I believe I was thinking more of Bartholomew than I was of

God. But he does seem so young; and he is so lovable. Look! See the brave little snowbird on the window sill. Wouldn't you love to take him in? That's the way my heart goes out to Bartholomew when I think of him lost among the silent men of Citeaux."

"And, Little Queen," said her father, "if you did manage to bring the snowbird in, you'd make him miserable. He likes it out there in the storm. God made him that way. Perhaps our little Bartholomew is a snowbird. But come, it's getting dark. Let's go down where logs crackle and flames leap, and see if we can't make it a happy New Year for all our serfs. I've invited them to the great hall for the evening."

Instantly Humbeline's mood changed. Throwing her arms around her father's neck she kissed him. "You'll never feel sorry for yourself, old Tawny-beard, simply because you're always too busy thinking of others. Come, let's go down!" she cried as she linked her arm under his and led him to the door. As she opened it, she said, "I'll have to be ten or twelve people at once tonight if all our dependents come. Some are so shy that they will be more restless than the snowbirds; while others—OH!" and she gave a trill of laughter that floated back from the stairway and filled her darkening room with silvered beauty.

"I Love the Guileless"

As Humbeline had said, Bartholomew had gone to Chatillon-sur-Seine with enthusiasm shining in his young eyes. He came to Citeaux the same way, and he kept that light shining in his eyes. Abbot Stephen Harding, looking on the thirty nobles who presented themselves that memorable morning in the spring of 1112, admired the stalwart, middle-aged Gaudry, felt his pulse quicken in sympathetic unison with the energetic, enterprising Bernard and Hugh of Macon, but he found his heart pulled to the youth who stood smiling and almost shy in the very center of the group. It was Bartholomew, the unsullied and unspoiled Bartholomew; and Abbot Stephen told his Prior that he imagined Nathaniel, the Apostle, had looked just like that to Jesus the day the Son of God had exclaimed, "Behold an Israelite in whom there is no guile."

Stephen Harding was English-born and English-bred; and since Englishmen have never been noted for their emotionalism, much less for sentimentality, this attraction of his to young Bartholomew of Fontaines demands explanation. And of it, some explanation was given at harvest time in 1113, when the Prior came to Abbot Stephen after a wearying day's work under a mercilessly hot sun. He bowed to his Abbot and after receiving permission to speak, said, "The field of barley is finished, Reverend Father."

"Finished?" exclaimed Stephen. "The community must have worked surprisingly hard then. I didn't expect that to be finished before tomorrow evening."

"They did. They worked extraordinarily hard. And surprise of surprises! Do you know who set the rapid pace? Bernard of Fontaines."

"Bernard!" gasped Stephen. "Why, only last week I had to take him away from the harvesting work because he couldn't keep up with the slowest. Poor boy, he is not physically strong, though his spirit is indomitable."

"Well, he was strong enough today to stay ahead of the fastest. I asked him where he got the energy and the skill. He only smiled and pointed to the skies."

"H-m-m-m," mused the Abbot, "that would be like him. I suppose he stormed heaven with prayers asking for strength enough to do his part in the heavy work of the harvest. He is an ardent soul."

"Isn't he, though? I like him more and more as time goes on. He is a born leader. He stands out above and beyond the entire group he brought in with him."

"Do you really think so, Father? I didn't find it that way at all. The one that attracted me most was his brother Bartholomew."

"Bartholomew?" came the incredulous cry from the Prior. "Why, he is so meek a mouse could run away with him."

"Don't you fool yourself, my good Prior. There is as much iron in that boy as there is in Bernard. The only difference is that Bernard's is a clanging iron; he makes more noise and attracts more notice. Look! Here is the way I usually divide men. When that group came to us a year ago, I immediately separated the dissenters from the assenters. Bernard and Hugh of Macon are the dissenters. Bartholomew, Guy and Gaudry are assenters.

"Roughly speaking I think all men fall under those two heads: the 'yes-men' and the 'no-men.' The first class see harmony and order everywhere, realize the innermost truth of things, and conform to things as they are. The 'no-men' are born to be in opposition; and it is only with the greatest difficulty that they ever subdue themselves into conformity. Bernard and Hugh are 'no-men'! They are controversialists and will always show best in adversity. External opposition and friction from some outside source seem necessary for their temperament. When they have it, it is a blessing for all those who have to live with them, for then their fighting instincts are directed against the enemy without and that keeps them from stirring up controversy and strife within. I have always found it fascinating to watch such men develop. They have to be watched; for they are dangerous minds and dangerous men."

"Bernard and Hugh, dangerous?"

"Yes, Bernard and Hugh! They are 'no-men' I tell you. They have an instinct for opposition. They are fighters, and that makes them very dangerous; for opposition can go into antagonism, antagonism into contempt and contempt into open rebellion and revolt. I have seen such natures so evolve. Ah, but when they are properly controlled and properly directed, then they become dynamic leaders and magnetic men. I'm praying that Hugh and Bernard get the control and direction. Hugh seems to have it; but Bernard is far too excessive yet to be safe. In another year maybe...."

"You study men closely, don't you, Reverend Father?"

"It's my duty. I have to. And let me tell you it's a difficult study. No two men are exactly alike even though all men will fall under my two main classes. I love the 'yes-men.' They are guileless and easy to get along with; they are happy souls who bring happiness to others. Bartholomew is a 'yes-man'; he is utterly guileless."

"But you don't find such men lacking initiative, energy, life?"

The Abbot smiled, cast a sly glance and one that was somewhat mischievous at his Prior and said, "I see my Prior studies men closely, too. Well, you have hit on their weakness, Father. They can be dangerous men also, for they are assenters, not dissenters, and their assent may be too easily given. They can become too yielding, soft, inconstant, and lack all steadiness of purpose. I have seen men develop, or rather, deteriorate that way, too. But I don't worry about Bartholomew; for as I said before, he has as much iron in his makeup as the fiery Bernard. Have you ever looked deep into that boy's eyes?"

"I can't say that I have."

"Then you're missing something, Father. There is a freshness there that makes mountain snow seem sullied and ocean's spray defiled; there is a smiling goodness there, rippling up from depths unknown, that makes sadness a curse and cunning a crime. I have seen a glowing ingenuousness there that is more refreshing than a summer's sea and more winsome than a rose. Study men's eyes, Father Prior; it will repay you. And I especially exhort you to look deep into the eyes of unspoiled youth; for there you will find a clarity that is clearer than an open sea or a cloudless sky. It will do your heart good. It will make you feel fresh, clean, joyous, happy and hopeful. I call such a sight the apparition of a soul. It seems as if the curtain of clay parts for a moment allowing the alert to catch a fleeting glimpse of the sublimity of the spirit. Young Bartholomew will give you such a glimpse, Father, if you are alert. That boy is utterly spotless; one of God's loveliest creations."

"But won't he grow conscious of my gaze?"

The Abbot laughed. "Of course he will, if you stare at him. But I said study him; I didn't say stare at him. You must learn to observe without seeming to observe. Manual labor gives you an ideal opportunity to study character."

"But how can I tell the 'yes-men' from the 'no-men'? Silence is the Rule you must remember."

"I'm not likely to forget it, Father. But you can tell the assenters from the dissenters without ever violating any silence. The 'no-men' are usually the active, energetic, enterprising. Look at Bernard. The 'yes-men' are less energetic, and utterly unenterprising. They have to be led."

"Then that takes Bartholomew out of that class; for while he is not exactly enterprising, he is far from an idler."

"You're forgetting that Bartholomew is a well-developed 'yes-man.' He's going to mature into a stable leader. He'll never shine as will Bernard, if Bernard develops correctly; but he'll be much less erratic, and much more dependable. You never see him doing the exaggerated things Bernard does, do you?"

"No, I don't. He's more temperate."

"Well, that's why he won't shine as will Bernard; but that is also why he'll be more dependable. Excessive men worry me. I never cared for extremists; perhaps it's my English conservatism. But I don't mind telling you that I prefer Bartholomew to Bernard, because I love the guileless."

"Flee Not"

What Abbot Stephen confessed in private to the Prior that golden afternoon in early Fall, he made known to the entire community one June morning in 1115 when he unashamedly wept as he said "good-bye" to young Bartholomew whom he was sending out with the rest of his brothers to found a new monastery. "Think of me, won't you, when you pray to God with more than usual fervor," sobbed the Abbot as he embraced the young monk who still had all the unsullied freshness of the boy about him. Bartholomew managed to mumble, "I will, Reverend Father," and wondered why he found it so hard to swallow and so difficult to breathe deeply.

The brothers and relatives fell in behind Bernard and left the cradle of their religious life singing psalms. They walked ninety miles due north from Citeaux, and on June twenty-fifth, took formal possession of the Valley of Wormwood with its thick overgrowth of brushwood, its tall trees and steep hills to north, south and west, and in its center the sparkling stream. Clairvaux was founded; and for the same reason that Stephen Harding had asked a remembrance, Bernard appointed his younger brother sacristan. He knew that Bartholomew was especially blessed with God's great gift of prayer.

The nine years that followed saw the monk living almost continually in the sacramental presence of his God. Bartholomew loved the church and everything about it; so the time not given to work in the sacristy or the sanctuary was spent before a crucifix in one of the side chapels.

Then with a suddenness that shocked, Stephen Harding sent word to Clairvaux that he would like Bartholomew to go to la Ferté, the first daughter-house of Citeaux, and take the place of Abbot Peter, who had just been raised to the archiepiscopal See of Tarentaise. The ever-loyal Bernard did not hesitate a moment. He called his brother to him and said, "Bartholomew, do you remember when cousin Robert deserted some five or six years ago?"

"I do," came the quiet reply, but there was a question in the younger brother's eyes.

"Well, I wrote a long letter to him on that occasion, and I think one of the real high spots in the letter was the passage in which I exhorted him to, *flee not.*' My argument, as I remember it was, *'Flight is the sole cause of the loss of victory.'* I said something to the effect that, 'neither wounded, nor thrown to the ground, nor trodden underfoot, nor (were it possible) a thousand times slain, will you be defrauded of victory, provided only you *flee not.* Flight is the sole cause of the loss of victory! Not by death can you lose it; no, not by death; but only by flight! Nay, blessed are you should you die fighting, for then you will soon be crowned.' Do you admit such reasoning, Bartholomew?"

"You know I do, Bernard! Isn't that my private war cry, 'Fight! Not flight!'"

"Yes," answered Bernard with a smile, "and it's a cry that I've had to sound for myself a thousand times. But now, my brother, you must live your war cry. Abbot Stephen wants you to go to la Ferté."

"Oh, I'll go gladly."

"Not so fast, young fellow, not so fast! He wants you to go there in a very trying capacity. He wants you to go there to stay. He wants you...but just a moment," and Bernard got up, walked to the darkest corner of the room, and returned with a wooden cross about five and a half feet high. "What's this, Bartholomew?"

"A cross."

"It's a symbol, isn't it? What does it symbolize?"

"Suffering and death."

"Yes, but after death, the resurrection. Never forget that. Remember also that it is the sign of salvation. Do you know where I got this?"

"It looks like the one Abbot Stephen gave you when we left Citeaux."

"It is the identical one; and I need not tell you that it was a fitting symbol to give me. Some abbots are beginning to wear miters now. Well, let them. All of us carry staffs or crosiers; and it's a proper symbol. We are shepherds. But, Bartholomew, this," and he held out the cross, "this is the most fitting symbol of all; for an abbacy is a crucifixion. Are you ready for it?"

"Ready for what?"

"Ready for a crucifixion."

"What are you talking about?"

"La Ferté. Stephen Harding's wish. My brother Bartholomew's agony and death."

"You mean...."

"I mean that you are to be la Ferté's abbot."

"But, Bernard, I...."

"You must sound your war cry, 'Fight! Not flight!' You must now go over to your favorite crucifix and learn how to be a real man. Ah, I pity you, even as I rejoice. Now is the time to show your strong faith. Let me tell you, Bartholomew, you are going to martyrdom. Remember, then, the essential element in martyrdom. It is not suffering. No! It is faith. Look! Martyrdom is able to fulfill the function of baptism, isn't it? It can make a man a child of God; stamp him indelibly as Christ's own; wash away all stain of sin and robe his soul in grace. But what is it that works these marvelous effects? Again I say: It is not suffering; it is faith. For apart from the faith in the martyr, what is martyrdom but the suffering of a penalty? You are going to suffer, Bartholomew, but if you do it with faith and for the Faith, for the Author and finisher of our faith, then you have won the martyr's crown."

"You frighten me."

"Don't let that bother you. If you didn't feel fright, I'd accuse you of pride and presumption. This whole thing is sudden, Bartholomew. You'll have to start out tomorrow."

"Oh, then tell me all you can right now. You've had ten years' experience...."

"There's nothing to tell you, brother-mine. Nothing. Just be yourself. Words mean little with men. It is the life you lead that will talk to them; and they have exceptionally keen hearing for its messages. Just remember that it is by climbing, not by flying that we get to the top of the ladder. So climb with both feet; and teach those under you to do the same. Meditation and prayer are the two feet we all need; for it is meditation that teaches us what is lacking, and it is prayer that obtains for us the supply thereof. You have used those two feet well all your religious life. That is why I say: Just be yourself."

"Yes, but how shall I handle men?"

"By remembering that they are men. That was my first mistake. I thought they were angels. They aren't. They are only men and some of them only babies. The holy Rule tells you all, Bartholomew. Meditate it carefully. Take nothing else for your guide. Deal gently. Lay aside all harshness. But I hardly need tell you that, for God has given you a very gentle nature. There is one danger I warn you of: be careful when you meet the murmuring, discontented soul; especially when it breaks forth in abuse and insult of yourself. Remember then that you are a physician, not a lord; and prepare for that soul's delirium not punishment, but soothing treatment."

"You dwell long on tenderness, charity and consideration, Bernard."

"I do, Bartholomew. For I think that the ideal Abbot is he who can be a mother in his caresses but a father in his corrections. We are members under a thorn-crowned head, it is true; we are austere contemplatives, it is also true; but the truest of all true things is that we are only wayfarers, footsore prodigals limping our way home to God, exiles who are lonely, very lonely, and men who have sensitive hearts. Don't break them, Bartholomew. Don't even ache them. But attune them all to the great Heart of Christ. And you can do that through gentleness that is never weakness, kindness and consideration that is never sentimental, charity that is as virile as was the Christ. Oh, how I wish I could practice what I preach! Christ is our model. We are His followers; but I feel that I have not caught up with Him yet. But overtake Him we must!"

"Why? Who calls you harsh?"

"All my adversaries and many of my friends," laughed Bernard. "I'm too forceful, Bartholomew. Learn from me how not to act and speak. I am a firebrand and I sometimes set the wrong things flaming. However, you've been blessed with an entirely different temperament, and on it you've stamped a deeper and better character. Now that you are leaving us, I can tell you that you've been an edification to all as you worked and prayed in the sacristy and church. To me personally you've been an inspiration, a consolation and a source of envy. I'm going to miss you, Bartholomew; so will the rest of the community. But the price of victory is always sacrifice. I'm sure that God will bless Clairvaux for giving you to la Ferté.

"You may speak to Guy, Gerard, Andrew and Nivard; and don't forget to say 'good-bye' to Gaudry. He loves you much. And now I bless you with all the power God has given me. Put your hand in His, Bartholomew; and never let go. It is the only way for any of us to walk through this world, whether we be abbot or sacristan. And now—*Benedictio Dei omnipotentis....*"

Bartholomew dropped to his knees and Bernard put all the love of his heart into his voice as he called down the blessing of Father, Son and Holy Spirit on his younger brother; and when he pressed his hands on his head, Bartholomew felt all the glowing warmth of burning affection that was deep in Bernard's being for him. When he arose and embraced his brother he could not speak, but Bernard heard more in the pressure of encircling arms than he would ever have heard had not emotion robbed Bartholomew of speech.

"Un Vagabondage Magnifique"

A little over ten years later when all Europe was listening to the voice of Bernard and following his lead in the awful schism that rent the Church, Bartholomew was returning to la Ferté after having made a formal visitation of the first foundation that was his. In 1132 he had sent a colony to establish a monastery at Mazières in Burgundy. As soon as they left he was shaken by the realization that, although he was only thirty-five years of age, he was responsible for two monasteries: la Ferté directly as Abbot, Mazières indirectly as Father Immediate. With anxious solicitude he set out each year to visit his daughter-house, and always returned marveling at God's ways with and in souls.

In 1135 he rode back to la Ferté with his heart athrob with glowing gratitude, for he had found Maria de Merceriis in perfect harmony with everything in Citeaux. And weary though he was from the fatiguing worry and work, he felt his spirits surge at the end of his long ride when he caught sight of the gleaming cross of his own monastery of la Ferté. "Ah!" he exclaimed, "your daughter is worthy of you. When I see the mother I congratulate her on her daughter; when I visit the daughter I congratulate her on her mother. And I do not do it to be diplomatic or courteous, but only to be honest and sincere." The smile that lighted his face then as he lifted it to the cross-topped steeple was a revelation. Bartholomew was thanking the Crucified.

At about the same time that he was chanting the praises of the daughter to the mother, Abbot Paganus sat in the reception room of Mazières and lifted a face that was lighted with a smile as revealing as Bartholomew's as he said, "Count Pierre, if you find my community fervent, don't thank me; thank the one you met here yesterday. Thank Abbot Bartholomew, for he taught me and many under me how to make life *un vagabondage magnifique*—nothing to live on, yet living splendidly; nothing to walk on, yet walking fearlessly; nothing to lean on, but leaning on God! Just about ten years ago he came to la Ferté and in no time he taught us lessons other monks don't learn in a lifetime. He had us cultivate the knight's instinct of being chivalrous towards God, the chivalry that has us bearing blows and arrows bravely; the adventurous spirit that has us looking on life as a journey glorious in its faith and hope. That just about sums up Abbot Bartholomew—an adventurous knight of God, glowing with a splendid faith and a glorious hope."

The Count was a tall man of stately build, and from his dark, piercing eyes excited gleams of merriment shot out from beneath black bushy eyebrows. These gleams lighted up his swarthy, aquiline features and added much to his words as he said, "That almost sounds like an address I could give my men just before battle. Odd, isn't it, that we men-at-arms credit you monks with so little martial spirit or chivalry?"

"No, Your Excellency, it is not strange at all, it is just one of those quirks common to human nature. We all believe that we have exclusive possession of whatever happens to be our individualistic profession. You men-at-arms think that you are the only martial men on the continent; while most monks think they are the only ones who have any real religion. You credit us with little chivalry; we are inclined to credit you with little religious virtue. And both of us are wrong! Why, Your Excellency, Abbot Bartholomew could wear that suit of mail that you have on with all the ease and grace that he carries his cowl, and could wield the sword by your side with all the effectiveness that he bears his crosier."

"It's hard to believe after meeting him and hearing him talk. I think he's one of the mildest and mellowest men I have ever met. Gentleness and kindness simply radiate from his whole person."

"That's the satin sheath that scabbards the keen-edged steel. You must never forget that he was Bartholomew of Fontaines before he became Bartholomew of la Ferté."

"Then that's one of Tawny-beard's sons!" exclaimed the Count. "Oh, I wish I had known that yesterday. I met his father once, long ago. I was little more than a boy at the time; but his father made an impression on me that I have never forgotten. He appeared to me as the perfect knight. He impressed me as tremendous strength under absolute control. Ah! I think it was something like what you just said about his son—steel sheathed in satin. What an exceptional family that was!"

"You mean, 'that is,' don't you, Your Excellency?" asked the Abbot smilingly.

The Count looked surprised. "There it is again—that quirk, as you call it, in human nature. Just because they left Fontaines and entered religion, we talk of them as dead. And yet, Bernard is the voice of Europe; Gerard, his constant companion; and the other brothers leaders in the monastery that houses more knights than I can claim as vassals."

"Well, not quite that many, Your Excellency; but Clairvaux numbers many knights. And note that I don't say 'former knights.'"

"I was just going to remark that, my lord Abbot; and I suppose your explanation is, 'Once a knight always a knight!'"

"Precisely. They changed weapons and liege lord, that's all. And if you had listened to that mild and mellow Abbot Bartholomew as I had to listen to him every morning for nine years, you'd know that religious have to be fighting men."

"Tell me more about him," requested the Count as he drew his chair in closer to the table and pushed aside his helmet with its proud plume so that he could have clear vision of Paganus. "And tell me more about this life. Why do you have to be fighting men and yet call it *un vagabondage magnifique?* What are you anyhow, soldiers of fortune?"

"Soldiers of good fortune, Your Excellency," laughed the Abbot. "But don't misunderstand me when I call our life a 'vagabondage.' We don't roam. But we do cultivate the vagabond's happy spirit of abandon. And why not? We are God's soldiers. He is our provident King. But it's a hard life."

"What's hard about it, my lord Abbot—the fasts, labor and silence?"

"No. Those things are easy, Your Excellency. It's the blindness of it all."

"Blindness? What do you mean?"

"Well, perhaps I can best explain by telling you what happened to me just about ten years ago. I had been in the Order some eight years then and had given my best, or at least I thought so; when suddenly I seemed to awake, look around me with wide open and clear-seeing eyes, and realize that my life was empty. I began to reason with myself about myself and about everything in the life. I tell you, Your Excellency, it was a blood-chilling experience."

"How so?"

"Well, there I was, a man in middle age, who in a moment of youthful enthusiasm had flung away everything that man holds dear. I had left family and friends and fortune. I had left my station in life and my rank in society to pledge myself to live forever as a Cistercian monk. The idealists would call my act, *un beau geste, un geste magnifique;* but the men of hard-headed practicality would call me 'fool.' And that is just what I was calling myself. Oh, how stupid it all seemed! Singing psalms and starving oneself, grubbing away at the soil like a serf, living on wretched food, in wretched quarters, a wretched life; and yet, calling it all a tribute to the good God.

"Believe me when I say that my horizons were black. I thought of many of my friends, men of rank and distinction in the Duchy and the Church, good men, holy men, yes, even saintly men; yet there was nothing of this extravaganza about them or their lives. I began to reason that God never meant us to waste our lives or bury our talents this way; never asked this sort of service or demanded this type of praise. I began to think that I had been wrong from the beginning; deluded even as had been the followers of Peter of Bruys and Henry of Lausanne. I began to suspect that Cistercians were heretics who had confused John the Baptist with Jesus Christ. Our like loomed as a fanatical caricature of the life led by the Precursor in the desert—fasting and watching and waiting for the Lord, rather than a following of the meek, gentle and sociable Jesus. Let me tell you, it was awful."

The Count shifted in his chair and said, "It's awful just to listen to your account of it. But, my lord Abbot, you're simply whetting my appetite for your solution; for those same thoughts have occurred to me. Your life does not look like the life of Jesus who 'went about doing good.'"

"That's exactly what I was thinking those dark days, and had just about come to the conclusion that I had squandered the best years of my life, when I went to Abbot Bartholomew. I was a very unhappy man, Your Excellency. Oh, what a thought it is to think that you have thrown away your best years, ruined beyond repair the one life you have to lead! And yet, down deep in my soul there was the faintest whisper, saying, 'No. Your reasoning is wrong.' And it was that little whisper that made my days agony and my nights torture. However, I went to my good Abbot and talked to him as plainly, even more plainly, than I'm talking to you. There's something about Abbot Bartholomew that invites complete openness and inspires confidence. He listened to me as intently and as interestedly as you are listening, my Lord, and never once interrupted."

"Did you tell him he seemed like a fool to you and the Cistercians, deluded heretics?"

"I did, Your Excellency, and in words not as nice sounding as that. He listened, encouraging me to speak out my whole mind, and, let me tell you, I accepted his encouragement. I told him everything. When I had finished he simply shook his head and said, 'I'm glad. I'm very glad.'"

"What was he glad about?" asked the Count with some little indignation.

"That's what I was thinking at the time, Your Excellency; but he said it in such a sincere, friendly way that I just waited. I had not long to wait, for soon he said, 'I suspect that quite recently God said to the devil: Have you seen my servant Paganus in the monastery at la Ferté?' 'You mean that I'm being tempted?' said I. 'That's exactly what I mean,' answered Bartholomew, 'and that's why I'm glad. It proves that you are God's faithful servant. It proves that He can trust you as He trusted Job.'"

"That's clever," put in the Count, "very clever and very encouraging; but how many men will accept it? You can't level the whole host of reasonable objections that you raised with a mere reference to Scripture."

"No, you can't," replied Paganus, "at least not with men who really think. Some excessively pious souls with simple minds might be satisfied with that. But, you see, Abbot Bartholomew is more than merely pious. He is a saintly soul with sound sense. As you say, his opening remark was encouraging. It gave voice to that whisper I told you about in the depths of my being. I began to admit that maybe Satan was using his wiles on me. But I was far from satisfied. It did not level all my towering objections, as you said. But Bartholomew had not finished with me; he had just begun. He turned on me then and analyzed me for myself. He took me apart physically, mentally and morally, and showed me my whole make-up. Oh, it was superb. First he attacked the physical and showed me that I was weary and not too well, not in my best fighting trim. Then he told me that my heart was strong, my backbone rigid and my vitals manly, but my eyesight was poor." Paganus paused and looked away for a moment. It seemed as if he would relish the memory. But the Count had become too interested to allow him his reverie.

"You'll explain that, I hope," he prompted.

"Yes, Your Excellency," said the Abbot turning back to him, "I'll explain it as Bartholomew did. He told me that I had been looking at things in the wrong light and that it had distorted my vision. He said that the grass and trees look black in starlight, brownish in moonlight, but green in sunlight. He said I needed sunlight to see colors truly. Then he twisted the word and said, 'You need the light of the Son, the only begotten Son of the Father, He who said He was the Light of the world.' Then to explain that, he took me apart morally. He said I didn't lack love, nor was I wanting in hope; but he insisted that I was weak in faith."

"Yes, but our faith must have a rational foundation," interrupted the Count.

Paganus slapped the edge of the table with his open hand and smiled delightedly as he exclaimed, "Your Excellency, it is simply thrilling to see how our two minds run in the same channel! I answered Bartholomew that day by quoting St. Paul. I said, 'I'll grant you that, Reverend Father, but we must have reason for the faith that is in us.' As I said it I was thinking of all the reasons I had for the faith that was not in me."

The Count smiled at the play on words but urged Paganus on by asking, "What did Tescelin's son say to that?"

Before answering, the Abbot drew his chair in a little closer to the table, straightened out the folds of his white robe, smoothed out the black scapular over his chest and gave a little tug on his leathern girdle; then placing his two arms on the table he leaned forward and said, "I have shown you the kindly, patient, mild-mannered Abbot, Your Excellency; now I'll show you the saintly monk and the real man. Without a word of prompting from me, my Lord, he took my arguments individually, stated them more forcefully than I had stated them, and then took my breath away by admitting every one of them. He admitted that the food, clothing and quarters were wretched; he admitted that the work was degrading; even conceded that many of my companions were most trying. He asked me to hold out my hands, and when I did he said, 'They are empty, Paganus, absolutely empty and your years have been utterly wasted.' Then he turned away. I assure you I was puzzled. For a fraction of a second I suspected that Bartholomew of la Ferté was a disappointed man even as I myself, but the suspicion had not fully formed when I heard him say, 'if—if—if we use only the light of reason, or limit our vision to the public life of Christ.'

"Then he turned on me and said, 'Paganus, I don't like solitude. I'm a man. I love company. I don't like unseasoned herbs, coarse bread and watered wine. I have a palate and a stomach. I don't like hard manual labor. No. I'm lazy just as every man and beast I know is lazy. But, Paganus, I do love Jesus Christ! And that makes all the difference in the world. Your objections are unanswerable unless we look long at Jesus in Gethsemane and on Golgotha. He went about doing good, Paganus; but He also sweated blood, was scourged, mocked, spit upon, crowned with thorns and crucified. Sin did it. Yours and mine and the sins of the world. Sin still does it. If men and women were all as pure as angels and as honest as saints, there would be no need for la Ferté or Citeaux. But, Paganus, God is not being honored as He should be by the race He has elevated to the sublime dignity of adopted sons. That's why I revel in what I naturally hate.'"

"What a man! What a man!" exclaimed the Count spontaneously.

"After that burst of saintly passion, he turned on me again," went on Paganus, "and said, 'You think you have wasted the best years of your life. You have, as far as man can see and this world is concerned. But let me tell you this: You have given God your very best. You are trying to spend every breath of your life and every power of your soul in His service, cut off from all you might have legitimately enjoyed. He cannot be insensible to that, Paganus. Never! He must be touched to the very heart by it, else He would not be our God, but Moloch. But He is our God, and He knows that failing often and blundering daily we are trying to give Him our very best, and what is the result? Look, Paganus! What is the result? The result is the very best worship that this earth can offer Him! Your years have been as wasted as were Christ's three hours on the cross! You have lived eight years of faith, hope and love, and you have lived them in vigorous, manly action. Could mortal man ask for more? What a sacrifice! What a worship of God! What a life of love! It is sublime! Paganus, you have imitated the Savior of the world!'"

"Great heavens, you have!" came the emphatic exclamation from the Count as he pounded the table sharply with his fist. Then drawing his sword across his knees, allowing him to shift his position, he asked, "Did Abbot Bartholomew deliver it as forcefully as you have done?"

"More forcefully. He's mild, moderate, merciful. But he's full of fire once he starts talking of Christ or of the service of Christ. He's a fighter, Your Excellency. As I remember that day he closed by saying, 'Paganus, God gives the light of faith, but you have to give God the full force of your will and every ounce of your fighting energy. Light from God, fight from you; that's the combination that brings victory; the only combination. Fight! Not flight! is your war cry. Trust God, Paganus. That's the important thing. Trust Him utterly. And that, despite what some men say, is a terribly difficult thing for men with minds to do. I know that. I have experienced it. It's hard to go on blindly. Yes, it's very hard; but it's also heroic. And let me tell you the more you pray and give yourself into His hands the better you will see; but the more you reason and struggle to see, the darker things will grow.' And, Your Excellency, I have found that he was most right."

"But what does he mean? Are you to stop reasoning?"

Paganus laughed. "At certain points, yes. There are mysteries, you know, Your Excellency."

"Oh, I know that. But your Cistercian life is no mystery."

"No, but there are mysteries in it. Why should I be Abbot of Maria de Merceriis when I vowed to die a monk of la Ferté? That's a mystery of God's providence. Why should Bartholomew of Fontaines be sent from Clairvaux to la Ferté? That's a mystery of God's providence. Yes, and in every soul you'll find darker and more troubling mysteries. That's where we have to go blindly. That's where we have to be fighters and chivalrous men."

"I believe you," said the Count slowly. "Inaction is always harder on a person than action. The moments before a battle are always the most trying. Once we sweep into physical combat, things are easy. This life of the spirit must call for tremendous stamina. You've opened my eyes."

"Your Excellency, it is chivalry at its highest. Just look what a man has to do: He has to swear undying fealty to a Lord he has never seen with his physical eyes; live out his vassal life in the service of a Leader from whom he has never, and will never, hear a word; carry on an endless campaign for a Ruler he will never see this side of the grave. That calls for knighthood's highest chivalry. Why, Your Excellency, it would be comparatively easy for me to swear away my life to you. I see you. I know you, I admire you. I would battle for you savagely, for I know you reward valor handsomely. Ah! But vassalage to the King of kings as a knight of Citeaux calls for sterner stuff. It demands faith. Not the faith that moves mountains but a greater one—the faith that transforms men! Do I seem to be boasting?"

"Boasting?" roared the Count. "Boasting? I should say not. No, you're shaming me and many like me. We are such narrow-minded, self-centered and self-satisfied individuals that we measure all men by our own stinginess. I doubt that there are a handful of nobles in the Duchy who ever think of you as other than men who have been driven in behind these walls by some cringing fear of the afterlife. Few indeed are those who think of you as knights of Christ, spurred on by a flaming love, a love that has you flinging away life that God might be praised and men saved. I kneel to you, Reverend Father Abbot; I kneel to you in tribute of my admiration, yes and to ask absolution for my stupid and rash judgment."

"Rise, Your Excellency, rise. Remember that I have given you only what I received from Bartholomew of la Ferté. I have knelt to him in admiration and for absolution, too. He is another Christ. He is St. Benedict's abbot indeed."

"What is that—a warrior hidden in a cowl?"

"After a fashion, yes; but more winningly put by saying, a man with the mind and the manner of Jesus Christ. Abbot Bartholomew has never hurt the feelings of anyone under him, yet no fault has ever escaped correction. He is loved by all because he loves all. When I was coming here as Abbot he told me to take for my motto the words of St. Benedict's Rule: *Prodesse magis quam praeesse.* 'Strive to be a servant,' he said, 'rather than a sovereign. Strive to be what you are called—a father!' I'm sure that he gave me the secret of his life and his service in those few words."

"The more you talk," said the Count, "the more I admire the man. But tell me: Did he learn all these tactics from his brother Bernard?"

"No. As far as I can find out, Bernard's forte is love, Bartholomew's is faith. I asked him once who trained him most, Stephen Harding or his brother. All I got for an answer was a chuckle and the reply, 'Neither.' He then told me that he learned his deepest lessons while working as sacristan. He claims that there are two studies all should make: the crucifix and the consecrated Host. These root one and establish one in faith, he said; and once one is so rooted and established he will know how to thank God for the darkness that shrouds our whole life on earth and take it as a glorious opportunity to prove our trust in God."

"What a concept!" exclaimed the Count in open admiration. "And what a truth!" he added. Then in a more subdued tone he thoughtfully said, "How I have wronged you men in my own mind, and how I have neglected faith. My Lord Abbot, we take our great gift too lightly. You have opened my eyes this afternoon. The visions you've shown me are sharply contrasted. I look at you and Abbot Bartholomew in awe; I look at myself and many like me in shame. You have done yourself a harm by talking as you did."

"How so?" asked Paganus as he came around the table.

"I'm going to inflict myself on you more often, if you don't too severely forbid me; for I want to learn more of what real chivalry is. And I'm going to visit la Ferté at the first opportunity to learn more of Tawny-beard's surprising boy. Mildness personified hiding the passion of a frenzied lover. That's my summation of Abbot Bartholomew now."

"And a happy summation it is, Your Excellency. You have described him exactly. About your visits here, you are always welcome. I can always make time to talk of Christ."

Paganus held the door open for Count Pierre. The latter stopped on the threshold and looked at his bodyguard, four stalwart knights who had been awaiting him in this antechamber. "Men," he said, "we have met our betters in these monks. They live a higher chivalry than we ever aspired to or even dreamed of. They are the real knights. We are weak imitations. And Abbot Bartholomew whom you saw here yesterday is the champion of them all. Bow with me to your betters. We were at tournament yesterday; these men are at tournament every day. Let us bow," and five men in linked mail took off gleaming helmets and bowed to Abbot Paganus, and in his person to all Cistercians.

Just Ready for Life at Death

Paganus had caught the secret of Bartholomew's life in the *prodesse magis quam praeesse* of the Rule, and Count Pierre had characterized him perfectly in his, "Mildness personified hiding the passion of a frenzied lover." For Bartholomew had pierced to the heart of St. Benedict's legislation regarding Abbots, and had determined to be what he was called—a father!

It was not always easy; for his community was large, and that meant a variety of characters: some docile and perfectly tractable, others unyielding, and some stiff-necked. But Bartholomew accommodated himself to all and by his mildness and moderation finally made the stiffest neck supple and the most unyielding pliable. But he bought his victories with the coin few like to spend—unmitigated penances. He had not forgotten Bernard's parting words, "Not words but works win men"; so he disciplined himself into perfect control and always exhibited the majesty of calmness.

Of course he had a firm foundation in the temperament God gave him; but he had built on it; and he had learned how to build by his study of the crucifix and the consecrated Host. That is why they did not exaggerate when they said that he had three hearts: one of fire for God, another of flesh for his fellow man, and a third of flint for himself.

His was a long and fruitful abbacy; and just when he thought he was acquiring some virtue, just when he thought he could meet all men with kindness and listen to all with patience, just when he thought he was becoming fit for life, he was called by death.

When Count Pierre heard of his demise he exclaimed, "Just when a man is most ready to live, he is taken by death!" To which Abbot Paganus replied with a smile, "Don't lament, Your Excellency; for that is what we mean by 'ripe for heaven.' God takes His own when they are perfectly matured. Bartholomew thought that he was just acquiring virtue, but we who lived under him, knew that he was crowning life-long virtue with the aureola of perfection. Such holiness is not for this earth; he was too lovable a man to live here below. Death took him when he was just ready for life, as you say; but for the other life, not this."

In the Cistercian Menology for December 9, the ever amiable Bartholomew is called "Blessed." The Bollandists make mention of him on July 1.

As to the year of his going to God there is some obscurity. Fire, pillage, revolution have obliterated so many precious records! Manrique, Mabillon and Le Nain say he died in 1144, the same year as Blessed Andrew, his brother; but some others prefer 1158 or even 1160, and with greater probability because of some documents later than 1144 which bear his name.

The Poor Little Rich Boy

"You take heaven and leave me the earth."

Nivard took off his heavy outer cloak and laid it on a rock. "Spring is here," he said to his five companions, "it's too hot for that old thing."

"You'll catch cold," warned his cousin Maurice, "and Humbeline will put you to bed."

"Huh! Humbeline's only my sister. She can't command me," came the bold reply with something of a swagger to the shoulders.

Nivard had just celebrated his twelfth birthday, and being the baby in the family of Fontaines, had been petted and pampered as all babies of families are, and hence, somewhat spoiled. Standing now in his neat, knee-length frock of blue with its border of bright yellow silk and girdle of the same shining color, he formed a marked contrast to his five little companions. Everything about him bespoke the leader. His squat little body told of care and training and robust health, while the lift of his head as he looked at Maurice and the others told clearly that he was the son of the lord of the land.

It was early March in 1112, and a warm wind shook the yellow patches of last summer's grass and blew Nivard's long, silky, golden locks from off his ears. The six boys had been playing on the slope just in front of

Fontaines castle and the activity and energy demanded by the game, coupled with the smiling sun and the warm wind, had Nivard ready to defy Humbeline on the question of the outer cloak.

Maurice had found no ready answer for the boldly spoken "She can't command me." Furthermore, Nivard's defiant attitude of independence, as he stood with his hands on his hips and a challenge in his eyes, hardly encouraged a reply. The others knew that Maurice was right, but they dared not contradict the boy from Fontaines, so they simply stood about looking uneasily from Nivard to his cousin. The tension grew and no one knows how it would have ended had not a man's voice called out, "Nivard, come here!"

At the first sound of the call Nivard had sprung into action. The cloak was off the rock and around his husky little shoulders almost before the "come here!" had been spoken. There was a smile of triumph on Maurice's lips and those near him heard him say, "I told you so." But Nivard didn't hear him, for he had turned and spied his oldest brother Guy standing in the archway of the main gate of the castle beckoning to him to come up. Behind Guy he could just see the figures of Bernard, Bartholomew and Andrew. They were waving to someone in the tower window.

Nivard ran up the slope as fast as he could. It was October since he had last seen his brothers; so his sturdy little legs could not carry him up the slope fast enough. He reached the level and then, without checking his speed in the slightest, flung himself into his oldest brother's arms crying, "Oh, Guy, are you and the others home to stay? It's been awfully lonely without you."

"Home to get killed, it seems," said Guy with a grunt and a laugh. "You don't seem to realize, young fellow, that you're no longer a baby. The shock of your charge is enough to unseat the strongest."

"Oh, excuse me. Did I hurt you?"

"No, no, little man; not a bit. But do be careful in the future; you're getting big. And now I've got some good news for you." By this time the older brothers had come out upon the level before the main gate and were standing around Guy smiling down on Nivard.

"Good news? What is it? Going to stay home?" came the eager questions from the lad whose face was alight with joy.

"Oh," said Guy, "something bigger than that."

"What? Going to have a joust?"

"Something away bigger than that."

"Then tell me. Don't be teasing me." And a little foot stamped the ground.

Andrew put his arm around Nivard's shoulders and said, "That's right, little fellow, make him talk up."

Nivard circled Andrew's waist with his arm and smiling up at him said, "What is it, Andrew? What's the big news? Make him tell me."

"Tell him, Guy. Don't tease him," put in Bernard.

"All right," said Guy, "then come out here, Nivard," and he walked some ten or fifteen paces from the gate. Nivard and the others followed. Maurice and the four other children formed a little group of their own; not close enough to be intimate; not distant enough to be out of earshot. "See that magnificent castle?" said Guy as he stretched out his right hand toward the stout walls and the sturdy towers.

"Uh-huh," grunted Nivard.

"Well, one day it's going to be yours, all yours. Every stone of it from deep, dark foundations to the topmost tip of that tower." Then turning completely around and spreading his two arms in a wide-open gesture, he said, "And look at these lands! Look as far as the eye can reach, down that valley, up that slope and into those woods, then all that lies to the north: vineyards, orchards, pastures. Beautiful, isn't it?"

"Uh-huh," came the rapid reply.

"Well, all that will one day be yours, too; for you, my little brother, will one day be Lord of Fontaines! Bernard, Bartholomew, Andrew and myself are off for Citeaux today; Gerard will soon follow; we leave it all to you. Now isn't that news?" and he put his hands on Nivard's shoulders and looked expectantly into his boyish face.

The little fellow's mouth opened a tiny bit, forming a perfect O; his eyes searched Guy's smiling face; then he gave a quick glance at Bernard, Bartholomew and Andrew. They, too, were waiting his reply. So looking up again to Guy he said, "The castle, huh?" and his left hand went behind him in a half gesture toward the towers and walls at his back, "And all these lands, huh?" and his right hand swept under Guy's pointing to the valley below, "Are mine, huh? And all because you are going to Citeaux?"

"That's it," said Guy enthusiastically. "Isn't it great?"

"Great?" exclaimed young Nivard and his lower lip began to tremble. "Great?" he said again. "What's great about it? You take heaven and leave me the earth. I don't see anything great about it. It's not even fair. I don't want it!" and he broke from his brothers and ran toward the gate of the castle which shimmered through his blinding tears.

Guy and Andrew started after him but Bernard called, "Don't, Guy! Don't, Andrew! Let him go. We won't say good-bye. It would break his little heart."

Guy turned and came back saying, "I think you're right, Bernard." But Andrew hesitated. He looked after the flying form of his youngest brother and seemed on the point of starting after him again when Bartholomew said, "Come on, Andrew. If you go in there again you'll only set Humbeline into more hysterics, and that won't help Father a bit."

Andrew shook his head slowly but walked back to the group, and the four brothers took a long last look at the castle. It had been their birthplace. It had been their home. It held everyone dear to them. They looked silently, then as if by common instinct they turned together, walked down the hill resolutely and plunged into the woods without ever once turning their heads. It was their farewell to Fontaines.

Six months before, they had gone to Chatillon-sur-Seine. Some of the older members of the band had affairs to settle before they could say that they were absolutely free to apply for acceptance as monks at Citeaux; so Bernard had decided to hold them together at Chatillon and have them lead the routine of a religious life until all was in readiness. Today he and his brothers had come to say good-bye to their father, sister and baby brother. Tescelin had grown strangely silent and Humbeline, seeing the pain in his eyes, had flown into a rage and given vent to a tirade against Bernard for emptying the castle of all life and darkening the declining years of their father's life. It seemed that she had been suddenly transformed into a tigress, and as she stood with her arms around her aged father's neck and tears streaming from her eyes, she mercilessly berated Bernard for enticing all her brothers into what she called religious fanaticism.

Tescelin had soothed her somewhat by patting her raven black head and whispering, "Easy, child. Easy." Soon the full force of her fury reduced her to sobs that shook her whole being. Then Tescelin laid his cheek on her gleaming hair and said, "It's for God, Little Queen. It's for God." Bernard stood with head bent studying the palm of his right hand and not uttering a word. Humbeline looked at him with eyes that shone like stars, then leaving her father's side she ran to Bernard, threw her arms around him and sobbed. "All right, if God wants you, go! Go! And pray for us every day."

It had been a trying scene for everybody. The aged lord carried it off best of all, though perhaps his heart was the most deeply wounded. The encounter with Nivard had promised to lighten things up for a moment, but his tears and his flight sent the brothers walking down the slope in silence. Just after they entered the woods, however, Andrew spoke up saying, "Did you hear what that little tike said? 'You take heaven and leave me the earth. I don't want it. It isn't fair.'"

All laughed at his perfect mimicry of the boyish pout, and Guy exclaimed, "He's the wisest lad in the family." But if they could have seen him at that exact moment they would not have laughed; for the youngster had run into the courtyard, up the stairs and into his room sobbing wildly. Flinging himself on his bed he cried into his pillow, "Who wants the old castle and all the lands? I don't; I don't. I want my brothers."

When the first awful anguish had spent itself and he was reduced to the stage when dry sobs alone shake the whole frame, he rubbed the salt dampness from his eyes, saying, "It isn't fair. It isn't fair." Then suddenly he stopped, doubled his little fists, glared out through bedewed lashes and blurted, "I know what I'll do. I'll follow them. I'll be a monk, too. I don't want to be an old lord."

And off he would have started at the moment had not his door opened under the hand of his stately father who walked in, sat on his bed, took him by the two arms, and smiling a brave smile said, "Come, little man. Lords of Fontaines don't cry!" and two hearts that were lonely found comfort in mutual love.

"When Is One Old Enough?"

Tescelin had managed to soothe the wounded feelings of his son that night in early March, but May's blossoms had not showered the ground before Humbeline startled him by saying, "Nivard's lost."

"Lost?" gasped Tescelin. "What do you mean?"

"He hasn't been seen since early morning."

"What?" snapped her father, and bolting out of his chair was across the room in a few quick strides. "Come along, Humbeline; I'm going to investigate." Out to the stables strode the lord of Fontaines with his worried looking daughter a few paces behind him. Going straight to the last stall, he looked quickly and said, "Just as I thought. The roan's gone. Where's Louis Joseph?" Then in a higher, louder tone he called, "Louis Joseph! Louis Joseph!"

"Coming, my Lord," answered a thin voice from outside, and shortly an old retainer limped into the stable. "What is it, Excellency? Would you ride?"

"No," barked Tescelin. "But I would like to know who is riding the roan."

"Is the roan out?" asked the old man as he limped past father and daughter and looked into the stall. "Well, what do you think of that?" he gasped.

"Come, Louis," said Tescelin severely. "Don't shield the boy. When did he ride forth and which way did he go?"

"My Lord, what is it you ask?" replied the old man resting his hand on a post and moving some straw with his lame leg.

"You know what I ask. When did Nivard leave the castle?"

"Nivard? Isn't he in his room?"

"No, he's not in his room any more than the roan is in her stall."

"Could they be together, do you think?"

"Yes, I think they could be together and I think you know when they left together and which way they went together."

"Soon you'll be saying I know where they are. Come, my Lord, you don't credit me with second sight, do you?"

"Enough, Louis!" cried Tescelin sternly. "When did the boy leave?"

"Well, you see, Your Lordship, it was like this. I was combing your charger, and I was doing a very careful job. You know, he's a fine horse, Your Lordship. He calls for extreme care. Well, I was combing him carefully...."

"Never mind about my charger. Tell me about my boy," broke in Tescelin.

"Now, Humbeline, my little Lady, isn't it difficult to tell your father anything? He wants it all out of me before I have begun...."

"That will do, Louis. Where is your son?"

Louis Joseph saw that he had tried Tescelin to the breaking point so he very wisely called, "Gautier! His Lordship is waiting. Come quickly!" And just as a youngster about Nivard's age came running from the corner of the stable, the hoofbeats of a weary horse rang through the courtyard. Humbeline and Tescelin hurried to the door of the stable and were just in time to see Nivard slide from his saddle and lean wearily against the side of his roan as he patted her and said, "Well done, Lady. Well done!" Then without looking he called, "Louis Joseph! Gautier!"

The old man and his son stopped at the stable door and looked questioningly at Tescelin. He merely nodded and they went out to the roan. "Give her extra care tonight, won't you?" begged Nivard. "She's tired, hungry and thirsty. And so am I," he added as he staggered rather than walked toward the castle.

Humbeline started after him, but Tescelin stopped her with a gesture and the whisper, "Let him get into the castle first. That boy is very tired. He can hardly stand. We'll talk to him after he gets some supper. Marie will take good care of him, don't worry." Then turning on Louis Joseph he asked, "What time did that boy leave the castle?"

"At sunup, Your Lordship. He said he was off for Citeaux. I'm surprised to see him back. I thought we had another monk in the family."

"I'll monk you if you ever allow him to do the like again!"

"Yes, Your Lordship," answered Louis as he limped away, but once inside the barn Gautier heard him say, "Well, he'll be a monk yet; whether I allow him or you allow him. Mark my words."

Two hours later Nivard was standing before his father in the great hall of the castle. Humbeline was seated before the hearth with a bit of lace in her hands. The boy had confessed his running away, and told how Stephen Harding had allowed him to see Guy and Gerard, Bernard, Andrew and Bartholomew; then sent him off with a blessing, saying, "When you are old enough, you may come back."

Humbeline allowed him to tell his story, then laying the bit of lace in her lap, asked question after question about Bernard and the others. Nivard's answers showed that he had not studied his brothers very closely; for he could not say whether they were thinner or fatter or just the same; he could not say whether they were happier or more sober or just the same. In fact, his every answer, because of its indefiniteness, prompted another question, until Tescelin finally said, "Humbeline dear, this boy was interested in the life, not in those living it. I think we had better let him go off to bed. He has had two very long rides today. I think he'll sleep soundly. And as for you, little man, I'll see you tomorrow. You're in no condition to hear what I have to say right now."

On the morrow the Lord of Fontaines talked very seriously with his only remaining son. He told him much about life, society and the Duchy; conjured up scenes that would have thrilled any other lad of twelve; promised him much in the way of favor with his liege lord, the Duke; but in the end, for all his talk, he received the one question, "When is one old enough, Father?"

Tescelin laughed; but he saw that he had a new problem; the problem of distracting his young son and getting his mind off Citeaux. It proved to be one that taxed his ingenuity to the utmost, and even then, in the end, remained unsolved. For Nivard often said, "I'm growing older...," a statement no one could deny; but a statement that told everyone where his thoughts lingered longest. Humbeline used to greet his, "I'm growing older" with, "Every day and in every way, Nivard; but you're not old enough yet."

Then for some six months no one heard him say a word about his age. His father and sister should have been suspicious, but they thought that perhaps the spell of Citeaux was wearing off. But their thought proved most incorrect, for on the day that Nivard could bravely say, "I'm thirteen now, going on fourteen," he slipped out to the stables, cajoled Louis Joseph into giving him a birthday present by saddling his roan and allowing him to ride unattended in the woods. The old man needed little coaxing. He simply said, "The woods will be refreshing this time of the year—especially," he added in a whisper, "those down toward Citeaux. And it's a blessed birthday I'm wishing you, little lord-to-be, or is it little monk-to-be?" Nivard made no answer but did all he could to hurry the limping Louis.

Down the fifteen miles he rode and back the same fifteen. For Stephen Harding gave him the same kindly reception and the same kind of a dismissal. But this time Nivard perceived a more encouraging phrase in the dismissal, for Stephen had said, "When you're a little bit older, I'll receive you." It was a promise as far as Nivard was concerned. He felt that he was already a Cistercian. And the words, "I'll receive you" kept him straight in his saddle the weary ride home. When he was met by his father with Humbeline and Guy de Marcy, he did not even think of an apology or the necessity of offering an excuse; he simply shouted, "Father, Father, Abbot Stephen says he'll accept me when I get a little older."

Tescelin bowed to the inevitable then, and won escape from the persistent question of, "Am I old enough now?" by entrusting Nivard to a worthy priest who was to teach him his letters. It was the only solution, for Nivard looked upon his lessons as a kind of postulancy; and that silenced him. When the good priest finally learned that he was training the monk-to-be and not the lord-to-be, he understood why Nivard had asked more questions about religious life than about his Latin lessons. He also understood why there was that burning light in his eyes.

In 1116, when Nivard was able to say, "I'm sixteen, going on seventeen," he practically demanded his father's permission and Stephen Harding's acceptance; and his persistence won both. He rode the fifteen miles to Citeaux jauntily, and sent the roan back to Fontaines saying, "No more running away for you and me, Lady. I'm old enough at last."

Growing Like God

If Tescelin had found his boy impatient to grow old enough, Stephen Harding found him even more impatient to grow perfect. The Abbot had a hard time convincing the youngster that religious perfection, like all great things in God's world, is a matter of slow growth.

One day the Prior found Stephen smiling and shaking his head. When he asked the reason for the smile, Stephen answered, "Human nature." He knew his answer was absolutely true; he was smiling at human nature; but he also knew it was unenlightening to the Prior, so he said, "I took young Nivard of Fontaines out to my giant oak today. I tried to teach him an important lesson. I showed him my grizzly veteran and said, 'That was an acorn once, Nivard. Yes, just about a hundred years ago, about the time Guido of Arezzo invented staff-notating for the gamut. It took all those years for it to attain its present perfection. It could not always look at the tempest without fear, or laugh at the storms as it does today. No, indeed. It was a question of gradual growth; little by little; year after year. That's how God does things in the natural order; and that's how He will do most things in the supernatural order. Religious perfection is a matter of slow growth. If we yield ourselves to God's grace the way this acorn yielded itself to the sun, the earth and the rain, we shall grow. But if we are too much in a hurry and try to push things, we spoil God's work.

"Well, I went on with the lesson in that strain for some time; but 'sixteen, just going on seventeen' doesn't take that lesson well. Nivard didn't like it a bit. Just now I was laughing to myself as I realized that thirty-six or forty-seven does not take it a bit better. We are an impatient race of men, Father Prior. We want the harvest as soon as we have planted the seed. I find the tendency still strong in myself; so I shouldn't be intolerant with it in Nivard."

The Prior smiled at the thought of the gentle, genial Abbot being intolerant with anyone. And so would Nivard have smiled had he heard it, for Stephen Harding was the soul of virile kindliness. For a year he instructed, admonished, corrected and gently reproved the growing novice. Most of his reproofs were for the normal imperfections of youth—impatience and impetuosity. Then in 1117, after Nivard had paid his eternal vows to God, Stephen Harding did one of the nicest things in his saintly life: he sent the happy lad along to Clairvaux that he might live his vows with Bernard as Abbot and the rest of his brothers as companions. Nivard jumped with joy and when he first met Guy, he held out his two arms, turned a complete circle slowly, then said, "How do you like the robes of the would-be lord of Fontaines, Guy?"

"You're not the would-be, Nivard," said Guy merrily. "You're the would-have-been."

"Right! I would have been if I had been foolish enough to accept the Trojan horse you offered me. *'Timeo Danaos et dona ferentes.'* But as you see, I was every bit as wise as my oldest brother; I gave the castle and the lands away, too."

Later when Guy was talking to Bernard he said, "I'm glad we observe such strict silence, Reverend Father."

"Why?" asked Bernard. "Are you beginning to get prayerful?"

"No, but I think that if we didn't have such silence we would all have to listen to some very smart things from that baby brother of ours."

"Oh, don't worry about Nivard." Bernard spoke with both pride and humor. "He'll come along. Perhaps it's a shame we have such silence; for I think that some of my older brothers might learn a little by hearing smart things."

Bernard and Guy were both right. Nivard did come along, and Nivard would have said some very smart things, as their cousin Maurice learned in 1132, when he visited Clairvaux on his way back from Paris. He had been attending the schools there and, of course, felt quite superior to his cousins in the monastery. A little education is always such a very dangerous thing!

Without the semblance of an invitation he plunged into a description of events that were full of color, pathos, and dramatic interest. He told of the awful plague of 1130 that was known as the *Sacred Fire*. He pictured for Nivard the vast Cathedral of Paris thronged to the doors with praying people, while in the center three hundred plague-stricken wretches lay gasping for breath. Then he told of the entrance of the shrine of St. Genevieve and how no sooner had the shrine crossed the threshold than the three hundred dying victims leaped to their feet and showed themselves completely cured. Naturally, Nivard gasped at that.

Then Maurice changed tone and told of the coronation of young Louis VII by Pope Innocent II at Rheims in 1131. With a ready flow of picture-making words he skillfully and vividly drew the highly colored scene for the listening monk. He placed the Pope and the King on the dais, surrounded them with mitered heads and palliumed shoulders of thirteen archbishops, and filled in the foreground with the figures of two hundred and sixty-three bishops from all parts of the Christian world. Then he told how the Pope had dipped his fingers into the very oil that St. Remigius had used in the baptism of Clovis. Of course Nivard was greatly impressed.

Feeling sure of his audience, Maurice changed tone a third time and with a very, very superior air told of the lectures of the flashing Abelard and the brilliant Hugh of St. Victor. On and on he went, simply dazzling his cousin with his dramatic descriptions of fascinating happenings. When he felt that he had completely overwhelmed the little monk, he turned and very condescendingly asked, "And what have you been doing all these years, my cousin?"

Nivard smiled quietly and said softly, "Growing like God."

His words had just the effect he intended. His cousin sagged like a punctured balloon; the arrogant light went from his eyes and the commanding tilt from his head. The whole air of superiority which had pervaded his entire manner was blown away by the little more than whispered, "Growing like God."

Nivard chuckled lightly as he said, "Sit down, Maurice; and don't look so surprised; for I have some really marvelous things to tell you and I want you to react."

"But—but—but—" sputtered his cousin, "you've— you've uttered blasphemy! You say—you've been— growing—like God."

"Sit down. Sit down," urged Nivard, "and I'll tell you all about it. Better to hear such blasphemy from the lips of a simple monk than the heresy you've been listening to from the lips of the brilliant Abelard. But I uttered no blasphemy," laughed Nivard, "Though perhaps I am guilty of an inaccuracy. I should have said: '*Striving* to grow like God.'"

"That's as bad," insisted his cousin censoriously.

"Maurice," began Nivard easily, "I cannot match your scenes with color or drama, or, perhaps, even with interest. I've been fifteen years in this Valley of Wormwood, and as far as the outward detail goes, I've spent my years in the dull monotony of singing, reading, working and praying. Every Monday was just like Sunday, and every Thursday just like the Tuesday before it; next week will be essentially the same as last week was, and ten years from today will be exactly like today. I've been doing the same thing, in the same way, in the same place with the same men for fifteen years."

"That's killing!" exclaimed Maurice.

"I thought you'd say that," replied Nivard. "But I say it's quickening, enlivening, completely transforming."

"Prove it," snorted Maurice. "To me it seems more like stagnating, moldering, and slowly corroding."

"Well, Maurice, to be brief, I spend seventeen or eighteen hours every day in prayer and penance. Or if you want to make it most brief, I spend my entire day at prayer."

"That's impossible!" came the haughty reply. "No one can keep constantly concentrated, and prayer without concentration is not prayer."

"How long can you hold converse with—oh, say a man like Hugh of St. Victor, or even Abelard?"

"Ah!" exclaimed Maurice with a show of his former enthusiasm and superiority, "I could talk all day and all night with such men. Oh, Nivard, what minds they have! Yes, indeed, I could talk with them endlessly."

"Would you have any difficulty keeping concentrated?" asked Nivard quietly.

"With Abelard and Hugh of St. Victor?" snorted his cousin. "Ha! It's easily seen that you've never heard them. Why, Nivard, they are so enlightening, so absorbingly interesting, so completely captivating that it is practically impossible to become distracted while in contact with them. They have minds that scintillate."

"So you could talk all day and all night with them?"

"I could spend my whole life in converse with them!" came the unconditioned reply.

"I see," said Nivard with a slow nod of his head. Then he added quietly, "Well, now, Maurice, don't you think that God has a mind at least equal to Abelard's?"

"Huh? What?—God?—Abelard? What are you saying? What are you talking about?"

"Prayer, Maurice, Prayer! Prayer is converse with God."

"God doesn't speak."

"God has spoken through the mouths of patriarchs and prophets, and lately through His only begotten Son," came the even reply. "And doesn't the universe say anything to you, Maurice? Don't birds or flowers, or whispering woods or singing waters? Don't the stars, the moon, the sun or the sea? Don't you ever hear God in the world of nature? I do. If you don't, I'm glad I went to Citeaux instead of to Paris: for I hear things you must be deaf to. I see things that you must be blind to. I find God where you find only earth and sea and sky."

"You're dreaming, Nivard," snorted his cousin. "Don't be a romantic fool, even though a pious one. Life is real. Life is action. Life is social. Man needs contact with man, and mind must be sharpened by contact with minds. You're mentally deteriorating because of lack of friction. That's your trouble. It is only out in the bustle of life that man matures and ripens. It is only out there in contact and conflict with intelligence that minds grow. Activity is what you lack; and because of that lack you'll never become like God, as you so blasphemously boasted; for He is pure act."

"Oh! So you do know something of God. Good! Do you happen to know much about His only begotten Son?"

"Of course I do."

"Do you know where He was born? Do you remember how He spent the first thirty of the short thirty-three years of His life? Do you by any chance recall where and how and why He died?"

"I'm a Catholic," snapped Maurice with an indignant toss of his head.

"If so, then why deny that I'm growing like God? He was born in obscurity; lived all but three short years in obscurity; then died the death of the infamous in order to win grace for men. That's history. Now look at the parallel: You'll admit my obscurity, won't you? You've already branded me as infamous. All that remains is that you allow that I'm winning grace for men." Nivard had struck the table sharply as he ticked off the points of the parallel. Then looking keenly at his cousin, he asked, "Well, what do you say: Am I growing like God or not?"

Maurice could only answer by clearing his throat and saying, "Ah-h-m-m-m,"

"You see, Maurice," Nivard said in a more friendly tone, "effects are always more arresting than their causes. A rose can send you into rapture, I know; but you wouldn't give so much as a second glance to its seed. This tremendous monastery of ours delights your eye with its harmony, proportion and perfection of detail, doesn't it? But you should have seen it in the process of construction. What an unsightly mess! Shapeless stone here, there and everywhere; lumber of all lengths and thicknesses littering the whole valley; loose dirt here, broken rock, gravel and plaster there, bent, twisted and rusty iron down yonder. Oh, awful!

"It's the same with life, Maurice. You admire the man who has attained sanctity. You reverence the one who has really caught up with Christ. The finished character pleases you immensely, but the process of construction, the things that go to make up the saint, the giant strides over hills and mountains and down through those dark, deep valleys, that are required of all who would overtake Christ—those things you despise. It's a sorry mistake, Maurice; and a very common one. People want the finished product, but they refuse to pay the price that will produce it. It's sad. Sad for them. Sad for Christ. It's a form of blindness."

"What are you insinuating? Do you mean to say that we all should become hewers of wood and drawers of water? Do you mean to insist that all France should turn Cistercian? Do you think that only those who become plowboys and psalm-singers and morose, melancholic, misanthropic dwellers in deep valleys or miasmic swamps can serve God? Have you lost all breadth of vision or was it completely stifled at birth? Must we all shave our heads to save our souls? Bah!"

"You wouldn't look so handsome with that flowing mane of yours cut off, Maurice," Nivard said happily as he felt his own thin monastic crown and shaved head; "and your soft, white hands would get terribly blistered and blackened if you had to dig dirt or saw wood. No, I don't think you'd do as a monk at all. Nor would I advise any of your particular cast of mind to attempt it. I've seen dozens of your temperament come here and leave here. It did them little good. I'm afraid that in later life it will do them much harm. It is not good to be haunted in your down-going years by phantoms of what-might-have-been. No, Maurice, I don't want the world to be a monastery; but I would have everyone in the world monastic minded. So would God. A learned man like you catches my meaning. You know what *'monos'* means: one, alone, solitary! Therefore to be monastic minded means to have grasped the full meaning of Christ's words, *'ONE thing alone is necessary!'* The trouble with most men, Maurice, is that they think life is a goblet to be drained. It is not! It is a measure to be filled."

"With what?"

"With what God gave you—love!"

"Love?"

"Yes, love! And first of all love for God. What have you given God during all your years in Paris?" The question came like a flash. Nivard had dropped his easy manner of address and his whole body grew tense.

"Why—I—What have I given to God?" faltered Maurice.

"There it is!" snapped Nivard, striking the table with his fist. "You have to grope. You stutter. The question startles you. Giving to God is a novel idea to you, isn't it? Ah, what a shame! For years you have been at the schools learning terms about God, but not learning God. Maurice, don't you know you were created only to give?"

"Only to give?" came the incredulous exclamation.

"Yes, only to give!" repeated Nivard. "To give glory to God. To give God love. What did Jesus Christ do on earth, Maurice?"

"He saved mankind."

"Uh-huh," said Nivard, shaking his head sadly. "I thought so. Did you ever hear that He gave satisfaction to God?"

"Of course I did; but they are the same thing."

"They are and they aren't," said Nivard with feeling. "We have selfishly insisted that God became man for man. It's true; but it's not adequate. He became man for God! That is the part we too often forget."

"What difference does it make?" asked his cousin haughtily.

"This," came the fiery reply. "You think He came as Savior only, forgetting that He came as model, too. He came to show us how to adore, how to fulfill the only end of our creation, how to give glory to God. That's the big difference it makes, Maurice. It makes us realize that we are adorers, glorifiers of the all-glorious God. It makes us realize that God made us for Himself, not for ourselves; that our prime function is not so much to save our souls as to know, love and serve God. You've heard all the terms before, I know, Maurice; but you haven't grasped their truth! We were created to give love to God. That's why I say that for fifteen years I have been growing like God. I've spent those fifteen years as Christ spent His thirty-three: 'doing always the things that please the Father,' not the things that please me!"

"You're looking at man from God's angle," said Maurice pensively.

"Right!" said Nivard, "I'm looking at man from God's angle because there is no other proper angle from which to view him. But don't mistake that I'm also looking at God from man's proper angle, at the same time. Maurice, Maurice, have you ever given a thought to what a disappointment our day must be to God Almighty? Look at us! The Church is in schism; petty rulers are at war; and society is being infected with anti-clericalism. What is God getting from the race He made to His own image and likeness, the race He created out of nothing for the prime purpose of manifesting His glory and communicating His goodness? What a miserable mess it is! There are monks who live in no monasteries; abbots who rule no community; monasteries that are utterly unmonastic. Men who have vowed to live the lives of poor men are rolling in wealth; men who have vowed to live the lives of pure men are unchaste; men who have vowed to live the lives of vicarious victims seek nothing but their own ease, comfort and sensual self-indulgence. Oh, it's a horror!"

Maurice looked at his cousin who had become flushed as he depicted the world, and then very quietly said, "One very important thing I learned at Paris, Nivard, is that it is most dangerous to make unqualified, universal and sweeping statements. They can too easily be denied."

"Thanks for the correction, Cousin," snapped back Nivard, "but since you've asked for the details, take them: Cardinals of holy Mother Church wrangle, and for months we, the sheep, are lost, for one shepherd says Innocent is Pope while the other says, 'No! Anacletus is!' What follows? The Church is rent from top to bottom. Why? Pride. Avarice. Men are greedy! Kings, emperors, barons, dukes and counts usurp the powers of the Pope and appoint Bishops, Archbishops, Abbots and parish priests. Why? Pride. Avarice. Men are greedy!

"Roger of Sicily gathers his army to uphold the cause of Anacletus. Why? Is it principle? It is not! It is policy. The coronet of the duke is too small for his head; he wants the crown of a king. That's pride. That's avarice. That shows the man is greedy! William of Aquataine stands out as the only ruler in France who has not submitted to Innocent. Why? Is it principle? It is not! It is prejudice. His favorite, Gerard of Angouleme, was stripped by Innocent of his power and dignity as apostolic delegate; so William retaliates by repudiating the lawful successor to Christ the King. That's nothing but pride. That shows the man is greedy! Money and false ambition are ruling the Church.

"And what is Arnold of Brescia, disciple of your brilliant Abelard, doing? Attacking the whole ecclesiastical structure by sowing the seeds of anti-clericalism. Many prelates are too wealthy. No one denies that. That's why Citeaux was founded. That's why Clairvaux flourishes. We are a protest against the lack of poverty and the want of humility in the Church and in the world. But look what Arnold of Brescia wants to do! He wants to separate the temporal from the spiritual, utterly divorce Church and State; really take soul from body. The man is mad. There are a few facts for you, Maurice; and given by one who hasn't been out in the world for over fifteen years."

His cousin shifted about in his chair uneasily so Nivard pushed on. "Now perhaps after those particulars, you'll allow me to make a general statement. Man is proud. Man is avaricious. Man is grasping, greedy and blind. Money has mesmerized him and the lust for power has deprived him of sight. He forgets that he has not here a lasting city. He is lost in the concerns of this world to the utter forgetfulness of the concerns of the other world. Man is neglecting God, Maurice, and hence, in his stupid selfishness is actually neglecting himself."

Nivard paused. Maurice, who had been spellbound by the vivid picture of actualities drawn by this cousin of his, who he thought knew nothing of actuality, was keen enough to realize that Nivard had seen more deeply than he himself had ever seen; and he was honest enough to admit it. "Nivard," he said in the humblest tone he had used all day, "you're opening my eyes. We do use terms and neglect their truths. We are giving God little glory indeed."

"You are giving God pain!" exclaimed the young monk who was now lost in his own thoughts of God and the world. "I'm afraid, Maurice, that there is much learning in the world, but little real wisdom. I'm very much afraid that people are confusing means and ends."

"You mean...."

"I mean that they are making an end out of things that are only means to a higher end. Look at this life of mine. What do you see? What have you seen? You looked only at the means, Maurice. You saw the manual labor, the silence, the solitude and the psalm-singing. You looked and saw only the husk; and from that false view you drew your conclusions. Could they be other than false? The things you saw are only means, not ends. They are to help me grow like God. Why, the whole monastic life is not an end in itself. Never! It is only a means to bind me closer to the God who made me. That is why I

say that you and all the world will right yourselves when
you learn how to distinguish means from ends, learn
how to use means as means while looking steadily to
your end. You don't have to change your state of life,
Maurice, in order to save your soul and glorify God. No.
But you and millions like you have got to change your
state of mind!"

"You think we should become more God-minded."

"I know you should. I know you must! You can pur-
sue your studies. Stay on at Paris under the learned lights
of the day; but have a different motive for sharpening
that mind of yours. Remember it belongs to God! The
world is all right, Maurice; it is the people in the world
who are wrong. They do the right things often, but from
the wrong motives. They seldom do things for God; and
that's bad for them and bad for Him. Poor God! He gets
small return from His mighty investment of creation."

"You sound sorry for God. That's an odd concept."

"I'm broken-hearted for Him!" said Nivard with a
noticeable catch in his voice. "That's why I swore my five
vows. That's why I swore to live poor and pure and obe-
dient to an Abbot, to change all my worldly manners and
to die a monk in this monastery. Think of it, Maurice! He
created whole hosts of angels; and many of them rebelled. He created a man and a woman; and they sinned.
He redeemed the whole race of mankind by a birth in a
barn and a death on a cross; and mankind goes its selfish, sinful, God-forgetting way. Oh! Poor God. Millions
have the name of Christian; but how many real Christians are there? Our civilization is called a Christian civilization; but where is the peace that should stamp the
followers of the Prince of peace? Where is the love for
one another that should set off His disciples from the rest
of the world? Yes, Maurice, I'm heart-broken for poor
God. And I'm also full of pity for the blind race of men.
When, oh when, will they learn?"

"Perhaps if more of them heard you talk...," said Maurice timidly.

Nivard laughed. "No, Maurice, words are not the weapons for reform; example is. I have hopes, high hopes for the immediate future."

"Based on what?" exclaimed Maurice. "On the schism, the heresy, the God-blindness of our day? How can you be so optimistic after drawing the awful picture of actuality that you just drew?"

"Maurice, hasn't it struck you yet that Citeaux, which does not teach or preach, is the coming teacher of the day?"

"You mean your brother Bernard's influence?"

"My brother Bernard's words would be worthless if people could not look at his life and see that he is seeking nothing but the glory of God and the good of man. My brother Bernard's voice would be sounding brass and a tinkling cymbal if in back of it were not Citeaux! Do you realize that we are not fifty years old as yet, still we have over ninety monasteries stretching from Scotland and Scandinavia to Italy and Spain? Do you realize that little Clairvaux, not twenty years old as yet, has twenty-three daughter houses? Poverty, purity and humility are waking the world up to its pride, its filth and its lust for wealth. The God-mindedness of men who grub away at the soil in silence and solitude is shaking this continent of ours and startling people into a recognition of their God-forgetfulness. Yes, my hopes are as high as the Himalayas."

"But again, Nivard, you sound as if you wanted to make the world one vast Cistercian monastery."

The young monk rested his chin on his hand and putting his elbow on the table looked at his cousin with piercing exasperation. "Maurice," he finally said, "you exasperate me. When will you grasp the spirit of things and forget the outward form? Look! My father died a lay brother. He spent only two years here at Clairvaux. But do you think for a moment that those two years are the sum total of his whole religious life? Of course not! He was God-minded all his life. He praised and glorified God when he was counsellor to the Duke of Burgundy and when he fought her just wars every bit as much as when he was a silent lay brother here in the monastery; for he knew the duties of his state in life. And my mother—she was a saint, Maurice! Nothing Cistercian about her except her heart. She was God-centered! She was a model mother because she knew that God wanted her to be that and just that. Fontaines castle was no convent, as you well remember; yet she sanctified herself there, and I have every reason to doubt that any of her sons or her only daughter will ever surpass her closeness to God. You can be a saint, and a great saint, as a student and a noble in the midst of society, if you will only change your mind and your motives. Live mindful of God, and do all things for His honor and glory and you have arrived. Do you understand?"

"Well—yes," came the hesitating reply.

"I see you don't, but I give up. Just let me tell you this: the monastery is *not* for all. It is essential for some, helpful for others, but it is not for all. As for myself all I can say is that I would have been the poor little rich boy if I had stayed at Fontaines, rich with the wealth of land and money, prestige and power, but poor in the things that are real riches. Here at Clairvaux, however, I am the rich little poor boy—I have God. I have all. I am growing like God."

"You make me slightly jealous," said Maurice as he rose to go.

"I only meant to make you a little judicious," smiled Nivard. "Remember what St. Paul said, Maurice, 'Therefore, whether you eat or drink, or whatsoever else you do, do all for the glory of God.' Put that into practice and

you'll be a Cistercian in the midst of the world. That's our
end—to glorify God; the specific means are only means.
I'm sorry Bernard is away; he would have been glad to
see you."

"I'm glad he's away," replied the cousin. "It was his
presence that kept me out of this valley so long. Everyone says he mesmerizes. I've heard that wives hide their
husbands and mothers their boys when they hear he is
coming. He has peopled this valley, but only by depopu-
lating many homes."

Nivard smiled broadly. "I see they still like to exaggerate in the world. Tell those wives that we don't want
their husbands, and tell those mothers that we don't
want their boys. We are not heart-breakers and home-
wreckers; we are only a recruiting agency for men who
want to grow like God."

They had walked to the front gate while discussing
Bernard; there they found Maurice's horse standing quietly. Nivard eyed the jeweled bridle and the highly orna-
mented saddle, then patting the horse's neck he said,
"Poor fellow! Everything about you bespeaks nobility, vi-
rility and strength, but they have dressed you up like a
lady's effeminate page. There's a fine example of the contradiction between externals and the real spirit, Maurice.
If I haven't lost my eye for horse-flesh, that's a splendid
beast. But the trappings are degrading. Meditate that on
your way home. Every time the sun catches on that
bridle or rebounds from that saddle ask yourself: What is
the spirit of Clairvaux and Citeaux? What lies behind the
external form? It may make you God-conscious. Well, be
off, cousin-mine. Thanks much for the visit. You've given
me a new stimulus to live for God alone."

Maurice mounted; then looking down on the young
monk said, "I'm coming again, Nivard. I want to learn
what fools we mortals can be. My thanks to you." With

that he turned his horse's head and Nivard watched beauty in action as the spirited beast with nodding head and tossing mane single-footed his way up the valley.

The Gentleman Robber

When Bernard returned from his campaigning for Pope Innocent II, Nivard told him all about Maurice's visit. Many times during the narration the Abbot smiled, and when Nivard closed with, "I sent him off with his silver bridle and star-spangled saddle to serve as a reminder that *unum est necessarium*," Bernard chuckled aloud.

"You were certainly generous with your doses, my good doctor Nivard. I hope you didn't kill your patient. It sometimes happens, you know, that a physician overdoses his patient and the last state of that man is much worse than the first. However, I'm glad you took Maurice down a peg or two. There was always something a little priggish about him. But now tell me: Did you ever hear of a gentleman robber?"

"There's no such animal," laughed Nivard. "A robber can't be a gentleman, no matter how courteous he is; and a gentleman is never a robber."

"Did you ever hear of Hugh d'Oisy?"

Nivard repeated the name thoughtfully, "Hugh d'Oisy...Hugh d'Oisy...Hugh...Ah! I've got it. Hugh d'Oisy is the scandal of Cambrai."

"Your tenses are wrong Nivard. He *was* the scandal. But I must confess that he was the most gentlemanly scandal I ever met. Urbanity marked his every word and gesture, courtliness dripped from him; he was courtesy incarnate."

"And yet a cutthroat," put in Nivard.

"So they told me," replied Bernard. "And so I told him when I met him last year. I gave him worse than you gave Maurice."

"What did you get for it? Did he give you a piece of his mind?"

"No, he gave me a piece of his land. He wants a colony of Clairvaux's monks to live at Vaucelles on the Schelde, not far from Cambrai."

"Are you going to accept?"

"Am I going to accept? The abbey is built! And you're going there."

"To a robber's roost, eh?"

"Well, you know, Nivard, restitution can be made by contributing to pious causes; and I really think that we fall under that category. At any rate give me your ideas on a master of novices. Sum him up in a word or two."

"He's one who weans."

"What?" exclaimed Bernard; and Nivard laughed at the surprised expression on his brother's face.

"I said he's one who weans," continued Nivard, "for his one big work is to wean postulants and novices from the world. And as far as I can judge, it's a man-sized job."

Bernard leaned back in his chair and looked at his brother with joy dancing in his eyes. "Not bad, little fellow, not bad at all. So to you the noviceship is just a process of world-weaning?"

"Exactly," replied Nivard, "and judging from some of the older specimens we have here, it is not always a successful process. A master of novices should get all worldly tastes and all taste for the world out of the system. If he doesn't do that, he's a failure."

"How do you say he should do it?"

"By giving them such sweet doses of God that anything that smacks of the world will disgust them."

"That's a large order," said Bernard with a calculating look.

"I know it is," replied the younger brother, "but there are some old monks in this community who are not perfectly happy today just because their master of novices failed to give them that taste for God. You know, Bernard, there are right ideas on God, and prayer, and sacrifice, and holy chivalry; and there are wrong ideas. A master of novices should give the right ones and blast the wrong ones to smithereens."

"Oh, you'd be violent about it, would you?"

"You just bet I would. Some people forget, or have never known that God is our Father! Now just recall our own father. Was there anyone more rigidly just than Tescelin the Tawny?"

"No, I guess there wasn't," said Bernard as he watched his younger brother closely.

"Well, would you ever be afraid to face Father? I don't care what you had done. Would you ever be afraid?"

"No," said Bernard slowly. "I don't think I would be afraid, but I know there were occasions when I was terribly ashamed."

"Ah, that's perfect!" exclaimed Nivard. "Afraid? No, not afraid. But ashamed? Yes, ashamed! Don't you see then, Bernard, how some people have overdrawn God? They picture Him as the Avenger. Oh, that's a horrible, an unjust and untrue concept. In the Old Testament, maybe; but in the Gospel as given us by Jesus Christ? Never! God is our Father. Get that idea into novices' heads and this hard life of ours is a glory! Excessive fear goes; burning love comes in."

"But fear is the beginning of wisdom."

"The fear you and I had of offending Father, yes; any other fear, no!"

"Strong on the fatherhood idea, aren't you?"

"Can't be strong enough!" said Nivard with feeling. "Just two capital ideas on God—He is my Father, and He is Sovereign. Then life is glorious and death more glorious still. As for judgment—why should I shrink from it when my Father is Judge?"

"H-m-m-m," mused Bernard. "Who was your master of novices, anyhow?"

"A woman," answered Nivard quickly.

Bernard's head jerked up. He flashed a sharp look at his young brother and found him smiling at the effect his statement had produced. "All right," said Bernard with a quizzical smile, "I'll ask the question you're waiting for: Who was the woman?"

"Our mother. Alice of Montbar. The Lady of Fontaines." Nivard said it with pride and triumph. "She gave us our foundation in the spiritual life, Bernard, by giving us right ideas on God. She was our master of novices, and a perfect one. What a training we got."

Bernard's eyes lit up as his younger brother enthused over the truth that their mother had actually trained them for the religious life. He smiled his beautiful smile and said, "Nivard, you startle us all with your unusual but absolutely true ideas."

Then Nivard, with a new tone of seriousness in his voice, said, "Bernard, you started this, so I think I can presume on the prerogatives of the baby of the family and tell you something I've wanted to tell you for a long time. I've insisted on right ideas about God, prayer, sacrifice and chivalry. Mother gave them to us. But sometimes as I listen to you in Chapter I feel like screaming as I used to when I wanted something very badly at home. Remember how I'd yell, 'Mother! Mother! Mother!'"

Bernard chuckled as Nivard reproduced his baby voice and pouty cry. "Indeed I remember. But why do you want to call Mother in Chapter?"

"Because of the way you preach," said Nivard emphatically. "Of course you know the community better than I do; and I suppose you know their needs; but sometimes you do not give clear ideas on God. You stress too much His vengeance. And with that flaming rhetorical style of yours, with your passion for hyperbole, you exaggerate, overcolor, overdraw. It will do no lasting good. Mother would never approve of it. I don't."

Bernard hitched his stool in closer to the desk and leaning on it he said, "You're not the first to criticize my style, Nivard. Many say I exaggerate. I suppose in my effort to be forceful, I overstate. But, you see, fear is necessary for some, and, at times, for all."

"I suppose so," answered Nivard, "but not all the time for everybody; and certainly never terror for anybody. Yet some of your sermons are calculated to strike terror into the simple. That's a wrong attitude for anyone to have toward God, Bernard. He is an all-just Judge, I know; yet I insist that He is our Father. Stir us up to chivalry rather than to servile fear and you do the better thing, the right thing. This insistence on the stern, forbidding Judge, the fearful avenger, the ever-watchful eye, the all-seeing spy does no good! It makes life a misery and death a torturing fright. Monks should not be moved by fear. Love, chivalry, devotion to the Father are the impelling forces."

"Well, don't tell me that I don't drive enough on love, Nivard."

"You can never drive too much on it, brother-mine. You asked me my concept of a master of novices. I called him one who weans, and you know why. He must break the postulants from worldly tastes and give them a hunger for God. Now, Bernard, that is a process of replacement. You don't take a baby from its mother's breasts by telling it that mother's breasts are insipid, tasteless, revolting. No. You give it some other food that will appeal as much, if not more, to its palate. Have you grasped that?"

"I think so."

"Well, never forget it! Sometimes when you talk about the pleasures of the world, about riches, position, ambition and power, you make me squirm. You decry these things in a way that is all but stupid. The pleasures of the world are real pleasures, Bernard; never forget that. You talk as if they were pain. Money is money, and it gives power. Position is position, and it gives influence. Prestige is prestige, honor is honor, and reputation is reputation. And calling them names does not change the facts! They are good. They can be great. And all your belittling of them sounds to me like the cry of 'sour grapes.'"

"I'm beginning," said Bernard with a good-natured smile, "yes, I'm beginning to have the slightest little suspicion that I do not exactly please my youngest brother with my sermons."

"Please me? Sometimes you almost make me sick. Look, Bernard! I can't stop a man from eating sugar by telling him that it's not sweet. All he has to do is taste it and laugh at me as a knave or a fool. So, too, with worldly pleasures; they are pleasures; else man would never go after them. Don't try to tell people that they are pain."

"Well, what would *you* do?" and Bernard stressed the "you."

"I'd break a man from sugar by giving him something sweeter. I'd give him honey. I wouldn't tell him sugar wasn't sweet. No. He could too easily prove me a liar. But I would tell him honey was sweeter and have him taste it to prove me right. That's what I'd do with novices, too. I'd wean them from the world not by telling them that the world is awful. That's a lie. I'd prove to them that the other world is more wonderful. I'd break them of their taste for excitement, tournaments, company, riches, ambition, and all the rest, not by saying that these things are bad—that's a lie—but by giving them a higher excitement, inviting them to a greater tourney, showing them greater riches and firing them with a higher ambition. I'd give them a taste and a thirst and a blazing yearning for God, their Father, and set them hurtling after Christ."

"Oh!" said Bernard, "my little brother can grow warm on the subject, can't he? Where did you get all your ideas?"

"By noticing your mistakes."

"Good for you!" exclaimed the Abbot. "I'm too rhetorical. I exaggerate. I insist too much on fear. I don't give the right ideas on God. What else?"

Nivard blushed, but his eyes were unblinking as they met Bernard's. "The baby of the family is talking, Bernard, because he loves you; a monk of Clairvaux is talking because he loves you and everyone in Clairvaux; a follower of Jesus Christ is talking because he loves God. Do you understand?"

"Perfectly, Nivard. I wasn't censuring; I was summing up. I always learn more from my mistakes than from my triumphs. I mean it. A frank friend is always more helpful than a whole host of false flatterers. What else have you noticed?"

"Well, before I answer, I want to correct one statement of yours. I didn't say you gave wrong ideas on God; I don't think you ever have. But I do think that you overdraw His justice at times, or rather that you fail to balance your picture with a touch of His mercy. But now I take you to task in earnest, as I say that if I were master of novices after right ideas on God, I'd give right ideas on self. And there I think you do err."

"How?"

"I am a creature, am I not, Bernard? A creature of God, a product of Omnipotence?"

"Of course."

"Then how can I be called 'nothing'? Did God create nothings? How can I look on myself as of no worth? Did Omnipotence exert Itself to call forth something of no worth? Did God become man and die for beings who are nothing and of absolutely no worth?"

"Just a second, young fellow," broke in Bernard. "When did I ever even insinuate such falsehood?"

"In your frequent insistence on humility," said Nivard with a show of fight. "You insist that it's a virtue which leads me to consider myself vile."

"And aren't you?"

"I am not!" came the instant reply. "Unless, perchance, the image and likeness of God is something vile."

"Hold on, Nivard. Aren't you forgetting the fall of our first parents and the consequent wound to our nature? Aren't you forgetting personal sin and its wound to God?"

"I'm very mindful of both, Bernard. But since when did a wound render one vile? And since when did the saving blood of Jesus Christ fail to wash away sin? I have been a sinner and still am sinful; concupiscence is in my make-up. But I have been pardoned and I'm striving to hold my evil tendencies in check. I am still a son of God and I'm striving might and main to overtake Christ. Yes, I am a son of God; a prodigal son, if you insist; but still a son. Now what's vile about all that?"

"Aren't you a beast?"

"Am I not a breath of God?"

"Oh, you're looking at it all from God's side?"

"I am not. But you're looking at it all from sinful man's side; and therein you're wrong. Bernard, is my soul vile?"

"No."

"Is my body vile?"

"It has vile tendencies."

"Has it? When our nature was wounded by Adam and Eve, I thought our intellects were darkened and our wills weakened. Isn't that the wound of original sin? And when God wanted to redeem the fallen race, wasn't it a human nature that He assumed? And wasn't it His human body that was crucified? What's vile about that? Nothing! I don't tell my body that it is vile. Never! I say to it: Remember, Dust, that you are splendor!"

"I'll grant you all that, Nivard," said Bernard as he sat back from his desk. "The human body is a masterly work of Omnipotence; the human soul, a breath of Divinity. But I'm vile because of the use I've made of that body and soul."

"All right," said Nivard as he crept closer to the desk. "That's one point gained. I'm not essentially vile, then. If I am vile at all it is because I have sinned."

"Precisely," snapped Bernard as he struck the desk. "God didn't make me vile; I made myself that way."

"Have those sins been forgiven?"

"I hope so."

"Well, where is the vileness, then?"

"We're wandering, Nivard. Humility is a virtue. It is the characteristic virtue of the Order. Humility is truth...."

"Well, tell the truth, then," broke in Nivard with flashing eyes. "Humility is our characteristic; but true humility, not vileness. Bernard, listen! Whose humility are we to acquire, yours or Jesus Christ's?"

"'Learn of me, for I am meek and humble of heart,' are Christ's words, not mine."

"You bet your life they are! Now tell me when, or where, or on what occasion did Christ say He was vile?"

"Did you ever read the line: 'I am a worm and no man'?"

"I did; and it fell not from the lips of Christ. Why, it is not even in the New Testament."

"No, but it is about Christ."

"Yes, but not as He was in Himself; nor as He ever made Himself; but only as He allowed brutal man to make Him in the passion and on the cross. No, Bernard, I can't agree with you at all. Christ's humility lies not in vileness; and it's His humility that we are to imitate. His birth was humble; His station in life was humble; His labor was humble; His death was most humble. And that humility we imitate perfectly, not by saying 'I am a nothing'; 'I am of no worth'; 'I am just a bit of vileness'; but by saying 'I am a Cistercian.'"

"What do you mean?"

"Bernard, you and I were born in a castle. Look what we live in now—the Valley of Wormwood. We were of noble extraction, destined for the place of nobles in human society. Look at us now—lower than serfs. We were so circumstanced that we need never soil our hands with labor or spend our days in any company but the best. Look at us now! Don't you see that our essential humility is in embracing this lowly state and loving it, not for what we are but for what Christ became! I am a slave, a soil-turner, a ditch-digger, a silent solitary because Jesus Christ was born in Bethlehem, lived in Nazareth and died on Calvary; and that's the only reason! Not because of what I have been or what I am, but because of what God is. You say humility is truth; I say it is love. You say it shows man his proper place—that of last, lowest and least. I say it shows him his proper place—that of a chivalrous knight giving his every breath to his Savior. Humility looks at God, not at man. And because by it man sees the supreme dominion of God, he acknowledges his absolute dependence on God. That's my concept of humility. It's a virtue that puts me on my knees to adore the one Supreme Being; to thank Him for what I am; to ask

Him for what I need; to tell Him I'm sorry for what I've been. It's a virtue that makes me an adorer! Your concept makes me...well, I don't know what; it makes me sick."

"There is a lot in what you say, Nivard; but our Order is the humility of abjection."

"I know it is; but what does that abjection consist in?—Telling lies about the creature that God has made? or in the labor of serfs; the garb of the poorest of peasants; the food of swineherds; the bed of an outcast; the position of a nameless slave?"

"Virtue is in the interior, Nivard."

"Yes, and Cistercian humility is in the full-hearted, head-long flinging of oneself into these lowly and humiliating things, not because I have deserved them—that would be but justice—but because Jesus Christ took the same before me."

"You're back to love again," said Bernard frowning.

"Of course I am; and any virtue that does not bring me there or spring from there, is not virtue. Humility is only a means, Bernard, to make us like Christ. Listening to you, I often think it is a means of making us lower than snakes. But suppose I'm all wrong and you are perfectly right, will you tell me how the constant insistence on and continual consideration of my vileness helps me in my endeavor to become like unto God?"

"Certainly; it keeps you from the fountain head of all sin—pride."

"It puts me in the workshop of the devil—sloth! For if I should ever convince myself absolutely that I am nothing; that I can do nothing; that I am only vileness— why should I stir? With what am I going to strive for perfection?"

"With the power of God; and that is precisely my whole point in preaching humility the way I do. You talk as if you did something, Nivard. You talk as if sanctity depended on you."

"Stop there, Bernard," broke in his younger brother, "and let me make two statements I want you to ponder. The first is this: Manichaeism teaches that the body is vile—and that is heresy. The second is this: The Church teaches that man can really merit. Hence, if sanctity depends on God entirely, as you seem to insinuate, and heaven depends on sanctity, then I can't merit heaven— and that's heresy. Think them over. But now it's getting late. Just let me say that even if you were absolutely right, you would be wrong to preach it all the time."

"Why?"

"Because it depresses, discourages, disheartens, and the devil likes nothing better than that trinity. Lift me up, Bernard; encourage me; inspire me; send me out to work with my heart singing and my head ringing with the consciousness that I can give great glory to God in this Cistercian life. That's what your Chapter talks are supposed to do. You're here to edify—that means build up—not to break down. And your insistence on my inherent vileness breaks down. If I were master of novices I'd strive for three things...."

"Will you please change one word in that last sentence, before you go on, Nivard?"

"Which one?"

"The very first. Change 'if' to 'as.' Say: As I am going to be master of novices."

"But, Bernard...," gasped the younger brother as he grasped the edge of the desk with both hands.

"But, Nivard...," laughed Bernard.

"Oh, no, Bernard, not that. One in the family is enough to do the training. You're Abbot here; that's enough of the Fontaines' flavor. Please."

"Oh, not here, Nivard. Up at Vaucelles, on the property given by the gentleman robber, Hugh d'Oisy. But complete that sentence, will you? I'm anxious to hear it."

"Ha, but I'm not so anxious to complete it now," mumbled Nivard with a stunned look in his eyes.

"Oh, come on! You had me fascinated; I thought you'd be delighted with the news. It gives you an opportunity to put all your theories into practice; a chance to avoid all my mistakes."

"Yes, but it takes me away from you and Andrew and all the rest."

"Oh, let's not talk about that. Give me those three points, please! You've opened my eyes to a whole lot this afternoon; don't close the curtains now just when I am getting the best view of the day. Come on!"

"Well, Bernard," began the younger brother, but the life had gone from his voice and the light from his face, "briefly I'd give them...."

"You *will* give them," corrected Bernard.

"I'll strive to give them," resumed Nivard, "right ideas on God, right ideas on self, and right ideas on devotion."

"Oh, I'm sorry I broke in when I did. I'd love to hear your fiery self on the matter of devotions."

"Well, substantially it is this, Bernard: No display. Nothing showy. As little external as possible. We are a fervid people, Bernard, but that doesn't necessarily mean that we are fervent. I'll strive to develop in my novices a deep, strong, virile, quiet, concealed devotedness to God. I'll aim at cultivating devotion and cut to the very minimum ostentatious, external, pious practices. I don't like them, for I don't trust them. There is something instinctive in real men that has them paying their deepest devotion and giving their most profound affection as quietly and in as concealed a manner as possible. My novices' deepest devotion will be a chivalrous service to God. No noise. But something steady, strong, silent, stable and sound. More like the rock on the eternal hills than the waving flower of the spring or the summer's lightning flash."

"And how do you plan to develop that?"

"By giving the noviceship an *esprit de corps*." Nivard showed a little more animation now. "Bernard, Bernard," he called, "we are knights of the Most High God. Chivalry toward our Sovereign is the spirit that should animate us all. We should be one in heart and mind as well as in external observance. Into the marrow of our bones should be shot that anxiety to give and give and give to God, our Father. And here is where our characteristic humility comes in. You can't have humility without humiliations, you say; and you're right. But what humiliations? Those of our life, our labor, our food, our dress, our lodging. And why take them with open arms and flaming hearts? Not because I have been a sinner. No. Not because I am vile. Certainly not! But only, only, only because Jesus Christ had a crown of thorns, pierced hands and feet, and an open side; only because He was stripped naked—Oh! that, to me, is the crowning agony of the whole Passion. Think of it! God Almighty stripped naked by His creatures! That's why I strip myself naked of name, family, fortune, fame, position and every possibility of acquiring anything in this life but the glory of God. And any other humiliation that comes from men I embrace, and willingly embrace, because—as I told Cousin Maurice—God the Father gets such a miserly return from His prodigious investment of creation. Angels fell. Adam fell. Men crucified Christ at 33 and still crucify His Church in 1133. It's God! God! God! with me, and it will be with my novices!" Tears were falling fast from Nivard's eyes as he struck the desk with his fist, saying, "God! God! God!"

Bernard put his arm around his brother's neck, laid his cheek close to Nivard's and through a mist that suddenly set the room shimmering before him, said, "Do it! Do it! Do it all for God and He will bless you here and hereafter. Baby brother, you've taught me one of the greatest lessons of my abbacy. Chivalry to God is our spirit." Then sitting back he wiped his eyes and said, "Just one last note and your plan is perfect. Do you remember my sermon in Chapter, *Respice Stellam. Voca Mariam?*" Nivard nodded his head. "You plan a chivalrous novitiate. Good. Then give them a Queen to love. Give them Mary. Have them give to Jesus through her; and have them win from Jesus the same way. In difficulty, doubt, trial or temptation have them look up to the Star, call upon Mary. She'll never fail them if they never fail her. You leave tomorrow, Nivard."

"So soon?" exclaimed the younger brother.

"It's better that way," said Bernard who was all business now. "See our brothers this evening. You may speak to them all. Say good-bye. It may be your last; it may not be. That's all in the hands of God. Don't make the mistakes I've made. I'll visit you when I can. Go now. I'll see you in the morning; and thanks for some splendid ideas and some real inspiration. You'll make a good master of novices, Nivard. Hard but not harsh; gentle but very firm; fiery but in no way exaggerated; and best of all— virile; God bless you." And he raised his hand and traced the sign of the cross over his youngest brother.

Unfulfilled Promises

Nivard left the following morning, and for three years inspired the novices at Vaucelles with such fervor that many in the Order were saying that he surpassed his brother as a moulder of men. He insisted on his right ideas and generated his *espirit de corps*. Vaucelles became the talk of Clairvaux and Citeaux whenever Abbots and Priors met. The community there was more of a unit than any other, and all who visited the monastery marveled at the air of energetic alertness that pervaded the place. Nivard had trained up chivalrous knights of God, and the discerning found them more truly humble than many at Clairvaux.

It was a revelation to Bernard. He began to believe in his younger brother's program of encouragement and laughingly called him 'one who weans.' In 1135, after his return from Italy, and after he had seen to the beginnings of the new buildings at Clairvaux, Bernard went to Vaucelles. In the course of his stay there, he one day called Nivard aside and said, "It looks to me as if you are too successful as a master of novices, Nivard; I'll have to remove you."

The younger brother laughed and said, "That's a new cause for removal—success. But you're the Abbot."

"Oh, there's nothing so very new about it. Didn't you ever read the line, 'Because you have been faithful over a few, I shall place you over many'?"

"Come on; I'm waiting. What is it?"

"Well, Duke Conon of Brittany...."

"Another 'gentleman robber'?" asked Nivard with a smile.

"No, not this time; but a warrior chief. He wants a monastery established in his domain. He has promised the land, buildings, cattle and a share in the upkeep. I'm too busy with the affairs of the Pope to go myself. You go there as Prior. Do some more weaning, and generate some more generously chivalrous souls who will give glory to God."

"Ah ha! I've converted you, have I? Or do you still insist that man is vile?"

"Your memory is vile," said Bernard quickly. "I'm glad Duke Conon lives so far away; babies of families are such persistent little animals. I hope you find de Buzay to your liking. Get there as soon as possible. I'll visit you when I can."

It was as sudden as all that. Nivard didn't mind; he was the soldier ever ready for battle. He took his group of twelve and made his way to Brittany. He found the land donated by the Duke at de Buzay, but he found no Duke; for that gentleman was busy with a war against a neighboring sovereign. The buildings were only fair. There were no cattle. And the land had never been tilled. Nivard looked at the monastery and then at his community. He smiled. They smiled in return. "We'll have an opportunity to give something to God in this place or I miss my guess. Are you ready?" Every face lit up. Every head nodded, and two or three rolled up their sleeves. "Good!" said Nivard. "God will get something from you men."

How right he was Bernard learned only three years later. In 1138, one year after the awful schism ended, the Abbot of Clairvaux managed a visit to de Buzay. His mouth opened and his forehead came down in a frown when he looked at Nivard's haggard face, threadbare robe and toil-worn hands. "What have you been doing? Going in for extra penances? You look wretched."

"I feel fine," came the cheerful reply.

"Where's the community?"

"Out in the woods picking berries."

"Berries?" exclaimed Bernard. "Why berries?"

"Must keep body and soul together somehow, Bernard," laughed Nivard. "Berries have been very helpful this year."

"Take me out to the barns," said Bernard in a severe tone.

Nivard shook his head. "No, you bit of vileness, I'll not take you out to the barns; for the very good reason that there are no cattle for you to inspect."

"No cattle," gasped Bernard. "Then what have you been living on?"

"Berries," smiled Nivard.

"But...," began Bernard.

"No buts," said Nivard. "The situation in brief is this: The ground was never tilled before. It is yielding better every year, but the crops are still thin. The duke furnished no cattle and contributed nothing to our up-keep. In fact, I haven't seen him in person since we arrived. He's been at war for three years."

"And so have you." Bernard was angry. "But it's over for you right now. I'll see Conon tomorrow and tell him what I think of his unfulfilled promises. But you, Nivard—why didn't you send word? Our life is strenuous, but it never means starvation.· I'm disappointed."

Nivard scratched his head, frowned deeply, looked at Bernard quizzically and asked, "Didn't I hear someone, somewhere, at some time say something about what a shame it would be to have weak members under a thorn-crowned Head? Didn't I, or is my memory playing tricks on me? I thought it was a scrawny fellow with big eyes and light, golden hair whom people call the Abbot of Clairvaux."

"Oh, Nivard, there are limits to everything," said Bernard in an aggrieved tone. "This is destitution, not poverty."

"What was Calvary, Bernard? What is chivalry to an outraged God? None of us died. We all suffered, it is true. But I think that by it we helped end the awful schism. Your little brother must have some part in your wonderful works, you know."

"All right, Nivard, I'll grant that you played your part. But the schism is ended now; and so is this situation going to be! I'll see the Duke tomorrow. You can prepare to bring the community back to Clairvaux. De Buzay ceases to be a Cistercian foundation because of unfulfilled promises."

Bernard was angrily indignant and fully determined to close the foundation; but he wanted to tell the Duke a few things before he did so. At the very moment that the aroused Bernard told Nivard to prepare to return to Clairvaux, Ermengarde, the mother of Duke Conon, told her son that the great Cistercian Abbot was at de Buzay and that courtliness demanded that he should go there and pay his respects to the most powerful man in Europe. The Duke was more interested in his war than he was in courtliness, but he gathered an escort quickly and galloped to de Buzay.

He came to be courtly, but he was given no opportunity to show it, for the moment Bernard laid eyes on him, he blazed away. The Duke faced more real fire in those first ten minutes than he had faced in the three years of his war. Bernard told him that Cistercians were angelic, but they were not angels; that they had bodies of blood and bone that had to be fed. He told him many more things, then turned and said that a man was worth as much as his word, and only that much; then he ended by saying, "You have proved yourself worthless, for your word has been worthless. This community returns to Clairvaux and this land returns to a man who cannot keep his promises."

The Duke then proved himself more of a man than Bernard expected. He beat his breast, acknowledged his fault, and accused himself of being selfish. But then he pleaded earnestly to be given another chance. "My Duchy needs a monastery more than it needs me," he said. "And I need men who will pray even more than I need men who will fight. If you won't have pity on me, at least have pity on my people."

Bernard was unmoved. "We'll pray for your people at Clairvaux," was his only reply. But then Nivard stepped forward and quietly said, "I have a company of chivalrous knights of God, here, Bernard. They have been through the hardest campaign possible and are still in the very best of spirits. They tell me that they are willing and even anxious to stay. Why not give His Excellency a chance to prove he is a Duke and us a chance to prove our love for God?"

What could Bernard do? The monks stayed. The Duke kept his promises and de Buzay flourished.

Hidalgos Seek Heaven

In 1146, Bernard called "the one who weans" to him and said that he was going to make a builder out of him. "Guy has gone to God," he said, "so I think you had better go to Normandy. They tell me it is a beautiful country. Go there, and find near the city of Vire a plot of ground on which they want us build the monastery of Soleuvre. See that it is built in strict Cistercian simplicity. You know our lines. See to it also that the community observes all our customs. No use in having the monastery strictly Cistercian if the monks aren't that way. And be quick about it all; for I may need you for a bit of work across the Pyrenees before the year is out. A Spanish princess by the lovely name of Sanchia met me in Germany and pleaded with me to send a colony south. I may do it. If I do, you go."

Nivard smiled. "From 'one who weans' I become a builder; and from a builder, what? A mountain climber?"

"Yes, and a mountain descender; for you will have to scale the Pyrenees, go down through Navarre, across Burgos and into Palencia. Sanchia is the sister of King

Alfonso. She says she has a heritage in Palencia called St. Peter of the Thorns, "espina" in Spanish; she wants us to settle there. You like thorns, don't you?"

"Yes, and I like Spain. I hear Alfonso is waging a splendid war against the infidel."

"Oh, Nivard!" cried Bernard, putting his hands to his ears, "don't talk to me about wars. This crusade is driving me crazy. I toured all France and emptied town after town of its fighting forces. I did the same in Germany. It's a stirring sight to see whole multitudes ablaze with holy ardor. It's thrilling to hear them call for the cross; and yet, my heart aches when I give it to them. For of the thousands and hundreds of thousands that have marched away, not all will return."

"*C'est la guerre!*" cried Nivard. "And what a glorious way to die. For God! For God alone!"

"Oh, I know," said Bernard with a shake of his head, "but what of the wives and mothers who are left behind and do not die?"

"Sad for them," said Nivard, "yet a glorious sadness: for thanks to their sons and husbands Holy Mother Church will be freed from the infidel."

"Let's not discuss it, Nivard. I'm weary of it all."

"Well, cheer up! At least your campaign in Germany allowed you to meet the Princess Sanchia and may allow me to set Spanish hidalgos seeking heaven."

"You're an irrepressible optimist, Nivard. Go on to Normandy. I'll let you know whether Spain needs one who weans or a gleaner. From what I have learned of the land, I think it needs a gleaner—someone to glean souls for God. Monasteries are relaxed, I hear. But, be on your way. We'll see what the future holds."

Not a month of 1147 had passed before Bernard sent Nivard scaling the Pyrenees. Palencia, situated in the northeast of Spain, gave Nivard a new country and a new climate; and he reacted to it. He grew young and enthusiastic again, and gave Spain its most edifying community of chivalrous monks. Nivard was now at his best. All the extravagances of youth had been tempered, the excessive energy of early middle age was under perfect control, and the mistakes made at Citeaux, Clairvaux, Vaucelles, de Buzay and Soleuvre were serving as guideposts.

Nivard was mature. He had ripened under the most favorable conditions for man to ripen—those of adversity. He was now a master, sure of himself, sure of his way, sure of his Cistercian life. The questions of earlier days had all been answered and he had put the answers to the severest test this earth offers—that of practical application. He was now the truly chivalrous knight of God. About him there was no display, no noise, nor any noticeable externals; but there was a devotion as steady as the stars and as deep as the sea. The baby of Fontaines family had grown to the full stature of noble Christian manhood and stood now a credit to Tescelin the Tawny and Alice of Montbar and a glory to God.

In Spain he proved himself a gleaner as well as one who weans; for he not only set Spanish hidalgos seeking heaven, but he shook the complacency out of many a monastery that was satisfied with half measures and mere gestures in the service of God. But all was not done without pain. No, nothing great is ever done that way. Espina lived up to its name and pressed thorns into Nivard's brow when its example of chivalrous service drew the monks of Tholdanos to cut themselves off from the monastery of Caracetta, upon which they were dependent, and put themselves under the authority of the Cistercians.

It so happened that the Infanta Elvira had founded Tholdanos and did not like 'her monks' to go to those of the King's sister. Spanish fevers began to rise. Caracetta's Abbot strenuously objected, and poor Princess Sanchia was torn between her many loves. She was devoted to Caracetta and its black monks; she loved the Infanta Elvira; and was proud sponsor of everything Cistercian.

Nivard, of course, was embarrassed. Strife between black and white monks was nothing new to him, but he did not like being the occasion of friction in the royal family. He suffered. And when Sanchia wrote to Bernard, he advised his brother to put entire confidence in the good lady and settle the whole affair in accord with her wishes.

When Bernard wrote this to the princess, Nivard became even more dear to all in the royal palace of Castile. Sanchia and the Infanta appreciated the delicacy with which he had yielded to their wishes and the chivalry with which he had prompted Bernard to remove all possibility of friction in the royal household. Alfonso, when he heard of the trouble, called it a tempest in a teapot and a bullfight without a bull, but said that Nivard was a courtly caballero.

The King was right, and not many years after Tholdanos became affiliated with Citeaux without offending even the black monks of Caracetta.

The Noblest Knight of Spain Is Dead

Not many years afterwards the Iberian Peninsula was completely dominated by the spirit of Citeaux; for Alfonso of Portugal far outdid his namesake of Spain. Not only did he ask for monks and donate monasteries, but he actually made his whole realm feudatory to Clairvaux. Princess Sanchia in Castile lifted her lovely Spanish eyes to heaven when she heard it and felt a legitimate pride in having turned the attention of the peninsula to the white monks of Citeaux. She then whispered warm thanks to God for Nivard; because it was he who had captivated all Spain by his charming simplicity and religious chivalry. Portugal was but following the leader.

One day Alfonso of Spain came upon his sister in tears. "Sanchia," he said softly, "Sanchia dear, what is wrong? Tears in a noblewoman's eyes? What is it?"

Then Sanchia lifted her head and the King saw beautiful dark eyes shimmering in luminous loveliness. When she allowed her long lashes to meet for a moment, two tears of crystal splendor formed and fell. Lifting a bit of dainty lace to them, Sanchia said, "Majesty, the noblest knight of Spain is dead."

"Who? Who?" asked the King in unaffected anxiety.

"Nivard of Fontaines," came the reply, which for all its sadness held rich warmth of admiring affection.

"It can't be!" gasped His Majesty. "He seemed so young a man."

"He was over sixty. But his heart was young and his spirit so happy! Oh, I feel sad, Alfonso; won't you sit with me a while and chat about the last of the family of Fontaines. Spain loved him so."

"And Spain will ever love him, Sanchia. We do not forget! He set our hidalgos seeking heaven, he took souls and made them swords, then took those swords and made them chivalrous knights of God. He made my kingdom God-conscious. How can I forget? How can they forget? He was the most natural supernatural man I ever met. Simple, sincere, straight as a rapier! I accept your title, for it is true. Nivard of Fontaines was the noblest knight of Spain."

"Oh, I'm glad to hear you say that. I never knew you appreciated him so highly."

"The Cistercians are changing Europe, Sanchia. The end of this century will be the antithesis to its beginning, and all because a few men had the courage of their convictions, and stripping themselves of all useless and unnecessary appendages, went down to bedrock. I think I've caught the spirit of Citeaux. I think I know its secret.

Poverty in its purest phase. Humility in its deepest depth. Simplicity in its utter nakedness. They take all manner of men and make them sincere with God; something I'm afraid only saints accomplish. We are seldom fully sincere, Sanchia. Somehow or other hypocrisy seems to be part of our very nature. These monks root it out of their being. I did not see enough of Nivard or Espina. Tell me, have I grasped him fully?"

"More fully than I have, I think," said Sanchia and her eyes were alight with happiness. "I did not see as much of Espina or of Nivard as I desired; for in his own chivalrous way he told me of Abbot Stephen Harding and how he forbade the Duke of Burgundy the freedom of the cloister on festival days. Nivard did it delicately; but I saw his point. I was welcome at Espina, but I must not wear out my welcome. You have analyzed more fully than I, Alfonso. I'm a woman. I sense things rather than reason them out; and I sensed sanctity in Nivard and his community. All I ever learned from him was that life was given us to make an act of love; and that, he said, really depended on an act of faith. He said a beautiful thing one day; he said, 'Faith lives on things that are most dark, just as hope lives best on the elements of despair.' I have thought of it often, and I find it most true."

"I imagine that that is an epitome of his life, Princess; for the religious life and the religious spirit fundamentally have got to be a flaming act of faith. What do those men live on? Only faith."

"Yes, but that makes their hope high and their lives one long act of love," supplied the princess. "Another beautiful thing he said, Alfonso, was, 'My Mother gave me my soundest training in how to grow like God. She laid firm foundations.'"

"Did he talk much about his family?" asked the King who saw that his sister delighted in this chat.

"No, although I questioned him often. But I learned a great deal from what was unsaid. There were lights in his eyes, and little pauses in his speech, and the quick intake of breath that told me more than his words. He adored his father. He called him 'God's nobleman.'"

"I have heard much of Tescelin the Tawny," said His Majesty thoughtfully. "The Duke of Burgundy said that he was the sincerest soul he ever encountered. Loyal to the last drop of his blood. Utterly fearless. Too honest to suit the Duke; and holier than any hermit. He must have been a rare character. He died at Clairvaux, didn't he?"

"Yes, as a lay brother. Imagine it, Alfonso, a lay brother! What an act of faith that was."

"What an act of love, I'd rather say," countered her brother. "It is almost past belief. That Bernard must have been Nivard's boast."

"Oh, no!" exclaimed Sanchia, and she managed the warmest, little throaty chuckle. "Bernard was not his boast, nor was he his favorite. He talked more freely and with much more loving enthusiasm about Andrew and Gerard. He said Bernard was an extremist. Oh, he was proud of him, but I really think he loved Andrew best of all. He used to call him 'the salty one.' He said there was hardly a person and certainly never an event or a situation that did not call forth some salty comment from Andrew. Nothing bitter. Nothing harsh. But keen, deep and, as Nivard said, 'salty.' Gerard, I guess, was the happiest and most good natured of the family. Nivard always referred to him as 'smiling, dependable Gerard.'"

"Of course, I don't know them well," said the King, "but from what I have heard, Humbeline is my favorite."

"She would be," smiled Sanchia. "You're a man, Your Majesty."

The King laughed. "There may be something in what you say, Sanchia; but think of the sacrifice she made. She was married; and I have heard, was the most envied woman in the Duchy."

"Oh," said Sanchia with grimace, "that's man's talk."

"Well, what did you hear about her from Nivard?"

"I might shock Your Majesty. I hope I don't break your idol. But you asked for it; so I'll tell you that Nivard more than once said that Humbeline was the greatest man of the family."

"Man? Why I heard that she was strikingly beautiful."

Sanchia smiled delightedly. "She was. Nivard admitted that and when a brother admits that about his sister, you can be sure that she was strikingly beautiful! But what Nivard meant was that she had more spirit than all the boys."

"Then she must have been something terrific," said Alfonso with a laugh that made melody, "for Bernard was a whirlwind if ever there was one, and Nivard himself was not exactly a spring zepher. What a remarkable family! The oldest boy left his wife and two children and the youngest gave up castle, fame, fortune, and all became...."

"Saints," said Sanchia.

"Well, I didn't intend to go that far, Princess," said the King smilingly.

"Oh, you can," replied his sister quickly. "Everybody in Burgundy calls them such. Why even Nivard used to call Bartholomew 'the saint.'"

"That may be family and local pride."

"Call it what you want, Alfonso, but I'm always going to speak of them as saints; and I'm going to boast that the ninth saint of the family of Fontaines was a Spaniard.

We adopted Nivard the moment he crossed the Pyrenes. Let Clairvaux have his body; Castile and Laon will keep his spirit. He was the noblest knight of Spain."

"Well, well, well," said the King lightly, "my little sister is ablaze. Sanchia, if Nivard can fire all Spaniards as he has fired you he'll be the patron of the kingdom."

"No," said Sanchia, "I don't expect that. I don't want that. But I tell you, Alfonso, he has already fired the people more than you suspect. When they hear that he is dead there will be a mighty demonstration. Prepare for it. Take part in it; for my little saint's act of faith is ended— he now sees! He spent his life preparing for death, and I'm positive his death will bring a new Catholic life to Spain. Thank you, Your Majesty, for a consoling chat. Let's pray to Saint Nivard for each other."

"I will, Sanchia," said the King as he took his sister's hands in his own and bending low, kissed them. "One thing Nivard has taught us all—chivalry is called for where we least display it. We should save our highest chivalry for—and show it to—God! He did it. I will strive to imitate him in that."

"God be praised," breathed Sanchia and majestically withdrew from the room.

Sanchia was right. Spain took Nivard to her heart. He was honored there with a more fervent and a more widespread devotion than was his brother, St. Bernard. She calls Nivard 'her saint,' and even in our own times, an Office is recited every February 7 in honor of the last of the family of Fontaines, the man who was, and taught others to be, chivalrous to God.

The baby of the family overtook Christ.

════ St. Paul Book & Media Centers ════

ALASKA
750 West 5th Ave., Anchorage, AK 99501; 907-272-8183

CALIFORNIA
3908 Sepulveda Blvd., Culver City, CA 90230; 310-397-8676
5945 Balboa Ave., San Diego, CA 92111; 619-565-9181
46 Geary Street, San Francisco, CA 94108; 415-781-5180

FLORIDA
145 S.W. 107th Ave., Miami, FL 33174; 305-559-6715

HAWAII
1143 Bishop Street, Honolulu, HI 96813; 808-521-2731

ILLINOIS
172 North Michigan Ave., Chicago, IL 60601; 312-346-4228

LOUISIANA
4403 Veterans Memorial Blvd., Metairie, LA 70006; 504-887-7631

MASSACHUSETTS
50 St. Paul's Ave., Jamaica Plain, Boston, MA 02130; 617-522-8911
Rte. 1, 885 Providence Hwy., Dedham, MA 02026; 617-326-5385

MISSOURI
9804 Watson Rd., St. Louis, MO 63126; 314-965-3512

NEW JERSEY
561 U.S. Route 1, Wick Plaza, Edison, NJ 08817; 908-572-1200

NEW YORK
150 East 52nd Street, New York, NY 10022; 212-754-1110
78 Fort Place, Staten Island, NY 10301; 718-447-5071

OHIO
2105 Ontario Street, Cleveland, OH 44115; 216-621-9427

PENNSYLVANIA
510 Holstein Street, Bridgeport, PA 19405; 215-277-7728

SOUTH CAROLINA
243 King Street, Charleston, SC 29401; 803-577-0175

TENNESSEE
4811 Poplar Ave., Memphis, TN 38117; 901-761-0874

TEXAS
114 Main Plaza, San Antonio, TX 78205; 210-224-8101

VIRGINIA
1025 King Street, Alexandria, VA 22314; 703-549-3806

GUAM
285 Farenholt Avenue, Suite 308, Tamuning, Guam 96911; 671-646-7745

CANADA
3022 Dufferin Street, Toronto, Ontario, Canada M6B 3T5; 416-781-9131